The Tewa World

Alfonso Ortiz

The
Tewa World

SPACE, TIME, BEING, AND BECOMING
IN A PUEBLO SOCIETY

The University of Chicago Press

CHICAGO AND LONDON

The University of Chicago Press, Chicago 60637
The University of Chicago Press, Ltd., London

© 1969 by The University of Chicago
All rights reserved
Published 1969
Second Impression 1971
Printed in the United States of America

Library of Congress Catalog Card Number: 72-94079
ISBN: 0-226-63306-3 (clothbound)
0-226-63307-1 (paperbound)

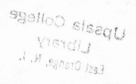

For Saya
before she returns to the lake

Contents

Illustrations

Foreword

Once in an anthropological blue moon the right person comes along at the proper time and presents us with an account of a particular tribe or a particular problem which moves us onto a new plateau. In this monograph on the Tewa Pueblos of New Mexico, Alfonso Ortiz has delineated their world view with the authority of a participant, and has related it to their social and cultural life with a clarity and economy which is as rare as it is impressive.

The Eastern Pueblos of New Mexico, who were first "discovered" by the Spaniards some four centuries ago, have managed to retain their cultural independence in the face of almost overwhelming political and religious pressures. The first reaction was militancy; the Tewa-speaking Pueblos in the Rio Grande valley to the north of Santa Fe took a leading role in the Pueblo Rebellion of 1680, which drove the Spaniards out of New Mexico for a dozen years. But the Spaniards were not to be denied. On their return the Pueblos were forced to submit and outwardly to conform. They became nominal Catholics, but they took their own religion underground and have maintained it to the present day, guarding their ceremonies and their inner life against the outside world.

The author of this volume, Alfonso Ortiz, is a relatively new type of social anthropologist—one who comes from the community that he studies and interprets. He was born thirty years ago in San Juan Pueblo, the largest of the six surviving Tewa villages in New Mexico. Such studies are particularly difficult for most of us since they normally require a certain degree of detachment, but under favorable circumstances the command of the language and the initial knowledge of the society and culture more than compensate. Here, for the first time, we have a view of Tewa life as seen from the inside.

The choice of San Juan as a basis for doctoral research was an obvious one. As the author notes, San Juan is the largest and most isolated of the Tewa Pueblos, as well as one of the least known. Earlier research by a number of students had indicated that the Tewa villages differed rather considerably from the better known Western Pueblos, particularly with regard to their social structure. Thus the basic feature of Tewa social organization was a division into "Summer people" and "Winter people" and a further tendency to fit various aspects of Tewa culture into this dual pattern. But the details were obscure and the data available often contradictory.

In the realm of anthropological theory there has been a revival of interest in dual organization in recent years, stemming in large measure from the theoretical formulations of Professor Lévi-Strauss and the ethnographic accounts of the Gê-speaking Indians of Brazil and their neighbors. The theoretical problems here are highly technical, but on an abstract level, at least, Lévi-Strauss has come to the conclusion that dual organizations really do not exist.

> I have tried to show that the study of so-called dual organizations discloses so many anomalies and contradictions in relation to extant theory that we should be well advised to reject the theory and treat the apparent manifestations of dualism as superficial distortions of structures whose real nature is quite different and vastly more complex (1963*a*, p. 161).

Lévi-Strauss goes on to express the hope that the "rare so-called dual organizations" still functioning may be adequately studied before they disintegrate.

The reader will soon discover that Alfonso Ortiz's account of Tewa world view more than fulfills this hope and expectation. Here the relationship between social dualism and symbolic dualism is analyzed in terms of the more fundamental problem of how a society can be divided and united at the same time. But dualism is only part of the Tewa picture, though a fundamental part; the way in which the dual organization ties the human categories together into a larger structure is an important part of the author's contribution.

The Tewa classify all human and spiritual existence into six categories, three human and three supernatural. These are linked into three pairs, so that at death the soul of each human category becomes a spirit of its linked supernatural category. The basic distinction is between the ordinary people and the religious leaders, between the Dry Food People and the Made People. Mediating their relations and guarding the ceremonies of the Made People are the *Towa é*, who represent native political officials.

These categories of human and spiritual existence have an intimate association with the Tewa world—the sacred mountains and hills in the four directions and the shrines just outside the village. In the origin myth the Tewa emerged from a lake far to the north and discovered the sacred mountains. After emergence they were divided into Summer and Winter people; they then migrated down both sides of the Rio Grande, making twelve stops before being reunited into a single community.

In the life cycle of an individual this tribal journey is symbolically reenacted in the rites of passage from birth to death. At birth the child is introduced into the society as a whole, but during the first year begins his recruitment into the moiety of his father. Here there are three rites which gradually give the child increasing adult responsibilities as a member of one moiety or the other. The moieties do not control marriage, and if the bride is of the opposite moiety she joins the moiety of her husband—"shaking off her blossom petals and replacing them with icicles," or vice versa. At death, however, the rituals emphasize the unity of the whole society, and the moieties are submerged in the distinction between the living and the dead. The soul goes to join its ancestors, either at the directional shrines or on the flat-topped hills or mountains, depending on its status in life.

There are important differences in the rituals with regard to the Dry Food People, the *Towa é*, and the Made People, which relate to their roles in Tewa life. The Made People control and direct all economic activities and most of the ritual. As representatives of the highest deities they stand at the apex of the social order. The moiety chiefs control the dual organization, each taking charge of the village for half of the year—from equinox to equinox in native theory—but the other groups of Made People are essentially mediators between the social and symbolic distinctions involved in the moiety system, and in this sense they transcend the dual divisions. The *Towa é* are likewise mediators between the Made People and the Dry Food People, but since they are recruited equally from both moieties they also serve to unite the society, through establishing a network of personal ties that cut across the dual organization. The role of the Made People is particularly apparent in the analysis of the annual cycles of ritual retreats, political events, and economic activities. Here, as the Tewa say, "all paths rejoin."

It is clear from this brief summary of Alfonso Ortiz's account of Tewa world view that the dual division is an essential component of Tewa life. The Tewa recognize both the social and the symbolic aspects of dualism, but they have more complex structures as well. Each of the six categories of human existence is conceptually distinct, but most of Tewa thought and action is organized according to the moiety division. Whenever any of the spiritual categories are impersonated in ritual, they represent one moiety or the other. The basic Tewa feeling for the equality of the moieties is demonstrated by the ways in which asymmetry is balanced over a period of time. Here is a classic account of the Tewa world view and the role of the dual organization in a functioning society.

FRED EGGAN

Preface

The ethnographic and historical record on the Tewa Pueblos has long been detailed enough to indicate that, despite the fact they are located along only a twenty-mile stretch of the Rio Grande and its tributaries, each village has always jealously guarded its autonomy; that as a consequence each has had a rather different history, has been subjected to different demographic pressures and political upheavals, and has been exposed to somewhat different external cultural influences. These and other factors have led to the loss of some belief or practice in each village, an occasional practice unique to one village, and to the differential weighting of one pattern or another from village to village. These differences in detail have long thwarted attempts at the formulation of meaningful general principles common to all, with the consequence that most studies, whatever their level or subject, have been particularistic to a fault, or general in their claims without accounting satisfactorily for local differences.

Yet this same ethnographic record was already deep enough to suggest, at the time I initiated research for this book, that there were general principles now or recently operative in all, and that if these were to be discovered it would most likely be in San Juan or Tesuque, the two most conservative villages. I decided to focus my attention on San Juan because, having been born and raised there, I had a solid base of knowledge upon which to build. But I have since checked the general pattern originally formulated for San Juan in the other villages, both from the ethnographic record and from inquiries in the three additional villages where Tewa culture still forms a viable system.

Thus, while I seem often to use the terms San Juan and Tewa interchangeably in this book, it is not because I regard San Juan as the only instructive variant of Tewa culture. Rather, I am using my more complete data on San Juan to illustrate the general underlying pattern. But what is the nature of this pattern? All of the Tewa have in common the six categories of existence, moieties, societies of Made People, and general economic, political, and kinship system; and from these general principles of social and cultural organization other similarities follow. All reflect a tendency to organize things—sacred mountains, hills, shrines, village houseblocks—in fours; they have in common the vast majority of rituals, along with the general choreographic patterns, musical traditions, and sacred symbols on which the rituals are based. The fact that these beliefs, ideas, and practices are often permuted in seemingly endless combinations from village to village should not obscure the fact that they form general classes and categories which conform, at an abstract but basically meaningful level, to structural principles common to them all. Among the Tewa, awareness of these more general considerations is restricted to only a reflective few, usually Made People, in each village, and no one of these is aware of more than a portion of the entire system of knowledge presented here.

This book was adapted from a study originally submitted as a doctoral thesis in the Department of Anthropology of the University of Chicago. It is based on field work that I conducted among the Tewa-speaking Pueblo Indians of New Mexico over a period of several years. I began the field work in the summer of 1963 while I was a participant in the Field Institute in Social Anthropology, co-sponsored by Harvard and Columbia universities, and I resumed it during the seven-month period between June 1964 and January 1965. During the first three of these months, I served as Field Director of the Museum of New Mexico's Field Institute in Ethnology. During the last four months a NIGMS Training Fellowship from the University of Chicago and an Opportunity Fellowship from the John Hay Whitney Foundation supported my research.

I was able to return to New Mexico for two months during the summer of 1965 with the aid of a grant from Project Head Start. Although I was conducting research for another study, the grant did make possible some additional investigations of the matters treated in this work. Finally, a faculty stipend from the Coordinating Committee on Foreign and International Affairs at Princeton University permitted me to recheck matters of fact in the field during the summer of 1967 and greatly facilitated the process of revision. The financial assistance from each of these sources is gratefully acknowledged. I am grateful as well to the Laboratory of Anthropology, Museum of New Mexico, for providing me with research facilities during the first two summers of field work, and to Benjamin N. Colby, then Curator of Social Anthropology, for making them possible.

My greatest intellectual debt is to the Tewa and to Fred Eggan, who, between them, made this study possible. The Tewa, especially the people of San Juan, have continued to give me friendship, trust, and cooperation in my new role as an anthropologist. Fred Eggan originally suggested that this study be undertaken and offered advice and encouragement throughout the period of field work. While the manuscript was in its various stages he spent many hours sharpening my sense of what is relevant and important in anthropology, and, when it was completed, contributed a generous Foreword.

I am also grateful to Edward P. Dozier and Nicholas S. Hopkins for extended critical comments which have greatly benefited the final product; to Richard I. Ford for assisting with botanical and zoological identifications and for sharing many insights with me during the years since 1962; to Antonio F. Garcia for helping me to formulate some of the lines of inquiry which were later to prove so fruitful in the field; to Raymond D. Fogelson, Paul Friedrich, David M. Schneider, and Nur Yalman for providing numerous fresh insights and encouragement while the first draft was in preparation; to Vera Laski, David W. Crabb, and Martin G. Silverman for reading the first draft and for discussing some of the issues with me; and to Clifford Geertz for exerting, albeit unknowingly, a substantial formative influence on the direction this work has taken.

As the reader will quickly gather, I am also indebted to Professors Claude Lévi-Strauss and David Maybury-Lewis, neither of whom I have yet had the pleasure of meeting, for a scholarly debate upon which I have intruded and from which I have profited enormously. Whatever value this work may be found to have as a contribution to the theoretical understanding of dual organizations is due entirely to the fact that they initially brought the discussion of the phenomenon to such a high level. My stance has often been critical, but the very frequency with which their names appear in these pages should be regarded as a tribute to the influence their thinking has had on my own.

Last but certainly not least, I wish to express my appreciation for the constant aid and comfort provided by my wife Margaret. She has been a full partner in this undertaking from the beginning; from the collecting and analyzing of data to typing the manuscript, correcting proofs, and, finally, preparing the Index. The finished product truly represents a joint effort.

I should like to add that this book is only the first of a projected trilogy of monographs examining data on the Tewa and other Pueblos for the light they might shed on issues of some consequence in modern anthropology. The second will be on ritual drama, and the third on mythology. In all of this my task is made much easier by Richard I. Ford's recent study, *An Ecological Analysis involving the Population of San Juan Pueblo, New Mexico* (1968). Ford presents a description and analysis of aspects of Tewa culture from a perspective complementary to my own and provides as well detailed historical, demographic, and other data on the Tewa that I have not included here. His work should be consulted by anyone wishing additional insights into the data utilized and the problems treated in this book.

The Tewa World

I
Introduction

This study represents an attempt to fill a serious gap in the ethnographic literature on the Pueblos of the American Southwest. As Fred Eggan observed more than a decade and a half ago: "Our knowledge of the eastern Pueblos is incomplete and often conflicting, so that it is not possible to speak with any certainty, even as to the facts" (1950, p. 304). Of the Tewa specifically, he notes that they are "the key group in any reconstruction of eastern Pueblo social organization" (1950, p. 315).

Of the six modern Tewa villages, San Juan was selected for this study for a number of reasons. First, it is the largest, with approximately 800 inhabitants (Ortiz 1965a). Secondly, it is one of the two most conservative villages, and it has long been regarded by the other four as the "mother village" in ritual and political matters. These factors, along with its northernmost location, furthest away from Keresan Pueblo influence, suggest that it might reflect an older or more nearly pure form of Tewa social structure and culture. Yet San Juan has never been thoroughly and systematically studied; in fact, no anthropologist has spent any appreciable amount of time there in more than four decades.

Aside from providing an opportunity to clarify the place of the Tewa in Pueblo culture generally, what other purpose in regard to contemporary anthropology might this study serve? To answer this question meaningfully let me refer to the observations of other writers on the Tewa. First, Elsie Clews Parsons concludes, in her detailed work on Tewa social organization, that "the most prominent Tewa social classification is the moiety, and for social organization the most significant habit of mind, the tendency to dichoto-

3

mize" (1929, p. 278). She goes on to observe that religious societies, deities, and even beliefs and practices borrowed from the Spaniards and other tribes "are fitted into this dual pattern" (1929, pp. 279–80). In another work, published a few years earlier, she observes: "This moiety system is indeed a substitute for clans in the social consciousness, where it holds the outstanding position clanship holds, let us say, among the Hopi" (1924, p. 336). Eggan, working from a larger body of evidence, summarizes the data on the Tewa as follows:

> The organization of social, ceremonial, and political activities in terms of a dual division, and the further conceptualization of this division in terms of winter and summer, and the associated natural phenomena, suggest a fairly long period of development [1950, p. 316].

More recently, Dozier observes: "The important sociopolitical and ceremonial organization of Tanoans generally [including the Tewa] . . . is a dual division of the society, usually referred to as a moiety" (1961, p. 107).

What these statements tell us, briefly, is that the moieties and the associated tendency to think in dualistically contrasting sets are basic in understanding the Tewa. Yet no one has ever made them the focal point of analysis in the many studies that have been carried out among the Tewa since the turn of the century. This then is the task I have set for this study: to derive as many implications as possible about the operation of these several forms of dualism in Tewa culture as a whole.

I might point out here that I follow Geertz (1965, 1966) throughout this work in my use of the concept of culture. For Geertz, as for me, culture refers to a system of historically derived meanings and conventional understandings embodied in symbols; meanings and understandings which derive from the social order, yet which also serve to reinforce and perpetuate that social order. More specifically I focus here on the more intellectual aspects of Tewa culture—on the ideas, rules, and principles, as these are reflected in mythology, world view, and ritual, by means of which the Tewa organize their thought and conduct. I believe further that the symbolic statements, representations, and acts reflected in Tewa mythology, world view, and ritual are more than epiphenomenal to social relations. Rather, as I shall attempt to demonstrate, they serve not only to reflect these social relations but to give them direction and continuity as well.

While I concern myself primarily with thought rather than

action, with the rules governing conduct rather than the conduct itself, there is such a goodness of fit between the two among the Tewa that such an approach does not serve to mislead. I believe, rather, that this approach serves to inform us in the most general and reliable terms possible about what holds Tewa society together and what gives it point and continuity. Nor do I ignore those instances in which there is not such a goodness of fit between thought and belief on the one hand and conduct on the other, for these instances often serve to lay bare some of the central concerns of Tewa life.

I seek, therefore, not only to provide a much-needed ethnographic description of the Tewa, written from this particular point of view, with these particular emphases, but also to derive implications for the study of social and symbolic dualism elsewhere. For the sake of convenience, I refer to all of the phenomena of dualism by the term *dual organization*, which I have elsewhere defined as "a system of antithetical institutions with the associated symbols, ideas, and meanings in terms of which social interaction takes place" (Ortiz 1965*b*, p. 389). I have also, in the same work, reviewed other definitions of the concept and illustrated the utility of the definition by reference to a few examples found in the literature on the eastern Pueblos. I continue to use this definition in this work, but I am careful to specify exactly the relation between the moieties and symbolic aspects of dual organization. In other words, I attempt, insofar as possible, to avoid the twin pitfalls of equating the two and of attempting to explain the one in terms of the other. Let us proceed now to a consideration of some of the major issues in the study of dual organizations, as discussed by Lévi-Strauss (1960, 1963*a*) and by Maybury-Lewis (1960). These two represent, Murdock (1956) notwithstanding, the principal polarizations of contemporary anthropological thought on the subject of dual organizations.

Turning first to Lévi-Strauss, we see in his papers an attempt to demonstrate, on the basis of examples taken from widely separated areas of the world, that dual organizations really do not exist. The core of his argument may be summarized as follows. First, he regards triadic structures and concentric dualism as more fundamental than dual organizations represented by his ethnographic examples. By triadic structure, Lévi-Strauss refers not only to a system of three parts but also to a system of two parts which are in an asymmetrical relationship. Thus, he regards as triadic phenomena both the sky, earth, and water conceptual polarizations which he derives from the Winnebago material, and the opposition between cooked

and uncooked food which he finds reflected in the literature on
Melanesia and Brazil (1963*a*, pp. 153–54). By concentric dualism,
on the other hand, he means any opposition between an inner and
an outer, as long as it is concentric (1960, p. 54).

In applying these concepts, Lévi-Strauss first establishes, through
a careful handling of his sources, that "triadism and dualism are
inseparable, since dualism is never conceived of as such, but only
as a 'borderline' form of the triadic type." He brings in his second
notion next: "Concentric dualism is a mediator between diametric
dualism and triadism, since it is through the agency of the former
that the transition takes place between the other two." He then
goes further: "Strictly speaking, any attempt to move from an
asymmetric triad to a symmetric dyad presupposes concentric
dualism, which is dyadic like the latter, but asymmetric like the
former" (1963*a*, p. 151). By this method, the culmination of a
complex intellectual exercise in the handling of ethnographic
sources, he submerges the dual organization. In doing so, he not
only fails to distinguish between social and symbolic phenomena,
but overrides what he calls, in one example, "the ecological-philo-
sophical distinction between cleared ground (i.e. 'culture'), and the
wilderness beyond the timber line (i.e. 'nature')" (1960, p. 46).
This failure to make analytic distinctions between different kinds
of phenomena in deriving his triadic and concentric models represents one of the major difficulties reflected in Lévi-Strauss's position.

A second difficulty, one which has been pointed out by Maybury-Lewis (1960) and Schneider (1965), is that Lévi-Strauss
tends to equate social structure with marriage systems. This point is
closely related to the preceding one, for his notion of the triadic
structure, or triadism, is based on his notion of "generalized exchange" (1963*a*, pp. 150–51). This leads him to assume that moieties,
no matter where they are found, will always be exogamous or
otherwise concerned with the regulation of marriage. A third
difficulty reflected in Lévi-Strauss's position is that he relies strictly
on societies with unilineal descent to justify his analysis. These two
points present problems, because the Tewa have never been known
to have any notion of unilineal descent, and Tewa moieties are
not exogamous.

In the end, Lévi-Strauss reduces all of his ethnographic examples
as resulting from a combination of five binary oppositions and
then uses the evidence to deny the existence of dual organization
(1963*a*, pp. 154–60). Since these interconnected binary oppositions
are based on some notion of marriage regulation and unilineal
descent, they cannot apply to the Tewa at all. All these points are

taken up in more meaningful detail in the following chapters, where I shall present the evidence on the Tewa. Indeed, I shall have occasion to refer to them again and again, by way of demonstrating why they present problems when the data on the Tewa is examined closely.

Turning now to Maybury-Lewis, we find much less to dwell upon because his own paper was intended primarily as a critique of Lévi-Strauss's position. Aside from a misunderstanding over the interpretation of data, he accuses Lévi-Strauss, on methodological grounds, of imprecision in defining terms, of ignoring the distinction between social and symbolic dualism, and of failing "to establish any adequate basis for his comparative analysis" (1960, pp. 40–41). Lévi-Strauss's pointed reply is that he wished to transcend the usual distinctions of terminology and concepts,

> and to put to test a kind of common language, into which the two forms of dualism (diametric and concentric) could be translated, thus enabling us to reach—not on the level of observation, of course—a "generalized" interpretation of all the phenomena of dualism [1960, p. 46].

What Maybury-Lewis does succeed in doing, however, is to point up the issues that Lévi-Strauss either ignores or overrides with his highly abstract triadic and concentric models. Maybury-Lewis's recognition of the first of these issues is reflected in his statement that

> the simultaneous awareness of the division and the unity of society is common enough in conjunction with dual organization and might be said to be the fundamental problem in their analysis [1960, p. 27].

He phrases another of the major issues, which he accuses Lévi-Strauss of failing to resolve, as follows:

> One of the purposes of his [Lévi-Strauss's] paper was to suggest a way in which the reciprocity characteristic of dual organization could be reconciled with the hierarchical superordination and subordination so often found associated with it [1960, p. 41].

He phrases a third issue, which he accuses Lévi-Strauss of ignoring, as follows: "One of the fundamental analytic problems in the study of dual organizations is that of the relation between social and symbolic dualism" (1960, p. 41).

Nevertheless, the difficulties inherent in Maybury-Lewis's position are more fundamental, for although he defines the major issues quite well, he fails to indicate how we are to go about resolving them. To illustrate with just one example, in his persistent concern with the dual organization as such—with the actual social segments comprising the dual organization—he offers no alternative method by which we might better understand what the total framework of integration is in a given society with dual organization. In other words, Maybury-Lewis seeks only what is sociologically relevant in the study of dual organizations, and this bent leads him to limit his discussion, like Lévi-Strauss, to dyadic, triadic, and concentric structures. Moreover, he ignores the time dimension by insisting on dealing with static structural models.

I can only note here, as in my discussion of Lévi-Strauss above, that the issues Maybury-Lewis raises and the difficulties presented by his position are best discussed in their appropriate context in the following chapter. What I hope I have indicated here is that there are unresolved issues of some consequence in the study of dual organization; issues that the Tewa data might serve to clarify in some measure. According to Murdock's (1956) estimates, I might point out, 10 to 15 per cent of all human societies known are or were characterized by dual organization in the sense in which the term is used here. At the risk of appearing redundant, let me restate the three major problems with which this work is primarily concerned.

One problem lies in attempting to reconcile the reciprocity which usually characterizes dual organizations with the asymmetrical relationships which are also often found associated with them. Another problem is that of determining the relationship between social dualism, which usually finds its institutional expression in moieties, and symbolic dualism. A more fundamental problem is that of understanding just how a society can be divided and united at the same time, and how it continues through time, given the fact of dual organization. It is to this third problem that the larger part of this work is addressed. I do not emphasize the dual organization itself, but seek instead the basis of unity in the society, given the dual organization. It is argued that non-dual aspects of society and culture have to be considered and analyzed, for no society is so rigorously dyadic that these aspects can be safely ignored.

To this end I outline, in the following chapter, a broad framework of analysis that does not deliberately overemphasize the dual organization. By a broad framework of analysis I mean that I begin by presenting one variant of the Tewa myth of origin, and then determine what part this myth plays in the Tewa world view. In this way we can attempt to understand how the Tewa perceive human and spiritual existence, and how they organize time and space within the geographical area they consider their world, utilizing their own categories, concepts, and distinctions. This is the key chapter in this work, in the sense that it sets the stage for a comprehensive discussion of what the dual organization means in Tewa society and culture.

The most important finding, the one which serves as a subsequent point of departure, is that the Tewa classify all human and spiritual existence into a hierarchy of six categories, three human and three spiritual, and that the spiritual categories are further associated with specific geographical points in the Tewa world. Moreover, these six categories are linked into three pairs; that is to say, the spiritual categories represent counterparts of the human categories, and at death the souls of each human category become spirits of its linked spiritual category.

After identifying these three pairs of linked categories, and indicating their relation to the natural world, I proceed to a more detailed discussion of their place in Tewa society and culture. Chapter 3 focuses on the first, or lowest human category and its linked supernatural counterpart, utilizing six life crisis rites that each Tewa normally undergoes in his lifetime as a basis for the discussion. In chapter 4, I analyze the intermediate human category and its similarly intermediate spiritual counterpart, focusing this time on the process of recruitment into the human category. In each chapter I build upon the understanding attained in the preceding chapters. I attempt to make this understanding reasonably complete in chapter 5, where I discuss in detail the highest ranked human category, and its similarly highest ranked spiritual counterpart. This time I not only focus on the process of recruitment into these categories, but attempt to determine their role in the annual cycle of ritual, political, and economic activities. Here, as the Tewa term it, "all paths rejoin," for only by reference to these highest categories of being can the rules governing conduct, thought, and belief in the Tewa world be fully understood, so thoroughly do they permeate the other categories.

What serves as the unifying thread throughout this work is that all six categories of being are divided into two parts. Those of the three human categories together constitute the Winter and Summer moieties, while the beings of the three spiritual categories together represent symbolic counterparts of the moieties. While each of the six categories is conceptually distinct from the others, most of Tewa thought and action is organized according to the moiety division, and whenever any beings of the spiritual categories are impersonated in ritual, they represent one moiety or the other.

Thus I can state quite simply that it is the moieties, rather than the categories, that are basic to understanding behavior. Why then do I emphasize the categories in the organization of this work? The answer is that because the Tewa use them to order all of human and spiritual existence, they serve for me as convenient analytic units. Thus by proceeding in terms of linked categories, I can keep the relation between social and symbolic dual organization constantly in the forefront of analysis. While each category sometimes varies independently of the other, some problems arising from the human categories are resolved or clarified by reference to how the Tewa conceptualize the linked spiritual counterparts. Thus we have the dual organization weaving in and out of the categories, becoming more relevant at certain times than at others. Yet it is the one concept which is relevant to all six, beginning even with the myth of origin. It thereby permits the data to be rendered into more order, in terms of the issues outlined in the preceding section, than any other single concept.

By this process, it is hoped, we obtain an understanding of how a society with dual organization achieves integration and continuity by overriding the division at crucial points in the life cycle, by devising systems of mediation when the division is potentially most disruptive, by making possible a network of crosscutting ties which transcend the division, and by equalizing the asymmetry within the division over a period of time. I am not attempting to state conclusions here, for the supporting evidence is yet to follow, and the conclusions are presented in more meaningful detail in the final chapter. Rather, I have outlined, in this section, the procedure by means of which I attempt to clarify the issues discussed in the preceding section.

One further point of clarification on procedure remains to be made. While it is traditional to present some historical summary in an introduction, insofar as the history of the people studied is known, I have refrained from doing so for two reasons. First, the history of San Juan and of the Tewa generally is largely inseparable from that of the Rio Grande Pueblo area as a whole, and the history of this area has been summarized with considerable detail by Aberle (1948), Dozier (1961, 1966), and others. For San Juan specifically, Aberle, Watkins, and Pitney (1940) have analyzed the available historical material to 1940, while I have elsewhere summarized subsequently published sources and added detailed demographic and other data on San Juan (Ortiz 1965*a*). As pointed out in the preface, moreover, Ford (1968) has presented additional ethnographic and historical information on San Juan which complements that given here.

The second and more important reason for the omission is that I do not wish to isolate historical facts of importance from their loci of relevance. I am concerned, throughout this work, not only with recorded history, but with myth, as indicated above, and with the archaeological record, insofar as it is known. Therefore, specific historical events are discussed where they are most meaningful, and no important area of understanding is sacrificed in the process.

2
In the Beginning

Within and around the earth, within and around
the hills, within and around the mountains,
your authority returns to you.

A TEWA PRAYER

The concern of this chapter is to outline the conceptual and symbolic basis of Tewa social behavior. First, the myth of origin and the early migrations of the Tewa is presented. It is a summary of the most detailed of seven recorded between 1958 and 1965, and it may be noted that most particulars are presented in others recorded by Parsons four decades earlier (1926, 1929, 1939). Next, the implications of the myth are examined in the context of how the Tewa conceptualize and classify their social, spiritual, and physical world today. Third, the key symbols and ideas which underly this system of classification and make it meaningful in behavioral terms are considered.

The Tewa were living in *Sipofene* beneath Sandy Place Lake far to the north. The world under the lake was like this one, but it was dark. Supernaturals, men, and animals lived together at this time, and death was unknown. Among the supernaturals were the first mothers of all the Tewa, known as "Blue Corn Woman, near to summer," or the Summer mother, and "White Corn Maiden, near to ice," the Winter mother.

These mothers asked one of the men present to go forth and explore the way by which the people might leave the lake. Three times the man refused, but on the fourth request he agreed. He went out first to the north, but saw only mist and haze; then he went successively to the west, south, and east, but again saw only mist and haze. After each of these four ventures he reported to the corn mothers and the people that he had seen nothing, that the world above was still *ochu*, "green" or "unripe."

13

Next the mothers told him to go to the above. On his way he came upon an open place and saw all the *tsiwi* (predatory mammals and carrion-eating birds) gathered there. There were mountain lions and other species of cat; wolves, coyotes, and foxes; and vultures and crows. On seeing the man these animals rushed him, knocked him down, and scratched him badly. Then they spoke, telling him: "Get up! We are your friends." His wounds vanished immediately. The animals gave him a bow and arrows and a quiver, dressed him in buckskin, painted his face black, and tied the feathers of the carrion-eaters on his hair. Finally they told him: "You have been accepted. These things we have given you are what you shall use henceforth. Now you are ready to go."

When he returned to the people he came as Mountain Lion, or the Hunt chief. This is how the first Made person came into being. On approaching the place where the people awaited, he announced his arrival by calling out like a fox (*de*). This is his call. The people rejoiced, saying, "We have been accepted."

The Hunt chief then took an ear of white corn, handed it to one of the other men, and said, "You are to lead and care for all of the people during the summer." To another man he handed another ear of white corn and told him, "You shall lead and care for the people during the winter." This is how, according to the myth, the Summer and Winter chiefs were instituted. They joined the Hunt chief as Made People.

Among the people were also six pairs of brothers called *Towa é*, literally "persons." To the first pair, who were *blue*, the newly appointed chiefs said: "Now you shall go forth to the north and tell us what you see." They went with the older one in the lead, but could not walk very far because the earth was soft. All they saw was a mountain to the north. They returned and reported their observations to the people. Next the *yellow* pair were sent out to the west, followed by the *red* ones who went south, the *white* ones who went east, and the *dark* (*nuxu in*) ones who went to the zenith. Each successive pair returned and reported that the earth was still soft. The yellow, red and white brothers reported seeing mountains in each direction, while the dark pair who went above reported seeing *agoyo nuxu*, a large star in the eastern sky. The first four pairs each picked up some mud and slung it toward each of the cardinal directions, thereby creating four *tsin*, or flat-topped hills.

Finally, the last pair of *Towa é*, the *all-colored* (*tsege in*) ones of the nadir, were sent out. They found that the ground had hardened somewhat, and they saw a rainbow in the distance. When they returned and reported this, the people made preparations to leave the lake. The Summer chief led the way, but as he stepped on the earth it was still soft and he sank to his ankles in the mud. Then the Winter chief came forth, and as he stepped on the ground there was hoarfrost. The ground became hard, and the rest of the people followed. The original corn mothers and other supernaturals, the predatory mammals, and the carrion-eaters remained beneath the lake. The *Towa é*, or brothers, went to the mountains of the directions to stand watch over the people.

As the people started southward many began to fall ill. The Winter and Summer chiefs decided that they were not yet complete; something else was needed. All returned once again to the home under the lake, and there the Hunt chief opened up Summer chief's corn mother. He discovered that the hollow core was filled with pebbles, ashes, and cactus spines. The Hunt chief replaced these with seeds and declared that one among the people was "of a different breath," or a witch, for the items discovered in the corn mother were recognized as items of witchcraft. This, then, marked the beginning of witchcraft and other forms of evil. In order to combat these and to make the people well, the *Ke* (medicine man) was created as the fourth Made person. The people then started out once again.

Before they proceeded very far south, they all had to return to the lake three times more, because the chiefs felt they were still not complete. At each subsequent return the *Kossa* and *Kwirana* (clowns), the Scalp chief, and the *Kwiyoh* (Women's society) were instituted, in that order. The *Kossa* and *Kwirana* were created to entertain the people when they grew tired and unhappy, the Scalp chief to insure success in warfare, and the Women's society to care for the scalps and to assist the Scalp chief. The people at last felt they were complete, and prepared to proceed southward once again.

Before doing so, the Hunt chief divided the people between the Summer chief and the Winter chief. Those who were to follow the Summer chief would proceed south along the mountains on the west side of the Rio Grande. The Winter chief and his group would proceed along the mountains on the east side of the river. The Summer People, as the former group came to be called, subsisted by agriculture and by gathering wild plant foods,[1] while the Winter People subsisted by hunting. Each group "took twelve steps" (made twelve stops) on this journey, and after each step they built a village and stayed for a day. "In that time one day was one year."[2] Those who died along the way—for death was now known—were buried near the village and stones piled over the graves.

At the twelfth step the two groups rejoined and founded a village called *Posi*, near present day Ojo Caliente. The village grew and prospered, and the people remained there for a long while. In time, however, an epidemic struck and the elders decided to abandon the village. Six different groups left and founded the six Tewa villages we know today. San Juan was founded first, so it became the "mother pueblo" for the other five.[3] Each of the six departing groups included both Winter and Summer people, so the chiefs and other Made People were replicated in each village. The origin and migration myth ends with an informant's observation:

> In the very beginning we were one people. Then we divided into Summer people and Winter people; in the end we came together again as we are today. But you can see we are still Summer people and Winter people.

In order to understand the transition from the mythical time before emergence to the present or historical time, let us explore the multiple symbolic referents of the Tewa concept of *seh t'a*. Here is a term which is truly pregnant with meaning. Literally translated, *seh t'a* means "dry food," from *seh* (soup, stew, or any other prepared dish), and *t'a* (hardened or dry). In ritual usage however, the range of referents of *seh* is extended to include all matter. Thus the origin myth compares the *ochu* (moist, green, and unripe) world before emergence to the *seh t'a* (dry, hardened, and ripe) world after emergence. When referring to the transition from one world level to another, then, *seh t'a* means "hardened matter," after the hardening of the earth upon the people's emergence from the lake.

Seh t'a is also used to distinguish older children from those up to the age of six or seven who have not yet attained the age of reason. Thus, to be not yet *seh t'a* is to be innocent or unknowing. I might sketch the general process of reasoning involved here as follows: to be innocent is to be not yet Tewa; to be not yet Tewa is to be not yet human; and to be not yet human is to be, in this use of the term, not entirely out of the realm of spiritual existence. The implications of this usage of *seh t'a* are presented in a more relevant context in the following chapter.

The term also embodies a sacred-profane distinction because what occurred in the lake, prior to emergence, is sacred. What has been occurring since is profane, because illness, death, and evil were introduced only after emergence.

But this distinction between the sacred and the profane is not as clear-cut as an orthodox Durkheimian interpretation would have it, because most Tewa myths and other oral traditions present the process of becoming *seh t'a* as a gradual one. It is a process which is said to have continued long after emergence. (Cf. Horton 1962, pp. 209–10 for a summary of the recent anthropological literature on the sacred-profane dichotomy).

Because of the number and complexity of its referents, I shall retain the literal meaning of the concept of *seh t'a* for the moment. Let us return to it now, by way of indicating how the Tewa view existence. Six levels or categories of being are recognized, as figure 1 illustrates. They are levels in the sense that they are discrete and

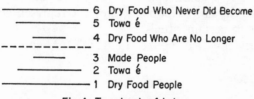

Fig. 1 Tewa levels of being

hierarchical. However, they are also cultural categories in the sense that they divide and classify *all* of Tewa social and supernatural existence. These categories, as such, are the primary concern of the remainder of this work; here the object is simply to identify them and indicate the larger system of classification of which they are a part.

Those of the first or lowest level are called, appropriately, "Dry Food People." These are the common Tewa who serve in no official capacity in the political or ritual system. The common Tewa are also called *Whe Towa* (Weed or Trash People), and *Nayi wha Towa* (Dust-dragging People), this latter term deriving from a prior practice whereby the common people swept the village before ritual and other festive occasions (cf. Curtis 1926). Both terms are intended to differentiate them clearly from the other categories. Level 2 indicates the *Towa é*, the social or natural counterparts of the six pairs of sibling deities who were with the Tewa before emergence. These constitute the core of the political organization of the Tewa. Level 3 represents the *Patowa*, or Made People. These include the members of the two moiety societies, the medicine men, the *Kwirana*, or "cold" clowns, the *Kossa*, or "warm" clowns, and the Hunt, Scalp, and Women's societies. They constitute a hierarchy of eight discrete but functionally interrelated organizations.

The next three categories may be regarded as supernatural counterparts of the first three. The "Dry Food Who Are No Longer" are the souls of the "Dry Food People"; that is to say, when a person of Category 1 dies, he becomes a spirit of Category 4. Level 5 represents the supernatural counterparts and patrons of Level 2. This category consists of the six pairs of sibling deities who were sent out to explore the world before emergence. Level 6, the "Dry Food Who Never Did Become," includes the souls of the Made people and all of the deities recognized by the Tewa, who were present before emergence. In other words, these deities never became *seh t'a* or dry food; they did not walk on the earth after it hardened. A whole host of spirits belong to this category, which is the Tewa counterpart of the more familiar *Kachina* of the Hopi. Like the Hopi *Kachinas*, they are represented by masked impersonators in certain rituals.[4]

Let us turn now to figure 2, which presents the principal

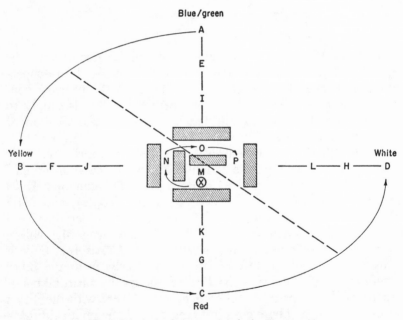

Fig. 2 Principal reference points in the Tewa world

reference points in the Tewa world as a series of tetrads or groups of four. It may be regarded as a counterpart, in the physical world, to figure 1. The color indicated is associated with each cardinal direction; and the arrows indicate the directional circuit, which usually proceeds sunwise and which usually also begins with north. The reasons for the reverse (anti-sunwise) circuit are given below. Taking the outermost tetrad first, the world of the Tewa is bounded by four sacred mountains, the same mountains which were seen by the first four pairs of sibling deities as they were sent out to explore the world in the origin myth.

Approximately sixty miles to the north of San Juan is *Tse Shu Pin* (Hazy or Shimmering Mountain); *Tsikomo* (Obsidian Covered Mountain) is about fifteen miles to the west; *Oku Pin* (Turtle Mountain) is about eighty miles to the south, and *Ku Sehn Pin* (Stone Man Mountain) is about twenty miles to the east. The northern mountain appears on topographic maps as Conjilon Peak; the second by its Tewa name, the third as Sandia Crest, just northeast of present day Albuquerque, and the last as Truchas Peak. The point of naming and locating them is to give proof of their objective existence, and to give some indication of the conceptual range of the Tewa world.[5]

These mountains are understood by the Tewa to be endowed with sacredness in several ways. First, a lake or pond is associated with each, and within this body of water live the "Dry Food Who Never Did Become," of the appropriate directional color. Secondly, there is a *nan sipu* or earth navel on top of each mountain, and within these live the *Towa é* who stand watch over the Tewa world.[6] The color classification is again replicated. The *Towa é* are distinguished from the spirits of Category 6 because they emerged with the people—or, more properly, led the way out— in the origin myth. Consequently, they are associated with the earth navels, which are represented by stone structures, rather than with the lakes or ponds.

The next tetrad (E,F,G,H) represents the sacred *Tsin* or flat-topped hills created by the *Towa é* of the directions. The northern hill is *Tema Yoh*, located just above the small Spanish village of La Madera. A few miles to the southwest is *Toma Yoh; Tun Yoh* is between San Ildefonso and Santa Clara Pueblos to the south, while *Tsi Mayoh* is near the Spanish village of the same name, east of San Juan.[7] Each of these hills is sacred because it is particularly dark and foreboding; each has a cave and/or tunnels running through it. All are believed to be inhabited by *Tsave Yoh*, the masked supernatural whippers who are impersonated by the *Towa é* and who constitute one of the Pueblo universals, being found in some manifestation from Taos to Hopi (Parsons 1929, p. 270). The *Towa é* of each directional color are also believed to watch over the Pueblo from these hills.[8] The question of how the

Towa é can be of the mountains and of the hills at the same time
is held in abeyance for now.

The third tetrad (I,J,K,L) represents the principal shrines of the
directions. First in the directional circuit is *Than Powa*, "Sun-
water-wind," represented by a pile of large stones at the northern
edge of the village. At the western edge of the village is *Awe
Kwiyoh* or Spider Woman, represented by a single stone; to the
south is *Nu Enu* or Ash Youth, also represented by a single stone.
Approximately one mile east of the village is a low hill with a
pile of stones on top; this is *Ti Tan He i* or "Large Marked Shield,"
the shrine of the east. There are numerous other shrines dotting
the landscape around each Tewa village, as is abundantly clear
from Harrington's (1916) account. But these four are the principal
ones of the directions, in the sense that regular, patterned usages
and meanings attach to these, and not to the others. Collectively
these shrines are known as *Xayeh T'a Pingeh*, "Souls-dwelling
Middle-places." Souls belong to a larger category of spirits and
man-associated objects called *xayeh*, which also includes fossilized
bone, sea shells, tools, weapons, and other objects rescued from
ruins; in essence, all objects which have been used by people are
endowed with sacredness because they are associated with the souls
and with the sacred past.

Three of the shrines are located in the middle of refuse dumps.
This follows from the ancient Pueblo practice, as noted in the
origin myth, of burying the dead near the village, and then leaving
a rock or pile of stones to mark the spot. Thus one informant
told me: "Long ago we buried the dead there and left a pile of
stones. Every pile of stones you see shows where the *xayeh* live,
for the dead have become *xayeh*." Parsons (1929, pp. 238, 244)
presents photographs of the northern shrine and notes that informants told her the shrines were on all four sides (p. 244). But
she did not discover that the shrines constituted a portion of a
complex and meaningful system of classification.

The final tetrad (M,N,O,P) represents the *bu pingeh* or dance
plazas within the village. All public rituals must be performed at
least four times, on each of the dance areas. Nor do the tetrads end
here, for there are other circuits within this circuit; in some rituals
the participants must face each of the four directions, and even
the accompanying songs are divided into four parts. The circuit
here is seen as proceeding from the south plaza to the west, then
north, and finally east; in other words north and south are reversed,
and the circuit becomes anti-sunwise. The Tewa explain this apparent discrepancy as follows. Long ago all of the houses of San

Juan were grouped around the south plaza; this was the only plaza. As the pueblo grew to the north, east and west, other dance areas were set aside in each direction. The available information from the mid-nineteenth century, consisting of photographs, church records, and the location of the church itself, tends to justify this claim, at least to the extent that there were no houses facing what are now the west and east plazas. Toward the end of the nineteenth century the north plaza was already in existence, as an undated photograph of San Juan published in Winship (1896) demonstrates.[9]

A more important form of objective proof is provided by point *x* on figure 2. It represents the *Nan echu kwi nan sipu pingeh*, or "Earth mother earth navel middle place." This is the sacred center of the village, and it is located on the south plaza. Ritual dances and other performances must continue to be initiated here, as the Tewa explain it, because this is the true center of the village.[10] I might go a little further and say that this is the center of centers, or the navel of navels. The construction of the respective earth navels will help to clarify this apparent play on words. Whereas the earth navels on the mountaintops are formed by a close arrangement of stones shaped like an open-ended keyhole (see footnote 6), the mother earth navel consists of a loose arrangement of stones forming a circle. Whereas the mountain earth navels are opened in only one direction, the mother earth navel is open to all four directions, for here the village exists all around it, rather than far off in a single direction. But while the mother earth navel is a sacred center like the others, it is also a condensation of the others. An example will serve to clarify this point.

Late each winter the medicine men of the village plant the seeds of all cultigens and those of plants utilized as food in the mother earth navel; this is how nature is reawakened each year. The medicine men are attributed the power to reach right into the ground to deposit the seeds deep within the earth. In fact, the Tewa believe that there is a shaft or tunnel within the navel which leads straight down into the earth. *Towa é* who have stood watch for the medicine men when they have performed this annual duty often claim that the latter all but disappear into the tunnel when planting the seeds.

Without belaboring the point further, let me draw the contrast —and similarity—between the two kinds of centers as follows. The mountain earth navels gather in blessings from all around and direct them *inward* toward the village; the mother earth navel is the *source* of all these blessings, so they are directed *outward* in all directions. By the system of ideas at work here, everything good and desirable stays within the Tewa world. This is how relentless and pervasive this tetramerous aspect of Tewa symbolic classification is.

Figures 1 and 2 may now be put together, keeping in mind that Categories 1, 2, and 3 become 4, 5, and 6, respectively, in the supernatural realm. We note that Level 6 on figure 1 is represented by the four sacred mountains of figure 2; Level 5 is represented by the sacred mesas, and Level 4 by the shrines near the village. To go one step further, we may draw the six levels of existence as the Tewa see them—as six differentiated but continuous levels.

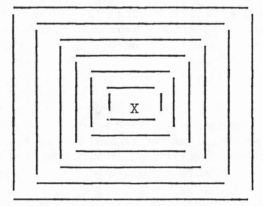

Fig. 3 Figure 1 and Figure 2 combined

Let X represent the earth navel, or sacred center once again. Now, since the outermost points on figure 2 contain earth navels as well as representing the dwelling places of the most sacred beings of the Tewa world, and since the sacred center itself is located in the conceptual center of the village, we seem to have an opposition between sacred and sacred. At least there is no simple opposition between the center and the periphery.

In justification of the foregoing interpretation of the Tewa system of classification let me add, first, that six levels of being are recognized because *all six* of them are simultaneously represented at some Tewa rituals. Secondly, one of my informants showed he understood the underlying dialectic of figure 2 by a remark which may be translated as follows:

> Remember that the words and the method of delivery of all prayers and speeches are the same; only the places mentioned are different. If you are a Made person you always pray to

and invoke the authority of the mountains, and the "Dry Food Who Never Did Become." If you are a *Towa é* you always mention the mesas and the *Towa é*.

Now that I have noted how human and spiritual existence is classified into six levels, and how these levels relate to the Tewa classification of horizontal space, I shall turn to the vertical classification. I noted that in the origin myth there is no mention of multiple underworld levels as among the Hopi, Zuni, or even the neighboring Keresan Pueblos (cf. White 1964). Rather, the underworld was like this one; it was broken in topography. Thus the Hunt chief's encounter with the animals of prey is to be understood as occurring on a different elevation of the same world level. Informants were rather explicit on this point. Moreover, there is no mention of multiple underworld levels in the several origin myths recorded in San Juan since the 1880's (Bandelier 1890, I:304–5; Parsons 1926, 1929). From all accounts available, the Tewa recognize only three cosmic levels; the below, the middle, and the above.

The above, like the below, is regarded as being like the middle, but there is relatively little concern with it; most of spiritual existence is attributed to the below, and all human existence occurs on the middle level. The celestial bodies, the more prominent of which are named and conceptualized as anthropomorphic, are believed to live there much as do the beings of the other levels, but as a sub-system of classification the above is almost undeveloped. The large historical and ethnographic record on the Tewa is also mute on this point. If the point that the Tewa are primarily concerned with the middle and the below may be accepted, we may now consider how the entire system of classification becomes meaningful to the Tewa in operational terms.

The quotation which opens this chapter now becomes relevant: "Within and around the earth, within and around the hills, within and around the mountains, your authority returns to you. . . ." This statement, a portion of a Tewa prayer, is one of the most recurrent whenever a Tewa addresses a spirit. The Dry Food person, whenever he approaches the shrines near the village to leave an offering, the *Towa é*, as he hands the symbols of his office over to his successor at the end of his term, and the Made person, whenever he has just completed any ritual involving the use of sacred objects, all recite this simple statement. At times the words "food" (white cornmeal) or "clothing" (feathers) are substituted for "authority," but whatever a person is returning, and to what-

ever category of spirit, it only returns after journeying through
the entire Tewa underworld. The elaborate conceptual distinction
between the three categories of spirit becomes, in a sense, erased.
To the Tewa this prayer is a simple formula to bring the various
categories of spirit together again. Thus, these categories, as the
three human categories, are not rigidly differentiated. This underlying unity helps to clarify, in part, how the *Towa é* may be of
the mountains and of the hills at the same time. Moreover, in the
origin myth they *saw* the former and *created* the latter.

The three principal sacred points at which one may communicate with a spirit are the lakes and ponds, the earth navels, and the
shrines. Although each of these is conceived to be a point of
entrance to the whole underworld, the first are used exclusively
for the spirits of Category 6, and the last for the *xayeh*, or souls.
The earth navels, on the other hand, represent an ambivalent category consisting of three different types. The first, as discussed
above, consists of those found on the sacred mountains and hills.
These are primarily associated with the *Towa é*, but one may place
offerings here to the other categories of spirit. The second type is
found on hilltops at about the same elevation as the sacred hills,
or in open places in the lowlands, but these are addressed exclusively to game animals. They are built near areas where the
species of game to which they are addressed are known to congre-
gate, or through which they are known to pass. These, too, are
keyhole-shaped, but smaller than those on the mountains. The final
type, of which there is only one, is, of course, the mother earth
navel at the center of the village.

The earth navels on the four sacred mountains are also symbolic
of something else. They serve not only as the entrances to the
below, but as the points at which the above, the middle, and the
below come closest to intersecting in each direction. This is rather
an abstract notion, but bearing in mind that the Tewa recognize
the three cosmic levels, let us look at two examples which lead
inescapably to the above conclusion. First, an informant once gave
this thoughtful response to my persistent inquiries regarding the
meaning of the earth navels:

> An earth navel is like an airport. You notice how airplanes,
> no matter where they go, always have to return to an airport.
> In the same way all things—game, people and spirits—always
> return to the earth navel.

It would be difficult to find a better analogy for the symbolism of
the center.

The spirits of Category 6, as deities, are the sources of all of man's needs. Among the Tewa these consist of the twin concerns of rainfall and game, especially the former. A second example will further clarify the issue. During the autumn of 1964, two informants and I climbed *Tsikomo*, the mountain of the west. As we neared the top, one of them remarked at the number of trees which had been felled by lightning, and how much more rainfall there was at that elevation. These and the almost perpetual presence of clouds overhead were signs of unusual sacredness; the spirits were unusually active here because this was where they lived. In the Tewa's—as all Pueblo Indians'—unceasing quest for rainfall, that which seems to bring them closer to the source of this precious moisture, is endowed with unusual sacredness.

Inasmuch as the six categories of existence—one triad constituting the plane of being, the other triad the plane of becoming—are fundamentally cultural categories, the transition within categories and between planes must be made clear. The implications of the simple prayer and the symbolism of the center have been explored in some detail for just this reason; they render meaningful the entire system of classification as a system in operation.

The crucial question may now be posed: What has all of this to do with dual organization? Admittedly very little, for it is on this level that the dual organization is overridden and submerged. The dotted line separating north and east from west and south on figure 2 has a reality of its own, but this will only become apparent and relevant in the following chapters, as will the unconsidered aspects of the origin myth.

Nonetheless, enough has been said to confront two of the basic issues presented in Lévi-Strauss's analysis of dual organizations (1963*a*). First, he places too fundamental a reliance on his notion of "triadism," by which he means not only a system of three parts, but one of two parts which are in an asymmetrical relationship to each other. These latter he regards as "triads, disguised as dyads through the logical subterfuge of treating as two homologous terms a whole that actually consists of a pole and an axis, which are not entities of the same nature" (1963*a*, p. 154). Returning now to figure 1, we note that the most inclusive cultural categories recognized by the Tewa constitute a hexad, or a hexamerous structure, to keep the terminology consistent. If, on the other hand, we are concerned with only the social or natural categories, we would see it as a triad which is replicated in the supernatural realm. Yet an analysis based on only one triad would result in only a partial understanding of the many implications which each triad has for the other when all six categories are represented on the ground, as it were. The continuity between human and spiritual existence is too fundamentally rooted in the data, so that to consider less than all six categories is to run the risk of understanding nothing. The analogy drawn elsewhere by Schneider is relevant here as well:

> It is not possible to operate like those in the story of the blind men and the elephant and hope that if only we can put enough blind men on the elephant we will get a good factual description of the beast—the total elephant [Schneider 1965, p. 78].

The massive ethnographic record on the Tewa bears mute testimony to the truth of this point.[11] I can only conclude that if my task is to understand how whole societies and whole cultures operate, then Lévi-Strauss's triadic structure, the maximal structure he considered, which he regards as a "formula" (1960, p. 47) to explain away the dual organization, would only impose an arbitrary limitation on the facts at hand.

Lévi-Strauss's notion of "concentric dualism" is also crucial to the development of his thesis. By this he refers to one or another type of opposition between the center and the periphery which he finds reflected in each of his ethnographic examples. In each instance his argument is buttressed by a circular village structure; this is what is used to justify the concentric designation of the phenomena. Here again the Tewa present problems, for they do not have a circular village structure but one of four parts in which the corners are always kept open. This situation was true of San Juan even in 1598, as Villagrá, the chronicler for the Oñate expedition of that year notes:

> El Pueblo, no constaua ni tenia
> Mas que una sola plaça bien quadrada
> Con quatro entradas solas curios puestos,
> Despues do auerlos bien fortaleado,
> Con tiros de campaña, y con mosquetes.
> [*Historia de la Nueva Mexico*; quoted
> in Bandelier 1892, II:59]

For at least three and a half centuries then, the Tewa have constructed their village in quarters, just as they divide and classify the physical world by quarters.[12]

Nor is there any simple opposition between the center and the periphery in the Tewa world, as noted in figure 3. Rather, each point on each of the tetrads is sacred and meaningful, albeit in a somewhat different way, and no Tewa would say that the earth navel on the distant mountaintop is any less sacred or important than the earth navel at the center of the village. Moreover, we are already too well acquainted with the concept of multiple centers through the work of Eliade (1958, pp. 374–78, 380–82; 1959, passim) to let this remain an issue. It is to emphasize this point that figure 3 is sketched in just that form. The relation of the Tewa world to what is outside of it is further outlined briefly in note 19, chapter 5.

Let me summarize briefly what I have sought to do in this chapter, first citing the definition of world view I have found most useful in approaching the tasks set forth at the beginning of the chapter. Clifford Geertz defines world view as "a people's picture of the way things, in sheer actuality are, their concept of nature, of self, of society. It contains their most comprehensive ideas of order" (1957, pp. 421–22). I have attempted to determine, then, how a reasonable Tewa everyman would answer for himself questions such as the following. Who am I? Where did I come from? How did I get here? With whom do I move through life? What are the boundaries of the world within which I move? What kind of order exists within it? How did suffering, evil, and death come to be in this world? What is likely to happen to *me* when I die? The general point of view from which I have approached the hypothetical Tewa everyman is the "view of man as a symbolizing, conceptualizing, meaning-seeking animal which . . . cannot live in a world it cannot understand" (Geertz 1957, p. 436). And in so doing I have attempted to define, as Geertz would have it, the general fund of meaning in terms of which the Tewa interpret experience and impose order on their world. To be sure, I have done so in so general a manner that the Tewa everyman has been submerged in the process, but he will be regained in the next chapter and the two to follow.

To set the stage for the next three chapters I might point to an observation made by Eggan about the field of social anthropology more than a dozen years ago: "The interrelationship between ritual and social structure and the mediating role of myth represent the new frontiers of social anthropological research" (1955, p. 502). Anthropology has, during the ensuing years, begun to explore intensively this new frontier, as Eggan foresaw, but we still need more detailed case studies attempting to determine the nature of this mutual relationship. The need is especially great in the Southwest, which has not received as much attention during the past dozen years as during previous decades, and, therefore, has not shared in recent developments in theory as much as it might have. This first chapter, as the title is intended to communicate, is a beginning toward that end, a logical first step toward a direct confrontation of the larger problem Eggan poses. The Tewa themselves seem to anticipate the proper procedure for the kind of understanding I seek, as they preface their answers to most questions about their traditional culture with the words *heh pare owe,* "in the beginning."

Let us turn now to an emphasis upon the ritual and social dimensions of the problem I have posed, dimensions which could only be touched upon in a programmatic way thus far.

3

The Dry Food People and the Dry Food Who Are No Longer

In the very beginning we were one people. Then we
divided into Summer people and Winter people;
in the end we came together again as we are today.

A TEWA

In the preceding chapter I identified the six categories into which
the Tewa classify all human and supernatural existence, and I outlined the larger system of classification of which these categories
are a part. In this chapter I will consider in detail what implications the system of classification has in structuring the behavior of
the Dry Food People, or common Tewa. I also want to demonstrate the nature of the linkage between the Dry Food People
and the "Dry Food Who Are No Longer," and in this way return
to the unresolved implications of the dotted line on figure 2. The
reader is reminded that the Dry Food People do not constitute an
operational social group; rather, they constitute a cultural category
to which anyman and everyman belong at some time in their lives.

This being so, the procedure adopted in this chapter is to analyze
six rites of passage that every Dry Food person normally undergoes
in his lifetime, noting the differences between the moieties. I have
labeled specific rites by the phase that appears to be dominant
within them, following the tripartite diachronic classification developed by van Gennep (1960). Thus, in the following section
when I discuss the naming ritual and the process of recruitment
into the moieties, I label each a "rite of incorporation," because the
separation and transition phases which ideally precede incorporation cannot be as clearly delineated. This does not mean, of course,
that they are completely absent; only that they are not as clearly
evident as the final phase, incorporation. Van Gennep himself
cautions that this is often the case when specific rites are analyzed:

> Thus, although a complete scheme of rites of passage theo-
> retically includes preliminal rites (rites of separation), liminal

rites (rites of transition) and postliminal rites (rites of incorporation), in specific instances these three types are not always equally important or equally elaborated [van Gennep 1960, p. 11].

Since my primary concern is not the rites themselves but the part they play in the society, my simplified procedure may be accepted with the above qualification.

In the third section I discuss separately Tewa marriage and death rituals, emphasizing especially the separation and reintegration aspects of the latter. In the final section I return to the issue of what the dual organization means and does not mean in the lives of the common Tewa, for it is in an analysis of these six rites of passage that the dual organization comes most clearly to the forefront. In this way also, the myth of origin and system of classification outlined in the preceding chapter come alive, as it were, for the first pair of linked categories.

At birth each Tewa child is attended by two midwives, neither of whom need necessarily be related to him. These women take over the mother's care from the time labor starts until four days after birth. They hold no formal office in the ritual organization; rather, they are specialists in childbirth who have acquired their knowledge through years of practice. There must always be two in attendance at childbirth, but often someone from within the household assists the specialist, who is called the "umbilical cord-cutting mother." During this four-day period both mother and child remain indoors, and relatives and other villagers who wish to do so may visit. Each visitor symbolically gathers in, with both hands, all illness, sloth, and misfortune which may later befall the child, and casts it to the west, "beyond Mount *Tsikomo*, to the land of the Navajo." In this symbolic gesture the Tewa wish the child long life by taking all illness and evil and casting it out of the sacred world to the land of their traditional enemies.

At dawn on the fourth day after birth, the "umbilical cord-cutting mother," or naming mother, for convenience, and her assistant take the newborn child out to present him to the sun, and to bestow a name on him. This naming ritual is the first important rite of passage for each Tewa child, so it may be outlined in some detail. On the night before the ritual, a number of objects to be used are carefully set out by the naming mother. These include two perfect ears of corn—one white and one blue—a variety of ground plant medicines, a cigarette of native tobacco, a native hand broom, a small pottery bowl, and a variety of *xayeh*. The *xayeh*, mentioned in the preceding chapter, are man-associated objects which are endowed with spiritual value, because they are believed to be the tangible manifestations of ancestral souls. The particular *xayeh* used in this context include seashells, stone axes, arrow points, and a pair of long smooth pieces of white quartz, one of which is grooved so that the other fits over it. These last are called "lightning stones," because when rubbed together in the dark they glow and give off sparks.

Well before dawn that morning the naming mother arises, takes the lightning stones, and rubs them briskly together, "to cast lightning" (sparks) to the north, west, south, east, up, and down, in that order. This symbolic act is an attempt to induce rainfall, for rainfall is regarded as a particularly auspicious sign that the spirits are pleased with the child. Next, water is placed in the pottery bowl, and smoke from the cigarette is quickly blown over it, with the ashes also being flicked into the water. The various medicines are then put into the water, followed by the household ritual objects. At each step the items are first offered to the spirits of the six directions, in order to invoke their presence in the undertaking. Finally, just before leaving for the infant's home, she addresses other *xayeh* which are buried in the four corners of every Tewa home and which are called "life root giving stones":

> Give me wisdom and lead me to the place where
> the child of man, child of woman is
> You, male spirits, female spirits who watch over
> my home
> I have placed before you the food [white cornmeal]
> of tradition
> Make my heart right and guide my thoughts
> Take me to where the child of the spirits is.

This portion of the ritual is called *t'amu xeh piyeh*, "going forth at dawn with power." These preparations completed, the naming mother and assistant go out with the infant to greet the rising sun, just as its first rays appear over the Sangre de Cristo Mountains. The naming mother holds the infant and the two ears of corn, while the assistant makes a sweeping inward motion over them with the hand broom, to gather in blessings for the child. The infant and the two ears of corn are proffered to the six directions in the same order as above if it is winter, or between the autumnal and vernal equinoxes. A prayer is said softly as they turn:

> Here is a child who has been given to us
> Let us bring him to manhood and womanhood

You who are dawn youths and dawn maidens
You who are winter spirits
You who are summer spirits
We have brought out a child that you may
    bring him to manhood and womanhood
That you may give him life
And not let him become alienated
Take, therefore [proffering the child and the corn],
    dawn beings, winter spirits, summer spirits
Give him good fortune we ask of you.

If the rite is held during the summer, or between the vernal and autumnal equinoxes, the directional circuit begins with the south and proceeds west-north-east-up, and then down. In this case the summer spirits, who are identified with the south, are also named first. Otherwise, the rite is exactly the same for all Tewa infants.

When the prayer is finished, the name is bestowed by the naming mother, as she invokes Blue Corn Woman and White Corn Maiden, the original mothers who were with the people before emergence, and from whom it is believed each child acquires his soul at birth. They are symbolically represented during this ritual by the two similar-colored ears of corn. The name itself is selected from some natural phenomenon appropriate to the season, or some unusual occurrence of the particular morning, or the name of some distinguished ancestor is revived, in hopes that the child will later manifest the same good qualities. This is the name by which the child is known to the village in everyday discourse for the rest of his life. When the attendants reenter the house, they bathe the child for the first time. The ears of corn are placed on either side of the infant's cradle-board, and remain there for a period of twelve days. Afterwards they are carefully wrapped and stored for planting the following spring. The pot is also stored; it will always belong to the child, and it must never be used for the same purpose again. The duties of the naming mothers are now over, and they may return home. For their labors they receive large quantities of cornmeal and other foodstuffs, which they divide between them.

A few of the more significant implications of this rite may be drawn together before I proceed to the next. First, this is a "rite of incorporation" (van Gennep 1960) of the child into the society; in the words of the Tewa, it is intended "to bring the child in out of the darkness," where he has no identity. But it is a ritual recognition of his identity as a member of the whole society rather than of any subgroup within it, for I have said that the naming mothers are selected without regard to kinship relations. Moreover, as

Parsons noted in presenting a lengthy listing of Tewa personal names (1929), the names are generally—but not consistently—sex-specific and season-specific, but nothing else. In both respects the Tewa naming ritual contrasts sharply with that of their clan-based Keresan neighbors, where a sister, father's sisters or some other female relatives of the father confer a clan-specific name on the child. This point of contrast is significant, because I have noted that no social groups other than the Winter and Summer moieties were given explicit recognition in the myth of origin and system of classification.

The presence of two naming mothers, the use of two ears of corn, and the seasonal differences in the ritual permit another important observation. Blue Corn Woman and White Corn Maiden represent the mothers of the Summer and Winter moieties, respectively. They are symbolically represented by the two ears of corn, but also by the two naming mothers. That is to say, while the naming mothers are selected on the basis of ritual knowledge rather than moiety membership, there must be two because there were two original mothers. Yet they act together in this ritual because its purpose is to incorporate the child into the society at large. The dual organization is also recognized in the seasonal divergence, but it is almost a perfunctory recognition, since it is submerged in the purpose of the ritual.

Sometime during the first year of the child's life, the second important rite of passage—and the first leading to incorporation into his own moiety—is held. It is called "water giving," and it is held once each year by each moiety chief, in his own home. The Winter chief conducts his rite in October, the Summer chief in late February or March; in other words, each holds the rite during the period in which he serves as head of the whole village. Let me outline the Winter version, for convenience, and then compare the two. Four days before the rite is to be held, the Winter chief sends the *Towa é*, or political officials, of his moiety to notify the parents of eligible infants and those new brides of the opposite moiety who have married Winter men during the past year. The criterion of eligibility is that the father or husband be of the Winter moiety. I leave the brides for now, and consider them in detail when discussing marriage. On the appointed day, the mothers appear at the chief's home with the infants, and take their places standing along the walls of an outer room. All the mothers wear traditional black woolen dresses, with one shoulder bare, and white buckskin boots. Each mother also brings a basket of flour or bread to give to the chief.

Meanwhile, in the chief's private inner sanctuary, which also serves as headquarters for him and his assistants, he and the latter have been busy with preparations since the previous night. A sand painting has been carefully constructed on the bare earthen floor, and on it an altar has been built. This altar consists of the moiety fetishes in the chief's keeping: Rain Standing Youth, which is brought out atop a long pole during relay races at the summer solstice; a cholla cactus plant called "the grandmother," the white spines of which symbolize icicles; and a spear, called the "Ice Governing Stick," which is his primary symbol of office. There is also a pair of folding painted sticks, somewhat resembling a carpenter's rule; these are called "world lengtheners." In the center of the altar are the chief's corn mother, encased in a ring of eagle feathers, other personal figurines, and a terraced, elaborately decorated pottery bowl in which a medicinal mixture has been prepared. All of these are said to have been brought up by the Winter chief from the original lake home, along with the knowledge of their use and meaning. The chief and his male assistants are all dressed in identical white buckskin kilts which are fringed with metal tubes and have serpents painted across the front. Their moccasins are also white, but they have red tongues. In the sand painting, personal adornment, and painting on the ritual objects, red and white are emphasized. Other colors are used, of course, but these two are the ones specifically identified with the Winter moiety; white because it symbolizes winter moisture, and red because it is a rouge used by men in warfare and hunting.

When all other preparations are completed, one final character appears on the scene. There is the bark of a fox outside, and the Hunt chief appears at the door. He is dressed in long flowing buckskin, his face painted red, a feather of one of the carrion-eaters tied to his hair, and a long bow in his hand. This, as we will recall, is the picture given in the origin myth; it is the classic pose of the Hunt chief. He is told, in a ritual exchange with the Winter chief, that he is needed once again for water giving. After formally indicating his acceptance, he proceeds to take each mother and infant into the inner sanctuary.

As the mothers begin to arrive, two male *Sehshu*, or lay assistants of the chief, stand on one side of the altar and proceed to cast the two parts of the "world lengthener" toward each other, so that the ends almost meet, and then pull them back. This symbolic act is intended to insure a long life for each of the infants. At the same time two female *Sehshu* stand on the other side of the altar, waiting to receive the infants. By prior arrangement with the parents of each infant, all those within the inner sanctuary, including the chief, have agreed to serve as sponsors for one or another of the infants. The only requirement is that the sponsor come from among the chief and his several assistants; thus one of the men or women may serve as sponsor to several infants of either sex, while another may serve as sponsor to only one.

Once inside, the female *Sehshu* take the infants, while the mothers stand to one side. The *Sehshu* hold each infant while the Winter chief recites a short prayer over him, and administers a drink of the sacred medicinal water from an abalone shell, thereby welcoming him into the moiety. He also administers a new name, which is supplied by the sponsor, to each child. This "water giving name," unlike the one he uses through life, is moiety-specific; that is to say, it is the name of one of the spirits of the category "Dry Food Who Never Did Become." This new name is only used if the child, when he has grown up, impersonates the spirits of this category in ritual, or joins the Winter moiety society as a Made person.

When all of the infants have been given water and named, the rite is over. Each mother leaves her basket of bread or meal for the Winter chief, and he in turn gives her meat of some game fowl (usually migratory). The Hunt chief is, however, the one actually to hand it over. The bread and meal are later divided up among the Winter moiety society members, the lay assistants, and the Hunt chief, although the Winter chief keeps the largest portion.

The Summer moiety version of water giving, which is held in late February or early March, is structurally the same as the Winter, but it differs markedly in symbolism. The Summer mothers are barefoot when they enter the Summer chief's home, and their feet are painted yellow. While the Winter chief and his male assistants wear white buckskin kilts, their Summer moiety counterparts wear black woolen kilts. A sand painting and altar are constructed, but the principal object on the altar is a long wooden rainbow; this is the functional equivalent of the Winter chief's "Ice Governing Stick." A "world stretcher" is also present, as is the terraced medicinal water bowl, and a corn mother. The female counterpart to Rain Standing Youth is also prominently displayed. But in these complementary symbols the colors black, green, and yellow—representing rain-laden clouds, growing crops, and sunshine, respectively—are emphasized.[1] These are the colors associated with the moiety. The Summer mothers also present the

Summer chief with a sweet broth made from fermented grain, in addition to cornmeal or bread. The Summer chief in turn shares the broth with the mothers.

The principal difference, however, comes in the selection of sponsors. The Summer parents are not restricted to members of the moiety society and lay assistants, for they may select any Summer adult *of the same sex as their child.* In other words, they are restricted as to sex, but not, as with the Winter moiety, to any particular group of people within the moiety. A part of the reason for this interesting divergence is that while the Winter and Summer moieties are identified with maleness and femaleness, respectively, the qualities of both sexes are believed present in men, while women are only women; in other words, there is a clear relationship of asymmetry between the sexes which is expressed through the moieties. Let me try to clarify this point, for it is a recurrent one in the relations between the moieties. First, the chief of the Winter moiety is referred to as *father* during the period when he heads the village (from the autumnal to the vernal equinox) and *mother* during the other half of the year, when the Summer chief is in charge. The latter, on the other hand, is always referred to as *mother* throughout the year; he is never called *father.* Until it was understood, this point proved a source of considerable confusion during field work. Secondly, men may impersonate women in rituals, but never the reverse; thus, when the spirits of Category 6 are impersonated, men come as female spirits, while women are excluded completely. Thirdly, the standard phrase of encouragement to men about to undertake a demanding task is "Be a woman, be a man," while the phrase to a woman in similar circumstances is simply, "Be a woman." Fourth and finally, during the naming ceremony when the spirits are addressed, they are asked for assistance in bringing a male infant to "womanhood and manhood," while the request for a female infant is for assistance to bring her to womanhood only. As is obvious, they are quite consistent in making this distinction on several levels, in both group and individual rituals. Thus, by a process of reasoning which is by no means entirely clear, the Summer moiety represents sexual specificity, while the Winter moiety disregards the fact of sexual dimorphism in selecting ceremonial sponsors.[2]

The fact that the Hunt chief participates in both rituals introduces another important process, that of mediation. Within the society, he is regarded as *te pingeh*, "of the middle of the structure," which is to say that he is a mediator between moieties. He represents hunting, which is a general male activity. Thus, while the meat-plant food distinction between the moieties—as first noted in the origin myth—is present in the respective rituals, it is mediated by the undeniable fact that hunting is a general male activity. While the Hunt chief's role in the ritual is minimal in contrast to the importance accorded him in the myth of origin, he is still a mediator between the moieties.

In this rite then, the dual organization comes dramatically to the forefront, for, unlike the naming ritual, which is a rite of incorporation into the whole society, water giving is a rite of incorporation into the moiety.[3] The differences noted between the two rites are part of what forms the basis of dual organization, both socially and symbolically, among the Tewa.

The third rite in the general life cycle is a "rite of transition" (van Gennep 1960) within each moiety. It is held when the child is between six and ten years of age. The upper age is not a rigid limit, but the lower one is; that is to say, the child must be at least six years of age. Here one of the special significations of the term "dry food" becomes relevant. Two meanings other than the literal one were given in the preceding chapter, but there is a fourth and final meaning. Children who are less than six years old are said to be "not yet *seh t'a*," that is, "innocent" or "unknowing." This third rite, called "water pouring," marks the transition from the carefree innocent state of early childhood to the Dry Food People. Once again, for convenience, I shall follow through the Winter moiety version and then note the differences.

Winter water pouring is held every four years, shortly after the water giving rite. Once again the Winter chief and his assistants are in charge of preparations, which this time begin twelve days before the ritual. There are two principal reasons for the long period of advance preparations. First, the rite is held in the kiva, or communal ritual house. The kiva is the earthly representation of the original, primordial home under the lake, and like the latter, it is conceptualized as being twelve "steps" away from the village. It will be recalled that, in the origin myth, the Tewa took twelve "steps" in their southward route of migration to the village of Posi, from which they divided and founded the six modern Tewa villages. The present kiva is rectangular and incorporated into one of the village houseblocks, as Laski (1959) shows in a detailed map of San Juan. However, in an earlier village which was occupied during the period of Spanish exploration and colonization, informants point out an area in the center of the ruin as being the site of a *circular* kiva. They add that the "earth mother earth navel middle place" was in the center of the kiva floor, rather than outside, as it is in the present village. The ruin is shaped like a horseshoe, and the kiva could conceivably have once been twelve steps from the nearest habitation area. This matter of conceptualization can be pushed too far, of course, in the sense of demanding too much empirical evidence of its validity. But there is very often a good correspondence between what the Tewa think and what they do.

The second reason will clarify the issue further. Water pouring involves the appearance of impersonators of the deities of Category 6. Since these deities journey, symbolically, from the same primordial home, they too must take twelve steps. In fact, when their journey is traced during the ritual, they do make twelve stops, of which the kiva itself is the last. There is also some evidence that the original migration was made in several steps, for informants point out other ruins on either side of the Rio Grande, which they add were occupied by the Winter and Summer people during the migration. To be sure, the number of ruins does not add up to twelve in either case, but much of the message of the origin myth is clarified.[4] The symbolism of the number twelve also serves to emphasize the point that the water pouring ritual makes children Dry Food People, for the process as outlined in the origin myth is dramatically reenacted during the ritual.

To return to the preparations again, during the first eight days there are tryouts for those who are to impersonate the "Dry Food Who Never Did Become"; the kiva is cleaned and repaired; and items of ritual paraphernalia are assembled. These preparations do not include the children, but their involvement comes suddenly on the fourth morning before the ritual. At this time the boys are made to carry a load of firewood which they have chopped themselves, and the girls a basket of cornmeal which they have ground themselves, to the homes of their sponsors for water giving. They do this on each of the four days, and also refrain from bathing during the entire period.

Unless the sponsor has died in the intervening years, the same one is retained. Otherwise, a new one is selected by the child's parents, in accordance with the same rules as during water giving. This time, however, their relations are more intimate, for in exchange for the wood or flour the sponsor most instruct the child in traditional beliefs and practices covering most aspects of life in the village. He also feeds the child at least once each day, although the food is provided by the child's parents. On the fourth night, the deities come to the kiva, and the child may go to watch them, theoretically for the first time in his life. Heretofore, he has hidden under his mother's blanket, for he was uninstructed; henceforth, he will take a place of his own in the kiva, along with other children his own age. Only the members of his moiety attend. After the coming of the gods, the sponsor bathes the child, and this terminates their period of intimate association. The name of the ritual comes from the fact that the child is bathed by having water poured over him.

The following morning, in a classic manifestation of the principle of reciprocity, all of the people of the Winter moiety invite the Summer people to eat in their homes. The feasting continues all day. That night the gods come once again, but this time the opposite moiety is also invited to attend the ritual performance, where the Winter gods give them gifts of food. This completes the rite of transition from the ambiguous role of child to the general category of Dry Food People, but it is a transition which takes place within the organization of the Winter moiety. The actual change is reflected in the fact that the child is given sex-specific duties from this time on. If the sponsor is of the opposite sex, this kind of instruction is given by his or her spouse. In any case, sex-specific instructions are kept to a minimum, since members of the opposite sex may be and often are paired. What is important, however, is that the relationship between sponsor and child is continued and further solidified.

The Summer version differs markedly, even more than in water giving. It, too, is held two weeks or so after water giving, but only once every seven years. The explanation given for the discrepancy —if it may be called an explanation—is that the Winter people must hold their rite more often, because they are limited to the members of the moiety society and their assistants in their choice of sponsors. Summer parents, it will be recalled, may select any adult of the moiety who is of the same sex as their child; consequently, they may hold their rite less frequently. But this does not tell us why the numbers seven and four specifically are used. I could find only one possible answer after many years of analyzing the evidence on the respective rituals: the rites cannot be held in adjacent seasons because the energies of most of the people of the village go into planning and executing the ritual, and foodstuffs, bird feathers, and other ritual items must be set aside beginning a year in advance. While I cannot here go into the total pattern of consumption and exchange, it is enormous; thus, if the rites were held in adjacent seasons, they would be drawing from the produce of the same agricultural season. The subsistence economy simply could not take this kind of strain. Now, if we take the various combinations of numbers totaling eleven, we would find that only six and five would coincide less frequently than seven and four. Six and five are not used as sacred numeral classifiers, but seven and four most definitely are. Of these, four predominates overwhelmingly of course, but seven is important in the sense that there are seven directions, including the middle place. Thus in a complete classification of directional color symbolism, which is sometimes brought into play in myth and ritual, the seventh direction includes all of the other colors. This is a formal explanation which assumes that the Tewa were extremely rational in working out this system, but then why not? The problem was certainly real enough and important enough to them, since their survival might have depended on it. In any case, this at least gives us a rational basis—one rooted in the very stuff of Tewa culture—for explaining this particular asymmetrical relationship between the moieties.

Other differences are more straightforward and center on a more stringent set of obligations and restrictions on the Summer novitiates. They are prohibited from eating meat during the four-day period, while Winter children have no food restrictions. Since their sponsors are of the same sex, there is also more than token attention paid to the instruction aspect. The boys specifically have a yellow canary feather tied on some part of their bodies on the first day, and they must wear it for the four days. As one Winter informant summed it up, "The Summer people are *xe oh* (bound), right up to the Summer chief himself, while for us water pouring passes without our being aware too much of what is happening."

The gods who come for Summer water pouring are also different, and here a whole cluster of dual symbolic associations come into play. They come from the south, while those for the Winter moiety come from the north.[5] The former are called "warm" gods, and the latter are called "cold" gods; while the former emphasize green, yellow, and black in their masks and dress, the latter emphasize red and white, the same colors associated with the respective moieties in the water giving ritual. Moreover, each set of gods may only be impersonated by members of the respective moieties. On the first night, when only members of the appropriate moiety may witness the coming of the gods, the respective moiety chiefs "shout the emergence path," or trace their journey from the distant lakes. The Summer chief traces the journey as taking place through "yellow blossoms, amidst the chirping of orioles and canaries, and the singing of cicadas." The Winter chief traces the journey of the northern gods through "areas covered by snow, through the deep snow."

The following night, however, when both moieties witness the performance, two *Kossa* (sacred clowns) trace the journey of the gods. The *Kossa*, like the Hunt chief, are mediators between the moieties, and just as the latter mediates during the water giving ritual, the *Kossa* mediate in this ritual. It is moiety-specific on the first night, but it becomes a communal ritual on the second night, when the entire village may go, as the Tewa term it, "to seek life" (Laski 1959). In all other respects, the rituals are the same for each moiety.

Water pouring, then, makes children Dry Food People, and begins to distinguish them sexually by giving them appropriate duties and instruction. But the process is not completed until another rite of passage, called "finishing," is held. This, too, is moiety-specific, and again it is held in the appropriate season for each moiety. Like water pouring, it is connected with the coming of the gods, but it is comparatively simple and of short duration. The symbolic distinctions outlined above still obtain, but both versions of finishing are otherwise the same, so a synthetic sketch will suffice.

Finishing is held whenever there are enough children in each moiety who are ten years of age and older. It does not matter how many years elapse between rites, but the children must be at least ten years of age, and there should be at least fifteen or twenty before the moiety chiefs and their assistants decide to have the finishing rite. Thus, when the first plans are made for the coming of the gods, twelve days beforehand, the moiety chief in question announces that finishing will be held four days hence. Once again the *Towa é* of his moiety are advised to notify the parents of eligible children. The children themselves are not told of what is in prospect until the very evening of the rite, when they are told by their parents to bathe and not to go out again. After bathing they usually go to bed, while their parents quietly lay out a traditional ritual outfit, which consists of a breechclout and blanket for boys, and a black woolen dress for girls. Later in the evening the child is suddenly awakened and told to put on the ritual dress. The only explanation given is that he or she is being taken to *Sipofene*. In this instance *Sipofene* refers to two private rooms which are attached to the kiva itself. Each moiety has two such rooms, a small antechamber, and a larger, windowless inner room. Laski (1959) presents a sketch of these rooms and their relation to the kiva.

Shortly thereafter, the *Towa é* arrive to accompany the girls to *Sipofene*. Boys are taken by their ceremonial sponsors for water giving and water pouring, if the sponsors are male. Those Winter boys who have female sponsors are taken by their fathers. The girls are assured by the *Towa é* that they need not be afraid, and that they will be free to return home in a short time. Boys, conversely, are told that they will "become men" on this night, and they are carefully informed of what is to happen. As the girls arrive, they proceed down a ladder leading into the antechamber and remain there, while the boys and accompanying male adults go into the larger inner room. When all of the children have been gathered within, two *Kossa* of the moiety proceed to trace the journey of the gods associated with the moiety; this is done from within the inner room, which is completely shut off from the girls. Just as the twelfth stop—the kiva itself—is mentioned, there is a resounding thump on the roof. The *Towa é*, who are in the antechamber, quickly put up a blanket screen around the ladder. By this time the *Kossa* are also in the antechamber. When the blanket screen is removed, there stands the chief masked deity of the moiety. The *Kossa* address him solemnly, telling him that he has been called from his dwelling place beneath the lake to "bring the girls to woman-hood and the boys to manhood and womanhood." The girls are then lined up facing the god, and the *Kossa* hold up the arms of each while the god administers two light blows on either side of each girl's rib cage with two yucca blades. When all are thus whipped, they are taken back to their homes by the *Towa é*; the finishing rite is over for them less than an hour after they leave their homes.

The boys, meanwhile, have shed their blankets and are gathered around the moiety chief, who asks each of them in turn if he truly wishes to be finished. When each has answered "yes," he is made to promise that he will never reveal to any outsider or younger child what he is about to undergo and witness. The god then proceeds into the inner room, and repeats the whipping pro-cedure on each boy. This time, however, he swings the long yucca blades with all his might and huge red welts appear on either side of the boy's naked rib cage; some are even cut. When the last boy has been whipped, the god suddenly takes off his mask and stands there grinning at the boys. When the boys have gotten over their sur-prise at seeing a relative or neighbor behind the mask, they each try on the mask themselves and attempt to imitate the call and gestures of the now unmasked god. Everyone, including the boys themselves, laughs heartily at these initial self-conscious attempts to imitate the god. The mood of the occasion passes quickly from solemnity to mirth.

Very shortly, however, it returns to solemnity, for the masks of the other gods are removed from a hidden case at the back of the room. On this night, eight days before the coming of the gods, practice sessions for those who will impersonate the gods begin. The boys must also stay and try out, for this is primarily what finishing means for them; they are now eligible to assist and partici- pate in the coming of the gods. Heretofore, they have even been denied admission into the moiety's *Sipofene*; now they may pass freely in and out. At the end of the evening they are told by the moiety chief: "Henceforth the door is open for you here; do not wait to be called, but come of your own accord." These practice sessions and tryouts continue for four nights, at the end of which one or two newly finished boys may be selected to impersonate the gods in another four nights. In this case, they will remain in this same room, along with others chosen, for the next four days and nights, or until the ritual is over. The meaning of the finishing rite for girls, on the other hand, is more limited. They are finished, as one informant summarized it, "only so that they will know, someday when they get married, what their husbands mean when they say they have to attend to kiva duties." This is the only time in their lives that they will even get into the antechamber, for they may never impersonate the gods.

Finishing, then, is a further rite of incorporation, this time into the ritual organization of one's own moiety. During the naming ritual we noticed that the moieties were only symbolically recog- nized. During water giving and water pouring the moieties and other aspects of dual organization emerged clearly, but they were mediated by the Hunt chief and the *Kossa*, respectively. During finishing even the mediation is lost; at this point in the individual life cycle, the moieties emerge as most clearly distinct. Even the *Kossa*, who at water pouring could be of either moiety, must now be of the moiety conducting the finishing rite. The reason is simple; no person of the opposite moiety—not even Made People —may ever enter *Sipofene*. The kiva, to which each moiety's *Sipofene* is attached, is communally owned, and here the various mediating personnel and concepts may come into play. This is one important theme to which I should like to call attention.

Another is that while the process of recruitment into the moieties seems to be patrilineal, specific kinship relations play a very small part in all of the rites thus far discussed. The sponsors are prescribed within a very limited circle for the Winter moiety, and chosen on the basis of ritual knowledge rather than kinship for the Summer. Thus, it is the process of initiation—the rituals themselves—which seems to be crucial. Three brief case histories will clarify this point. The first concerns a Made person, assistant to the Summer chief, who had four daughters but no sons. He wanted to leave a male heir in his moiety, so when his oldest daughter gave birth to the second of four sons, he requested that the infant be initiated into the Summer moiety. The older son had already undergone the water giving rite, but into the Winter moiety, because his father was Winter. The mother herself had converted from her father's moiety to that of her husband. Now, when the old man made the request of his daughter, she consulted with her husband, and they both agreed to "give" the second son to the Summer moiety. Today, twenty-eight years later, this son is the only member of the immediate family who belongs to the Summer moiety.[6]

A second case occurred about thirty-five years ago, and involves the daughter of a male lay assistant to the Summer chief. While still a small child, she became ill with fever, and her parents feared for her life. Since the Winter chief and his assistants are believed to possess the power to cure fever, the father offered the girl to the Winter moiety if they would cure her. The Winter chief daubed a white claylike substance over the girl's body, and the fever subsided. She had already undergone the water giving rite into the Summer moiety, but renounced that by undergoing the Winter water giving rite the following year, in accordance with her father's promise.

The third and final case occurred about half a century ago. A boy, son of a female assistant to the *Kossa*, also became ill with fever and sores. He, too, was said to have been cured by the Winter chief's medicine. However, he was not only promised to the Winter moiety, but to the moiety society as well. He never became an assistant to the Winter chief because he moved out of the village, but he remains a member of the Winter moiety. More cases could be cited, but these three are chosen because they indicate the continuity of the practice through time, and because they all involved people who were prominent in the ritual organizations of their own moieties. These are the people who ordinarily would not wish to "give" their children to the opposite moiety.[7]

What is indicated is that there is no clear and unambiguous rule of recruitment into the moieties. The absence of a rule has always given a rather fuzzy quality to the Tewa data, but it is just this flexibility which has insured the survival of the system to the present time. In the past, whenever an epidemic or other crisis has created a numerical imbalance between the moieties, there is a subtle, long-term redistribution of personnel to reestablish a rough balance. One cannot shift moiety membership freely, of course, since it is a process which takes several years, but the above cases illustrate the conditions under which a shift is possible.

A third general observation regarding the entire process of recruitment into the moieties is that the symbols associated with the moieties themselves have a great deal of influence over behavior. The two children who were cured by the Winter moiety society are a case in point. The Winter moiety, it will be recalled, is associated with cold. The chief and his assistants are attributed the power to cause cold weather, and by logical extension, the power to cure fever. But in receiving this cure the patient remains abnormally "cold" for life. Thus, the two Summer people who were cured are also known as "those who cannot cook peas." Dried peas are the hardest of vegetables to cook, taking hours of boiling before they are edible. The woman believes in the power of this symbolism to such an extent that she always has someone else cook her peas. I have witnessed her complaints about this lost culinary art. The Summer chief has the opposite power, of course, but people's lives are rarely endangered by chills in this area.

A fourth general observation, which is by now obvious, is that the moieties also represent symbolic divisions of the world of nature. Thus the dotted line separating north and east from south and west on figure 2 now becomes relevant. I have noted that the deities of the respective moieties come from opposite directions and emphasize colors associated with the warm-cold and summer-winter antitheses. Even in the personal adornments and paraphernalia of the respective moiety societies, these symbols have been clearly evident. It is in the process of moiety recruitment and ritual that we see emerge not only the social dual organization which Maybury-Lewis (1960) regards as fundamental, but its close and indispensable link with symbolic dual organization. I proceed now to a separate discussion of marriage and death.

Tewa marriage practices are analytically disappointing in one sense, and unusually enlightening in another. In the former sense, one of the classic functions of moieties wherever they are found around the world, that of exogamy, is here absent. Here as nowhere else in the system, the four centuries of close contact with Spaniards and Catholicism have left their mark, for native and Catholic marriage practices are thoroughly syncretized. Parsons

(1924, 1929), Whitman (1940), and Dozier (1960), in their treatments of the subject, have found no clear correlation between marriage and moiety membership, other than a tendency toward moiety endogamy in two of the villages where factional disputes have occurred along moiety lines. Moreover, there is no clear postmarital residence rule, and the only restriction on the selection of a spouse is that he or she not be closer than a fourth cousin. This, of course, is also the rule of the Catholic Church. In fact, Parsons (1929, p. 33) notes that the Tewa interpret what definitely appear to be Catholic rules more strictly than the Church itself. Nonetheless the procedure is worth sketching briefly.

First, any young couple who wish to marry must have undergone the finishing rite. The issue is, of course, academic, for all Tewa children are finished by their early or middle teens. It is the prospective groom who initiates proceedings by notifying his parents that he wishes to marry. The boy's father drafts a go-between to speak to the girl's parents on his son's behalf. This go-between is most often the father's older brother, but in his absence the prospective groom's ceremonial sponsor may act. Ritual prominence and a knowledge of the formal ritual speaking style are the primary criteria for selection. The go-between presents the groom's request to the girl's parents, who then ask their daughter if she wishes to marry the boy. If she consents, a date is soon set for the wedding ceremony, which will take place with a gathering of all available relatives of both families at the prospective bride's home.

In the intervening days or weeks, the boy's relatives contribute household gifts, clothing, and jewelry for presentation to the girl. The girl's relatives contribute food, for they must feed the boy's relatives, in her home. On the appointed day, the couple sit together at one end of the largest room in the house, while both sets of relatives and ceremonial sponsors gather around. The ceremony begins when the bride's father asks the senior male present among his relatives to address the couple. The elder then proceeds to advise the couple on all aspects of married life except the sexual. The language is Tewa, but what is most impressive about this procedure is that Christ, his cross, the Virgin Mary, and even saints are invoked right along with, and sometimes in place of, Tewa spirits. The couple are told that they are now "taking up the way of God." The ceremony proceeds in this way, with elder male relatives of both families being asked to address the couple. When all the males who wish to do so have spoken, females get their turn. At the middle of each address, the couple are asked if they truly desire one another, to which they answer "yes." Repeatedly, the question is also put by each speaker to everyone present: "Is this not an occasion for which we should all be happy? Is this also not a matter of our desire?" The formal response, "It is so," resounds from every corner of the room or house. The attempt is made to achieve unanimity among all relatives present, and it is difficult to escape the impression that two large groups of bilaterally reckoned kin and ceremonial sponsors are being married. They are being united, of course, in the sense of joining forces to ensure the success of the marriage.

When all have been given a chance to speak, the bride's father turns to the groom's relatives and asks, "And who shall be our elder *Owha* (Catholic priest)?" A pre-selected elder, who may be the go-between or ceremonial sponsor, steps forth to assume the role of Catholic priest for the conclusion of the ceremony. He is appointed by the groom's parents, in consultation with their relatives. He admonishes the couple at length once again, after which he places rosaries around their necks. This concludes the wedding ceremony which is defined by the Tewa as native. All relatives then eat, first in the bride's home, then in that of the groom. At the end of the feasting period, the bride's father asks the "priest" if he will "continue to take the responsibility which you have assumed on this day?" The response is always "yes," and it means that the elder will continue to advise and assist the couple as long as he lives. Henceforth, all domestic quarrels may be taken to him for arbitration. Thus, the ceremony is partly a mock-Catholic rite and partly native, but it is difficult to draw the line between the two.

In addition to this "native" ceremony, there is a church wedding held a few days or weeks later, at which the reciprocal feeding of relatives is repeated. Sometimes the native and the church weddings are held a day apart so that the feasting will occur on the same day; in any case, the church wedding is always held, while the native one has often been dispensed with.

We come now to the more enlightening aspect of Tewa marriage, and here the moieties become relevant again. If the bride is of the moiety opposite to that of her husband, she must convert to his. She does this by undergoing the three moiety-specific rituals of water giving, water pouring, and finishing all over again, but into her husband's moiety. Whenever the water giving ritual is next held she is taken by her mother-in-law, just as infants are taken by their mothers, and she also acquires a new ceremonial sponsor and receives a new name appropriate to the moiety. If she already has a child by the time the ritual is next held—a not uncommon occurrence—both mother and child may undergo the rite at the same time. If, on the other hand, she has children by a previous marriage or by other fathers, they continue the process of recruitment into their mother's original moiety. In this event, their grandparents or other relatives see that they complete the process. The situation can be rather complex, but this second hypothetical situation is rare, since divorce and widow remarriage are also rare.

In any case, the bride may witness moiety-specific rituals with her husband after water giving. Conversely, she may not return to the rituals of her original moiety again. The next two rituals proceed for her in just the way they do for children. At water pouring she must take baskets of meal to her sponsor, and if she is converting to the Summer moiety she must undergo the same food restrictions. Only the instruction aspect is perfunctory. At finishing she undergoes an additional process which differs from that of the children. When the bride-novitiate into the Summer moiety stands before the chief deity of her new moiety, she is first whipped, then her icicles are symbolically shed. To take the place of the icicles she is symbolically sprinkled with *pose* (dew), and blossom petals; this brings her "to the side of warmth," or makes her a full member of the moiety. The Winter novitiate, conversely, has her blossom petals shed and replaced by icicles; she is brought over to the "cold" side. Converts by marriage, then, are treated like growing children in their new moiety; they are remade, as it were, into the symbolic image of its adult members.

But here again the rule is not a hard and fast one, for ritual once again intervenes to render the system flexible. If the bride belongs to one of the societies of Made People, she does not convert to her husband's moiety, even if her duties as a Made person do not conflict in any way with the ritual activities of her husband's moiety. The reason is the Made People have passed beyond ordinary existence and are no longer subject to the ways and rules of the Dry Food People. By undergoing a process of recruitment through their own distinct versions of water giving and finishing, they become "of the lake." The Made People are discussed in more detail in chapter 5, but here it may be noted that their immunity from the above procedure represents one of the few absolute rules in the Tewa system. As in the process of initiating children, just as we seem at last to have a clear and unambiguous process, ritual considerations come in to override it.

Nevertheless, what emerges clearly is that there has been heavy Spanish influence on Tewa marriage practices, and there is much more still to be learned concerning this rite. The fact that the

Tewa have an elaborate procedure for converting brides, for example, may represent a ritual survival of what may once have been a standard and uniform procedure for all brides; that is to say, the initiation process would solve the problem of how to integrate these new members into the moiety. In any case, we simply do not know, for the facts which would permit us to go further are not yet available; indeed, they may be unobtainable.

After marriage, men are eligible to become *Towa é* or other political officials. It is also after marriage that the finishing rites of the Made People are usually performed, although marriage is not a specific requirement for becoming a Made person. These two natural categories and their supernatural counterparts form the focus of the next two chapters, but it should be pointed out that it is after marriage that the transitions between the three general categories occur.

It is also after marriage that another important process of the general life cycle reaches its peak of development. First, let me review briefly the ties that ego has formed thus far. He has enduring mutual-aid and respect relationships with his naming mother, his ceremonial sponsor, and the "priest" who is appointed to advise him after matrimony. A woman who marries a man of the opposite moiety has, in addition, a new sponsor for the conversion process, although she retains her ties to her original sponsor. After the couple have children, they repeat this process for them, and a whole new set of ties may be formed which include them. During this time also, they themselves are eligible to serve as sponsors of one kind or another. If either or both join the Made People—and a person often joins two separate societies of Made People—he gets a new sponsor from each of the societies. These ties, too, are permanent, for one is a Made person until death. Even if we leave the Made People out of consideration, every Tewa has a minimum of three ties with other Dry Food People who may be outside his range of recognized relatives. Later on he may have a dozen or more such ties, depending on his personal qualities, and these ties extend even to other members of the nuclear family. This whole process is a by-product of the elaborate system of rites of passage— five thus far—of the Dry Food People.

All of these ties are enduring, and all are important, because ego may rely on the people involved and their families for a tremendous range and diversity of needs, just as they may call upon him, in their turn. Even those ties which transcend kinship and the moiety may be put into play in simple economic activities, if ego has no relatives of his own to help him. In fact, some of the ties may be formed with a view toward acquiring new relationships or cementing those which have become weakened. It is not unusual, for instance, for siblings all to have different ceremonial sponsors.

Through time, meaning the entire life cycle, the Dry Food person's progression through the system may be symbolized by a vine which branches out and reaches into almost every household in the village. In the absence of a rule of descent, it is this vinelike network of ties which gives the individual a sense of community. The cyclical nature of the rites of passage on which these ties are based insures, in addition, the continuation of the system. To avoid a programmatic statement which would clarify very few of the larger problems of kinship in this society, no more is said here and now. But the reader is referred to Parsons (1929), Dozier (1960), and Eggan (1966) for more detailed information on the current state of our understanding of Tewa kinship.[8] Let us now turn to "the supreme and final crisis of life—death" (Malinowski 1948, p. 47).

When a Dry Food person dies, senior relatives of the same sex as the deceased dress the corpse immediately in traditional Tewa— today only ritual—clothing. His moccasins are reversed, and a bit of food, whatever he most enjoyed eating in life, is wrapped in cotton and placed in his left armpit. These two acts are done because everything in the afterworld—the world beneath this one—is reversed. The amount of food will vary with the individual; if he has been highly regarded in life, only a small amount is placed in the armpit, for the road to the afterworld will be straight. If he was known not to have led a particularly virtuous life, more food is provided, along with extra pairs of moccasins, for the Tewa believe that such a person will take longer to reach the afterworld. His road will be rocky and winding; there will be many branches to confuse him; and he may have to battle many beasts of prey along the way. Yet he will always reach the afterworld, for a place of eternal damnation is not recognized in Tewa cosmology.

If other adult relatives from outside the household are not already present, they immediately drop whatever they are doing and come to the deceased's home with food. The senior male among them goes to the home of the head *Fiscal,* or Church warden, one of four such officials instituted by the Spaniards early in the seventeenth century (Parsons 1939). The general role of the *Fiscales* is discussed in greater detail in the following chapter; here I shall note only that they are adult Tewa males who assume a large part of the responsibility for the Catholic portion of the death ritual. Thus, the relative makes the visit to formally request the *Fiscales'* aid.

This is done in a highly standardized manner, followed whenever any Made person or civil official is approached with a request. First the relative apologizes for disturbing the peace of the *Fiscal's* home, and then asks: "Does our elder have a corner?" This means: "I have come to make a formal request of you in your official capacity. Will you grant me permission to speak?" The latter responds in the affirmative, and the relative proceeds. "As it has been left among us from the time of the earth's dawn, when all was young and green," and then makes his request. It may never be turned down, so the *Fiscal* immediately goes to notify his three assistants that they are needed "to rest and retire" the deceased.

The relative continues on his way to the home of the Catholic priest to ask him when the corpse may be brought to the Church for the requiem mass. It must be in the morning, for the Tewa believe that if one is buried after the sun has reached its zenith, there will be deaths "like an avalanche." The Catholic priests have always complied with this custom, since it does not conflict with Church dogma.

That night there is a Spanish Catholic-derived *velorio*, or wake, to which all members of the village come, if only for a few minutes. Non-Indian friends may also pay their last respects at this time. Relatives and close friends stay all night, and for them meals are served throughout the night. The principal activity during the wake is the singing of funeral dirges in Spanish. This is the *Fiscales'* primary responsibility, but any other man—Tewa or Spanish—may join in. Every few hours prayers are said in Spanish. If the deceased was particularly prominent and respected outside the village, Spanish penitentes from the neighboring area may come to lead the singing and prayers.

Shortly after dawn the next day, the four *Fiscales*, two from each moiety, go to the Church cemetery to dig the grave. When this is completed, three leave to take the corpse, first to the Church for the requiem mass, then on to the cemetery. One *Fiscal* remains inside the grave to insure that witches will not occupy it or plant evil objects within. The priest and most adult members of the community follow the funeral procession to the cemetery, where the priest completes the funeral rites of the Church with the sprinkling of holy water, a prayer, and finally by taking a handful of earth in his left hand and throwing it into the grave. The priest and all non-Indians leave at this point, and the *Fiscales* complete burial. But first, a bag containing the clothing of the deceased is placed under his head as a pillow, along with other most prized and personal possessions. For a woman this may be an item of jewelry, her corn-grinding stone, and the pot used at her naming ritual. For a man it may be his hunting bow, arrows, and a stone axe, in addition to the pot. These most personal of items henceforth become endowed with spirit through their former owner, who has become a spirit.

Thus, the middle portion of the death ritual, from the time the wake begins until the priest throws the first handful of dirt into the grave, is almost completely Spanish and Catholic. That is to say, it is the same procedure followed in the Spanish-speaking villages and hamlets in the area. But as soon as the priest leaves, Tewa ideas and practice take over once again. Even the head *Fiscal*, who is structurally a Spanish-introduced Church warden, now comes forth to perform a purely native act. When the grave has been covered, he stands at the head of it, like the priest, but he tells the survivors that the deceased has gone to the place "of endless cicada singing," that he will be happy, and he admonishes them not to let the loss divide the home. If the head of a household dies, the *Fiscal* asks them to recognize the next senior person of either sex as head. Afterwards, all the relatives gather again in the home of the deceased, and the same senior male who represented them before the *Fiscal* and the priest addresses them. He admonishes the relatives to close ranks and live as before, essentially repeating what the head *Fiscal* said at the grave.

During the next four days following death, the soul, or "Dry Food Who Is No Longer," is believed to wander about in this world in the company of its ancestors. After the soul is released from the body through the mouth, it is believed to go immediately to one of the four directional shrines, where it is met by the ancestral souls. From here they journey together to all points in the Tewa world, to the sacred mountains, hills, and other shrines. One story is cited by the elders to validate native traditions regarding the activities of the soul immediately after death. Long ago, a man from the village died. The relatives dressed him and held the all-night wake. The following morning, as the relatives were weeping and preparing to take him out of his home for the last time, he suddenly arose and asked for water. He reported that he had indeed died, that his soul had passed out of his body through his mouth, and proceeded directly to a shrine, and that a large group of ancestral souls were there to greet him and take him to all sacred points in the Tewa world. The souls also reported to him that some people who had died long before were not yet admitted to the underworld because they had neglected their ritual duties, and they showed him feather offerings, placed at shrines and earth navels, which were lying in the dust because they were not offered with proper humility. They then sent him back to convey these facts to the people so that they might live according to tradition. At this point he awoke. Most Tewa are familiar with this story, which is cited to justify their beliefs about the afterlife.

Because the soul is still wandering about in this world, the four days are also a time of general uneasiness in the village. There is the fear among the relatives that the soul may become lonely and return to take one of them with him. Children who were closest to the deceased, and who have not yet undergone water pouring, are most susceptible, because they are not yet fully Dry Food People; they are innocent and uneducated. Thus they are never left alone in a room during the four days. The house itself must not be left unoccupied at any time during the period, for the soul may return and try to reoccupy it. There must be at least two people inside at all times. The uneasiness permeates the rest of the village, because another activity in which the soul indulges is to go around and ask forgiveness of all those to whom he owes something, or whom he has wronged in the past. During this period, individuals will report strong winds whistling just outside their doors, "something" trying to enter their homes late at night, seeing the deceased in their dreams, or hearing voices. This is why the entire village should visit the deceased while he lies in state; not alone to offer sympathy to the survivors, but to make sure the deceased knows he is forgiven for past wrongs. Those who have wronged the deceased have less to fear, because the soul is not believed likely to delay his acceptance into the underworld by vengeance.

The period of uneasiness ends on the fourth evening, for at this time all relatives (*matuin*) gather once again to perform the "releasing" rite, a classic "rite of separation" (van Gennep 1960). Each household, which may include three or four generations, brings a basket of food and various side dishes. All of these are placed in a row in a room which has been cleared for the purpose. A new cooking pot is placed at the head of the row, and the senior male present sits on the floor before it. He takes a small portion of each kind of food from each basket and puts it into the pot with his left hand. Next he smokes a cigarette of native tobacco over the pot, and after finishing throws the cigarette into it as well. Then he rises, takes a short hand broom, and goes to each person present in the room, making an outward sweeping motion over each in turn. From here he proceeds to the fireplace, removes a piece of dead charcoal, and puts it under his tongue; then he wraps himself in a blanket, puts the pot under his left arm, and proceeds silently out the door. Immediately several other senior relatives, including the surviving spouse, if any, also wrap themselves in blankets and follow the first man a few paces behind; they, too, go silently. They are going to the nearest directional shrine to present the "feast" to the deceased and other ancestors who await there.[9] Near the shrine, but not on it, he drops the pot, breaking it and scattering the food. The others are now lined up behind him. Next he draws four lines in front of him with his left foot, and the others silently follow suit. After spitting out a portion of the charcoal in his mouth to the cardinal directions, he turns to go back to the house. The others also follow close behind, and still without speaking. A third of the way back, the lead elder stops, turns to the direction of the shrine, draws four more lines with his left foot, and spits out a little bit more of the charcoal. The others once again silently follow suit. The process is repeated two thirds of the way back, and a fourth time just before the door, and at each window of the house. After the last bit of charcoal is spat out and the final lines drawn, the lead elder at last softly utters a short prayer and reveals the purpose of the several symbolic acts:

> We have muddied the waters for you (the smoke)
> We have cast shadows between us (the charcoal)
> We have made steep gullies between us (the lines)
> Do not, therefore, reach for even a hair on our heads
> Rather, help us attain that which we are always seeking
> Long life, that our children may grow
> Abundant game, the raising of crops
> And in all the works of man
> Ask for these things for all, and do no more
> And now you must go, for you are now free.

With the soul now released, all those comprising the heretofore silent procession breathe a sigh of relief, and proceed to wash their hands in a bowl of water which has previously been placed near the door. As each finishes, he reenters the house and says to those within: "May you have life," to which the latter respond: "Let it be so." As the lead elder reenters he picks up the hand broom once again, pokes it into the fireplace to get ashes, and blows in an outward motion over the people, and at each of the corners of the house. This final symbolic act is intended to protect the house itself, first by invoking the protection of the *xayeh* (soul-associated objects) which are buried under the floor at each corner of Tewa homes. Secondly, the ashes are intended to invoke the protection of Ash Youth, a benevolent spirit of Category 6, who lives in ashes. The elder then announces to all: "Now you may eat." The food has not been touched, because they must wait until the souls have eaten. The tension is now all gone, and the children immediately leap for choice items brought by their relatives, for they cannot take their own things back home. What remains is eaten, and what remains after that is exchanged among the women of the various households represented.

Another story is widely cited to show why the releasing rite must be performed four days after a death. About twenty years ago, an adolescent girl died suddenly in Santa Fe, and was brought home for burial. She was buried in the village, but the releasing rite was not performed because her relatives were skeptical of native customs. Shortly afterwards, the surviving members of her household began to hear someone whispering and walking about in the house at night. This continued for so long that the house was finally abandoned, and it remains so today.

Some days after the releasing rite, just before the next festive occasion in the village, the two moiety chiefs go together to the home of the recently deceased. They ask those within to "leave all sadness behind, for he whom you miss so much is now at the place of endless cicada singing." They are invited to join in the festivities or the ritual now near at hand. This is a "rite of reintegration" (van Gennep 1960, p. 147) of the survivors back into the society. It is also the one occasion at which both moiety chiefs go to any private home in the village. In terms of the issues outlined in this work, the differences between the moieties are temporarily and dramatically put aside at this, the highest level, in the interest of reaffirming the solidarity of the whole against the permanent loss of one of its members. The fact that the soul is henceforth no longer regarded as a representative of either moiety, but as a member of the generalized (and transcendentalized) category of "Dry Food Who Are No Longer," is also directly relevant here. As during the naming ritual it is the unity, rather than the division, of the society which is emphasized by this joint appearance. I shall have more to say about this point presently.

The releasing rite is repeated for the deceased exactly one year after death, perhaps because it is also traditional to have a commemorative mass said in the Church at the same time. The same rite is also performed each year on All Souls' Day, but this time for the generalized ancestors.[10] On each of these occasions, however, the sadness and uneasiness is gone, and the festive aspects are emphasized. Only one person takes the pot of food to the shrine, for there is no fear that the soul may still be about. Both occasions are

instances in which Catholic commemorative dates are observed
with a purely native ritual.

The preceding two sections, from naming until death, have been
rather long and involved, so I should now like to call attention to
a few points relating these two rites, by way of summary. That
the two rites have much in common is obvious, since Ash Youth
is invoked on both occasions, and the pot buried with the deceased
is the same one used at his naming ritual. What is most striking,
however, is that other similar symbols are used in contrasting
fashion during the two rituals. The hand broom, which at birth
was used to gather in blessings from the directions, is used at death
to release the soul and speed it on its way to the afterworld. The
broom itself only represents the long wing-tip feather of the eagle,
but since only the Made People may use the latter, the broom may
be regarded as everyman's version of the feather. Another reversal
occurs in the symbolism of the smoke. Whereas the naming mother
smokes over the pot to simulate clouds in the hope of inducing rainfall, the elder male at the death ritual smokes to "muddy the
waters" for the dead so that he will not find his way back to the
living. The charcoal, on the other hand, is used to blur the image
the living have of the dead, "so that they will not see him clearly
in their dreams."

The symbolism of the number four here means that the dead
takes only four steps from the living; he goes only to the shrines,
or one-third of the way back along the path of emergence. This
is why there is only a four-day mourning period, and only four
lines are drawn between the living and the dead. The Made People,
as will be noted in chapter 5, take all twelve steps back along the
path of emergence; they go back to the lakes, so there is a twelve-
day period of mourning for them. Thus while the line between the
living and the dead is clearly drawn in several ways, the use of the
same symbols underscores the continuity between the two. We
may now proceed to a consideration of the general implications
that might be derived for the operation of the dual organization in
Tewa society and culture.

First, the general similarities between the naming and death
rituals give rise to what is perhaps the most important point to
be made in this entire work. It is that at the beginning and at the
end of life—when it matters most—the Tewa emphasize the solidarity of the whole society rather than the dual organization. Both
the social and symbolic aspects of the dual organization are real
and important, as we have seen from the four intermediate rites,

but during the naming and death rituals they are definitely played down. During the former ritual the Dry Food person's entry into the society at large is emphasized, and at death he passes not from his moiety but from the whole society. This is why I have opened this chapter with the concluding statement of the Tewa elder whose version of the myth of origin I outlined in the preceding chapter:

> In the beginning we were one people. Then we divided into Summer people and Winter people; in the end we came together again as we are today.

True to the underlying message of the origin myth which he interprets so well, the Tewa do begin and end life as one people. The term they use for the life cycle is *poeh*, or "path," after the two different migration paths the moieties followed after emergence. Thus, at the beginning of life there is a single path for all Tewa. At water giving it divides into two parallel paths and continues in that way until the end of life. At death the paths rejoin again and become one, just as the moieties rejoined in the myth of origin. While I do not mean to postulate a one-to-one correlation between all aspects of the myth and Tewa life today, it is sufficiently clear that the myth is both a "model of" and a "model for" (Geertz 1966, pp. 7, 29) at least the life cycle of the common Tewa.

As an issue in the analysis of dual organizations, the naming and death rituals are important in the light of Maybury-Lewis's observation that "the simultaneous awareness of the division and the unity of society is common enough in conjunction with dual organization and might be said to be the fundamental problem in their analysis" (1960, p. 27). These two rites, when viewed against the background of the myth of origin and the entire life cycle, provide the single most persuasive answer the Tewa have for the problem. This is a problem which Lévi-Strauss (1960, 1963a) also recognized, but which he, like Maybury-Lewis, failed to resolve. Indeed the answer can only be found when the framework of analysis includes the entire life-span of the average individual within the society.

But life as a member of Tewa society begins only after the child is named, and it is from this point on that the dual organization assumes paramount significance. The elaborate and lengthy process of becoming a member of one moiety or the other—from water giving during infancy to finishing at adolescence—convinces us of its significance. But even here problems arise when we observe that one is not born into a moiety but is recruited into it, and the basis of this recruitment is flexible at best. As I have observed, it is possible to change one's moiety membership, and many Tewa do so. There is no clear and unalterable rule of recruitment into the moieties, because there is no clear and unambiguous rule of descent. Moreover, the Tewa system has been functioning in just this way for at least a century—probably for much longer—because there is no evidence in the ethnographic record to indicate they ever had a unilineal rule of descent.

This point becomes important when we recall that Lévi-Strauss bases his analysis of dual organizations and his denial of their existence entirely on data from societies with unilineal descent. In other words, there is at least the implicit assumption that unilineal descent must accompany "so-called dual organizations" (Lévi-Strauss 1963*a*, p. 161), because he never considers the alternative possibility in what is purported to be a general formulation on the subject. Maybury-Lewis also apparently accepts this assumption because he raises no objection to it in his critique of Lévi-Strauss's formulation (1960). I need not belabor the obvious, since other specific points of criticism of both positions are more telling. The unalterable fact is that the Tewa have dual organization without unilineal descent. They have instead a process of recruitment flexible enough to permit the redistribution of personnel between the moieties, and thus insure a rough numerical balance between them through time.

Another significant issue is raised when we consider Tewa marriage practices. Several writers, notably Schneider (1965), have noted that Lévi-Strauss places too heavy a reliance on marriage systems in formulating conclusions about the operation of whole societies. The Tewa data suggest that, at least with regard to the study of dual organizations, Lévi-Strauss's emphasis on marriage practices is unwarranted, and serious doubts are cast on the validity of his conclusions because they are based on the assumption that moieties are always exogamous (1960, 1963*a*). While I cannot deny that the practices and beliefs have been altered through Spanish Catholic influence, neither can I deny that there is no direct evidence for the former practice of moiety exogamy by the Tewa, Fox (1967) notwithstanding. Once again, as with the absence of unilineal descent, Tewa society continues to function very well without exogamy. There is evidence neither for nor against the former practice of exogamy, but—and this is the crux of the issue —its former existence probably would not alter the system of classification or the emphasis on the solidarity of the society at crucial points in the life cycle. In short, the present analysis probably would not be substantially affected.[11]

Before proceeding to a consideration of what happens in the lives of the Tewa between marriage and death, let me attempt to establish the nature of the linkage between the Dry Food People and the "Dry Food Who Are No Longer." The nature of this linkage is most clearly established in the interplay between the shrines and the *xayeh* during the naming and death rituals. In the discussion of the life cycle the shrines came into play only at death, but they are important throughout life whenever the common Tewa feels the need of spiritual assistance. By visiting any shrine and placing an offering of feathers and white cornmeal on it, he can enlist the aid of the ancestral souls in his undertaking.[12] Moreover, the ancestors are present not alone in the shrines but, through their most tangible manifestation as *xayeh*, in the home itself. The *xayeh* are, in fact, the only ritual objects that the Dry Food People may utilize and keep in their homes; these are the only spirits to which they can appeal directly. The relentlessly tetramerous system of classification outlined in the preceding chapter reaches right into the home itself, because these spirit-associated objects are buried in the four corners of each Tewa home. In this sense it may be said that the ancestors are always present in the life of the Dry Food People. It is proof enough that the shrines and *xayeh* exist as tangible objects, but the naming and death rituals show in addition just how the linkage between the two categories works. This is another reason why I have emphasized these two rites.

Since most of the process of living takes place between marriage and death, I now turn to a detailed consideration of the human and supernatural *Towa é*, the next pair of linked categories in the Tewa system of classification. In this way we may attempt to understand just what the dual organization means and does not mean in the adult life of the Tewa.

4
The Towa é

For you, our elder, nothing is forbidden, either
here in the lake or among the Dry Food People.

A TEWA

The story of the *Towa é* must properly begin with the colonization and conquest of New Mexico by Juan de Oñate in 1598. After
establishing the first Spanish colony and first capital of New
Mexico at Yunque (old San Juan) across the Rio Grande from
present-day San Juan, Oñate proceeded to obtain the allegiance of
all the Pueblos along the river. He divided them into missionary
districts, and assigned a friar to each district. His original force
of four hundred men (Crane 1928, p. 97) was probably too small
to attempt a corresponding imposition of Spanish institutions of
local government at this time, but after the capital, and primary
base of operations, was moved to Santa Fe in 1605 (Twitchell
1912, 1:333), the group was augmented by new colonists and its
position strengthened. The move toward altering the political organization of the Rio Grande Pueblos soon followed. Bandelier,
citing an unpublished manuscript, notes that in 1620 the King of
Spain decreed that an election of officers should be held in the
Pueblos of New Mexico at the beginning of each year (Bandelier
1890, vol. 1, citing *Real Cédula Dirigida al Padre Costodio Estevan
Perea* [MS], 1620). Parsons, on the other hand, indicates that this
royal edict was handed down in 1621 (1939, 1:147).

In fact, it is really not known when the Spanish system of local
government was imposed, since most church and administrative
records in New Mexico were burned during the Pueblo Revolt of
1680 (Hackett and Shelby 1942). What is known, however, is
that Spanish and Tewa political institutions and concepts are now
merged to such a degree that no one has yet been able to disentangle
them in any analytically satisfactory way. The head of the group

I here call *Towa é*, for example, has been variously known as "War Chief" (Aberle 1948, p. 91), "Outside Chief" (Parsons 1929, p. 103) and "War Captain" (Dozier 1960, p. 153). The entire group has been dismissed as "half secular, half ceremonial officers" (Parsons 1929, p. 102), or as completely derived from the Spaniards (Dozier 1960). Moreover, this confusion and uncertainty has not been restricted to the Tewa, but is reflected in all of the literature on the Pueblos of New Mexico; no one has ever been able to explain their nature and their significance in the society. These are the same *Towa é* who occupy two levels in the Tewa classification of being. Until the issue is clarified I shall retain the more neutral native term, which means simply "person" or "persons." The spelling for both the singular and the plural is the same, with only a slight tonal shift differentiating the latter.[1]

Accepting for now that Spanish influence is apparent and relevant to understanding the *Towa é*, I shall proceed as follows. First, I will identify the three groups which today comprise the Tewa political system and take a detailed look at the process by which one is recruited into them. Next, I examine the conceptual basis of the differentiation into three groups. Thirdly, I trace the part each group plays in the system, their relations to one another, and their relations to other groups in the society. I conclude by returning to and clarifying the issue noted in chapter 2, that of the ambivalence of the *Towa é* as a category of being.

The *Towa é* today comprise the middle level in a tripartite political organization, just as they probably have for almost three centuries. Figures 4, 5, and 6 illustrate their structural relations to the two other groups, which were introduced by the Spaniards. The *Kwaku tsonin*, "Spanish officials," are first in the hierarchy as a group; it includes the governor, two lieutenants, and an *aguacil*, or sheriff. The *Towa é* are next, and they are six in number. The *Fiscales* (*Pika* in Tewa) are last because, as we shall see presently, they are functionally most limited.[2]

All fourteen officials are selected from among the Dry Food People and all take office on January 1. They serve a term of one year, but are subject to future reappointment. Upon taking office, each is given a metal-topped cane which serves as his symbol of office; this is the one symbol all fourteen officials have in common. The appointments are made by the two moiety chiefs together, in consultation with the other male heads of the Made People's societies. The appointees themselves are not notified of their selection until the morning they are to take office. This derives from

the fact that the offices involve a great expenditure of time and re-
sources, and scant compensation. Thus the appointee may be expected to protest his selection vigorously, and, at least in recent
decades, he may even leave town if notified of his appointment
ahead of time. The process of selection may be outlined in some
detail, as a way of showing the conceptual and structural relations
between the three groups.

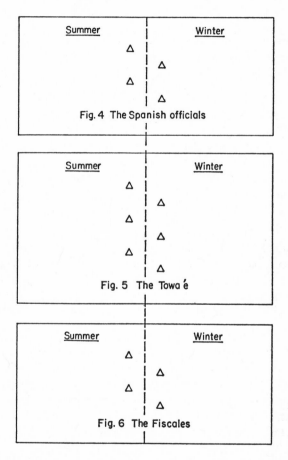

Fig. 4 The Spanish officials

Fig. 5 The Towa é

Fig. 6 The Fiscales

As the year draws to a close the two moiety chiefs begin to draw
up a mental list of those whom they wish to appoint to the various
offices for the following year. Let us return to figures 4, 5, and 6,
which permit us to assume, for convenience, that the head of each
group is presently of the Summer moiety. This in fact is the case
during 1968, so the Winter chief will select the head of each group
for 1969, hypothetically as follows.

On December 29 the Winter chief goes to the home of the Summer chief. After a ritual exchange of greetings at the door, he is asked to sit down and smoke. When he has done so, he tells his colleague that it is time once again to choose those who will help us "open the village and the plain" (start the year). The Summer chief agrees, and after a few moments' contemplation the Winter chief presents his nomination for governor:

> to carry on the work of our elder *Yosi Rey* (God and King). My pains and the weight of my thoughts have gone toward thinking of the children (villagers), that he might help them, and that we might place them on his back. What do you think, younger sibling older than I?

Usually the Summer chief will have no objections, so he in turn offers his nomination for "*Santu tenente*" (holy lieutenant). When the four officials of figure 4 are nominated, the Winter chief again opens the nominations; this time for the officials of figure 5. He presents his choice for *Towa é sehn*, "to head those of our *Towa puxu* (traditional ways)." When all six *Towa é* are chosen, the Winter chief presents his nomination for *Santu Pika mayo* (holy Fiscal major), the head of the third group:

> We still need those of the entrance to the *misa teh* [mass kiva or church], so that when our elder *owha* [Catholic priest] has need, they shall come forth. No one wants anything to happen, but we also need these to take to rest [bury] any children who may leave us during the year. I believe [names him] will help the children.[3]

The *Fiscales* (figure 6) are nominated in alternating order, like the two preceding groups, with each chief selecting two.

Shortly afterwards the other male heads of the five Made People's societies arrive at the Summer chief's home. Only the *Apienu*, head of the Women's society, is absent, for women do not participate in these deliberations. Following another period of smoking and small talk, the moiety chiefs present their nominations to the assembled Made People:

> These are the children whom we have selected to help us open the village and the plain. The "Dry Food Who Are No Longer" and the "Dry Food Who Never Did Become" [naming some] have weighted their thoughts in the children's direction.

Next, one of the others, usually the head medicine man since he stands third in the hierarchy, says, "So these are the ones," and indicates his acceptance. All the others usually concur, but any one of them protesting vigorously can negate one of the nominations. This protest comes rarely, however, and then only if the Made person can show proof that the nominee is unworthy, or that he would be placed under an intolerable burden if given the office. When unanimity is achieved, the gathering breaks up.

The following evening (December 30) the moiety chiefs together go to the home of the governor, where the *punan* (previous governors) are also assembled, and present the selections; they are selections now because nothing can reverse them.[4] They state: "These Dry Food People [naming all fourteen in order] shall govern us during the year which is now at hand." The chiefs emphasize that the selections are also those of the other Made People and of the spirits. They also repeat, in meticulous detail and with an impressive display of memory, the entire dialogue resulting in the choices. The dialogue is actually not as difficult to remember as one might expect, because it is delivered in a highly standardized oratorical style, adopted on all ritual occasions. This is how we know the nomination and selection process occurs as outlined above, although only Made People are actually present during the deliberations. The intent of this visit is merely to notify the governor and *punan* of the selections.

The following evening (December 31) the governor gathers in all members of the three groups and informs them of their replacements for the following year. He says: "These [naming all fourteen in order] are the ones you will bring in tomorrow. But do not say anything, for they may hide or run away."

Next, the governor and his first lieutenant go to the home of the Summer chief, the same chief who appointed the governor to office. The other twelve officials remain at the governor's house. When they arrive they ask the Summer chief if they may speak. After the request is granted, either may address the Summer chief:

> We have sat on cloud blossoms this year and dropped over our heads these duties. Now, the authority of the blue saints of Hazy Mountain, the yellow saints of *Tsikomo*, the red saints of Turtle Mountain, and the white saints of Stone Man Mountain returns to them; once, twice, thrice, four times, within and around the earth, within and around the hills, within and around the mountains, it returns to them. So also the authority of the blue *Towa é*, the yellow *Towa é*, the red *Towa é*, the white *Towa é;* it returns to them within and around the earth, within and around the hills, within and around the mountains, it returns to them; once, twice, thrice, four times. . . .

This retires the governor and his lieutenant. After the Summer chief thanks them for serving, they return to the governor's house where the other officials wait. Here either the governor or his lieutenant repeats everything that happened at the Summer chief's home, saying that on behalf of all assembled therein, they have returned their authority to the Summer chief and to the spirits. This retires the other twelve officials, but before the gathering breaks up the same man who has thus far done the speaking adds this last statement:

> By token of the fact that we have sat on cloud blossoms this year, and dropped over our heads these duties, may the authority of the Made People [naming them in order] go once again around every corner of the village. Therefore, tomorrow you will bring those who are to relieve us here. Each one of you will bring your counterpart.

The final step, installation, occurs in two parts. On the morning of January 1, the still unsuspecting selectees are accosted in their homes by those they are to replace. The retiring official says: "I have come as *toro sendo* (drafting elder); you are needed at the home of our elder, the governor." No further explanation is needed, and the replacements usually come along to the governor's home with only mild protest. When they arrive at the governor's house, all the retiring officials, previous governors, and heads of the Made People's societies are gathered there. This is where the selectee may protest vigorously; he may say he has a large family to support, or that he knows nothing of the requisite duties. He may even lodge bitter protests against the way the village is governed. Throughout all of this the Made People remain quiet, even when they become the objects of protest. Occasionally one will say, "Be as woman, be as man," meaning, in this case, "Be an adult Tewa and accept your responsibility." If counterprotests are to be made, and angry words are to be spoken, it is the retiring officials or previous governors who do so.

All protest is futile; in the end, often late in the afternoon, each official kneels before the Winter chief and is sworn in with a prayer. The governor, his assistants, and the *Fiscales* are sworn in in the name of God, the saints, and the three kings; the *Towa é* in the name of the spiritual *Towa é*. These latter usually offer only token protest, and they are the first to accept the new positions. Protest is expected from the Spanish officials and *Fiscales*, for reasons noted below, and they are the ones who may keep deliberations going all day. As each is sworn in, the Winter chief gives him the metal-topped cane symbolic of his office. These were originally given to the village by the Spaniards. The governor gets three, the second one coming from the Mexican government, which succeeded the Spanish, and the third representing a gift from President Abraham Lincoln. Only the governor carries his canes with him whenever he acts in an official capacity outside his home; the others remain hanging on the walls of their holders' homes during the entire term of office. This completes the first part of the installation process.

The second part begins the following day (January 2) when all fourteen officials gather in the home of the new governor, at his request. At his request also, each has brought a small bundle of feathers which he breathes on and places in a basket on the floor. When all are gathered, and all have placed their feathers in the basket, the new governor addresses them:

> I have called you here with the clothing (feathers) of the "Dry Food Who Are No Longer," the "Dry Food Who Never Did Become" because our elders (the moiety chiefs) are going to work to put us on top of cloud blossoms. And toward our elder *Yosi* (God) it has also been established from long ago, so there must be a mass. It is all a matter of one wing.

When the governor has finished speaking, the basket of feathers is passed around, and everyone breathes on it once again. The first placing of breath is to place one's individual identity on his own feather bundle, so that the spirits will know whom it is from. The second placing of breath symbolizes the collective identity of the group. To place the new officials "on cloud blossoms" means that supernatural sanction is invoked for their authority, and it is legitimized. The chiefs, as mediators between the supernatural and the people, are the ones who must invoke this sanction. Thus, the governor and his first lieutenant carry the basket to the Winter chief's home so that spiritual sanction may be invoked. Right afterwards they go to the priest's home to buy a mass for the new officials, so that the priest may invoke the blessings of God and the saints. The Feast of the Three Kings (January 6) is traditionally set aside for this mass. Then and only then is their authority completely official; this double spiritual sanction assures the new officials of obedience from the people.

This process of recruitment, from nomination to installation, contains in microcosm an answer to the nature of the whole system, and the relations of the three groups within it. Note, first, that each of the three groups is conceptually distinguished from the others during the nominating dialogue. The governor is identified with God and the three kings, while his assistants are identified with the saints. The *Fiscales* are identified with the priest and the Catholic Church, and the *Towa é* simply with native or traditional ways. Let us consider the Spanish officials and *Fiscales* more closely.

The governor's initial identification with God and the three kings, and the subsequent invocation of them during the installation ceremony for the two groups, reveals an interesting process of analogical reasoning. What is really intended is that the Spanish officials and *Fiscales* should take office in the name of God and King, as elsewhere in Spanish America. These, being abstract entities, are difficult to reconcile to the Tewa system of classification and categories of being. Thus the symbolic referent for King is fixed on the Feast of the Three Kings (January 6), because the authority of the Spanish officials becomes legitimized by the mass on this day, at which time they formally take office.

Similarly, the concept of the Christian God is relevant in only one sense. While the governor is identified with God, and both groups of officials take office in his name, neither God nor the three kings are given a place on the hills, mountains, or in the lakes, because they are alien to the Tewa system of classification, including the categories of being. More specifically, the concept of the high God is incompatible with this system of classification, and the three kings are relevant in only a special and limited sense, as substitutes for the more abstract concept of the Spanish King.

The issue is clarified considerably by reference to the saints, for we have saints being mentioned for the first time, and, like the *Towa é*, they live on mountain-tops. The saints have been partially reconciled to Tewa thought and belief in the sense that the Spanish officials and *Fiscales* have saints of the directional colors as spiritual patrons, just as the *Towa é* have their spiritual counterparts. To carry the logic a little further, since both groups are more political than ritual, like the *Towa é*, they are of the mountains, and not of the lakes with the "Dry Food Who Never Did Become." The informant quoted on page 22 actually went on to say: "And if you are a Spanish official or *Fiscal* you also mention the mountains, but instead of *Towa é* or 'Dry Food Who Never Did Become,' you invoke the saints." The point was held until now for a very important reason, and here the qualification that the saints were only partially reconciled to the system of classification becomes meaningful.

Although the Tewa recognize that the Catholic saints are named, no particular ones are attributed to particular mountains, no particular ones are assigned a given color, and, unlike the spiritual *Towa é*, they do not occur in pairs. Moreover, there are no earth navels, shrines, or other visible monuments dedicated to saints, and they have not found their way into Tewa mythology *at all*. Finally, they are not given a place in the categories of being at any time other than with reference to the sanction for the authority of the Spanish officials and *Fiscales*. They have been denied assimilation in this deeper and more meaningful sense.

What remains, then, is the general concept of saint as a spiritual sanction for the authority of the two groups, rather than "God" or "King." These latter have no counterparts in Tewa thought and institutions; they are not "good to think" (Lévi-Strauss 1963c) as symbols. But again, the saints are only "good to think" in a special sense; they are "colored" rather than specifically identified.[5]

I come now to the *Towa é*, and to explain their place in the system I must return to the days immediately preceding the nominating process, where a subtle but crucially important process of classification is in operation in the minds of the moiety chiefs. While drawing up their mental list, the chiefs classify the nominees by specific qualities and types of knowledge. The nominees for Spanish officials are those who have demonstrated ability in dealing with the outside world. The primary requirements in the past were that the nominees know the Spanish language and Spanish institutions. Today, some degree of formal education and knowledge of English are added. The nominees for *Fiscales* are those well versed in Catholicism, in addition to knowing the Spanish language. This is the one group into which Spanish-Americans married, and Spanish-Americans living in the village may be appointed; this is the one catch-all group. The nominees for *Towa é*, on the other hand, are those known to have a firm commitment to and knowledge of native ritual. As a group, these are the ones who are most integrated into the native culture by any criterion of judgment. This pattern of selection, which emerges strikingly over a period of years, permits us to understand the points on which the *Towa é* were distinguished.

I noted that they offer little protest and accept their office before the other groups. Protest, at times loud and angry, is expected of the others, for this is customarily Spanish. The *Towa é* selectees, on the other hand, emphasize their lack of knowledge of native ritual, particularly of the complex speech and prayer cycles. They approach their imminent installation with humility rather than anger; this is customarily Tewa, as I shall have occasion to note when discussing the Made People. Moreover, the *Towa é* do not require the sanction of the mass on January 6 for their authority. They are installed in the name of the spiritual *Towa é*, and supernatural sanction is obtained just as soon as the moiety chiefs offer the prayer feathers to the three categories of spirits. In fact, two *Towa é*, one from each moiety, stand guard at each of the chief's homes during this process, which begins on January 2. They take office immediately, while the installation process is not completed for the others until January 6. To clarify the issue in just one more way, while the governor's office has been successfully refused twice during recent years (1952 and 1965), it is almost inconceivable for the office of *Towa é* to be refused; informants cannot recall an occasion on which it was done. Quite simply, considerations of temperament, experience, and family background structure the selections and preclude this possibility.

I come now to the point, which is that just as the Spanish officials and *Fiscales* are clearly and unambiguously recognized as Spanish-derived, so also are the *Towa é* clearly and unambiguously recognized as native. However, it still remains to be demonstrated that the spiritual *Towa é* are represented in some tangible form in Tewa society, and that there is a meaningful relationship between them and the human *Towa é*. After all, are not Spanish canes the only tangible symbols of office that the *Towa é* receive? To take the first aspect of the problem, the spiritual *Towa é* are represented in tangible form by three identical anthropomorphic fetishes that are in the possession of the Scalp, Hunt, and Medicine societies, respectively. There is also a shrine dedicated to the *Towa é*, which is located on a hilltop approximately two miles north of San Juan. This shrine may be visited by men engaged in hunting or warfare, by anyone suffering from a persisting ailment, and by the *Towa é*. By leaving an offering at the shrine the Tewa believe that they may obtain the protection and benevolent intercession of the *Towa é*. There is, then, a relationship between the three societies of Made People mentioned above and the *Towa é*. This is why, according to the Tewa, these three groups possess the *Towa é* fetishes.

The fetish in the possession of the head medicine man may also be used and invoked by those serving as *Towa é* whenever there is a communal cleansing rite. This rite is planned and directed by the medicine men, and held whenever some misfortune, such as an epidemic or drought, endangers the village. At this time two *Towa é* accompany the medicine men on a witch hunt around the village and act as their lookouts and protectors. In preparation for the witch hunt, the medicine men achieve a clairvoyant state by taking herb medicines. Since these are denied the *Towa é*, they achieve the same effect by taking the *Towa é* fetish in their hands and holding it up to the cardinal directions, "so that it will lead them to the witches."

Similarly structured relationships may once have existed between the *Towa é* and the Scalp and Hunt societies, but I cannot demonstrate this, because organized war and hunting activities are too much a thing of the past. The one example does, however, demonstrate the conceptual linkage between the spiritual and human categories of *Towa é*. The latter are the living, functional representatives of the former. The latter may once also have had their own symbols of office, but when the Spaniards introduced the canes, along with the custom of replacing the *Towa é* each year, the fetishes may have been placed in the hands of the permanently organized societies of Made People. This point cannot be proven either, of course, but a careful consideration of the part each of the three political groups plays in the society will further clarify the issues under discussion.

As soon as the process of installation is completed, the conceptual differentiation between the three groups becomes an operational one, for the paths of the three immediately and completely diverge. All fourteen officials never again meet or act as a group until they are to retire and deliver their replacements to the governor's home at the end of their common term of office. Furthermore, the *Towa é* and *Fiscales* are no longer hierarchically subordinate to the governor; he cannot tell them what to do after they take office. To state it another way, the system, as a system, is ternary only this one time. The separation is effected as follows.

First, the Spanish officials conduct all of the village's business with the outside world and perform those duties which became necessary after the advent of the Spaniards, and later the Americans. These include the maintenance and supervision of an elaborate system of irrigation canals, in cooperation with neighboring Spanish-American farmers, with whom the village shares the entire irrigation system; the control of stock and grazing rights on village lands; and the rental of land and other village property to outsiders. They also represent the village in dealing with other tribes and the federal government.[6] The *Aguacil* (sheriff) is specifically empowered to punish minor abuses of those things within the group's control and to bring more serious offenders before the governor, who may fine them.

The *Fiscales*, on the other hand, maintain the church and mission grounds and assist the priest on festive church occasions. In the past they also forced people to go to church at the point of a whip and taught catechism to the children. For this last purpose they had a house where the lessons were held. I have already noted in the preceding chapter that they also took charge of the Catholic portion of death ritual and formal burial in consecrated ground.

The *Towa é* have still another discrete and more demanding set of duties. They serve as protectors of the Made People by standing guard at all of their retreats, and they always accompany any Made People who have to leave the village. When the medicine men are performing a communal cleansing ritual, for instance, the *Towa é* accompany them on a witch hunt which may lead outside the village. They also keep the kivas in good repair, just as the *Fiscales* maintain the church and mission grounds.

However, their primary and most time-consuming duty throughout the year is to coordinate, on the ground, all rituals planned and directed by the Made People and participated in by the Dry Food People. Song practice sessions are held in the home of the head *Towa é* for several nights, beginning twelve days before each ritual. His five assistants, in turn, have the task of calling upon and bringing in all eligible male participants, by force if necessary. When actual practice sessions begin, about eight days before the ritual, the *Towa é* continue to insure full participation, but in addition they must open and heat the kiva where the sessions are held. On the day of the dance itself, they help to dress and decorate the participants, accompany them to the kiva, and police the dance while it is in progress. Throughout the year they may also whip any Dry Food person who neglects his ritual duties, just as the governor and *Aguacil* punish those who, for instance, neglect their duties in maintaining the irrigation canals. The place of the *Towa é* in the society will not become fully meaningful until the next chapter, since they are so closely associated with the Made People; but this summary does indicate that their duties fall strictly within the culturally defined traditional.[7] This is why I have elsewhere referred to the *Towa é* as the "internal organization" as opposed to the Spanish officials whom I called the "external organization" (Ortiz 1965*b*).

Let me now focus on some of the other issues set forth at the beginning of this study. To do so, I return just once more to the nomination process and to figures 4, 5, and 6, where I noted that the moiety chiefs, acting for all of the Made People, made the selections. First, the method of alternation permitted the Winter chief to select the head of each of the three groups from his own moiety, just as did the Summer chief the previous year. Thus, if each official represented on the figures is moved horizontally across the dotted line, we have the structural alignment for 1969, although the people will not be the same. Secondly, because there are an even number of officials (fourteen), each chief gets to select the same number, and the whole system works out to a neatly asymmetrical relationship between the moieties. Over a two-year cycle, it becomes symmetrical.

But why is the system structured in just this way? Here the dual organization finally becomes relevant. In the myth of origin I noted that the supernatural *Towa é* always acted in pairs. On the ground, the members of each of the three groups also act in pairs, one from each moiety. Every time the *Towa é* act in an official capacity, they go in pairs, as when they go to stand guard at the moiety chiefs' homes when the prayer feathers are offered to the spirits on their behalf. They do this a total of sixty-four times during the course of the year and, in each case, there is one from each moiety. When the first and second become tired, the third- and fourth-ranked *Towa é* replace them, and so on; the cycle may even be repeated if the situation demands the presence of the *Towa é* for a prolonged period.

Similarly, it has been noted that during the process of retiring from office at the end of the year, the governor and his first lieutenant together went to the home of the Summer chief. The new governor also took his first lieutenant when they delivered the prayer feathers to the Winter chief's home, as well as when they went to the priest to ask for a mass. Even the *Fiscales* must always go in pairs (at least), whenever they dig graves or assist the priest. In each instance the pair always includes a member of each moiety.

To understand why both moieties must be represented, we must return again to the recruitment process. While the moiety chiefs select the officials from the Dry Food People, they themselves do not formally go out and notify them, or bring them in to be installed. Instead the retiring officials do this, while all of the Made People remain in the background and largely refrain from speech, even when they become objects of protest. To the Tewa the Made People, as a category, are seen as mediators between spiritual and human existence. They are part-time priests who transcend ordinary existence, and, as such, they are regarded with ambivalence by the Dry Food People. Their role, in the most general terms, is to keep the seasons progressing normally and to concern themselves with peace and harmony in social relations. This is why they must not display anger or interfere directly in the affairs of the

Dry Food People; to do so would be regarded as an arbitrary application and abuse of their power.

Since they themselves cannot go out among the Dry Food People, some link or system of mediation is needed between the two categories. The *Towa é* and the other officials provide this link, and because they may intervene directly in the affairs of their fellow men, they are referred to here as a political organization. All three groups temporarily undergo what van Gennep (1960) calls a "rite of transition"; that is to say, they wear their authority over their heads—a symbolic reference to the wearing of *Kachina* masks—and they are symbolically put on "cloud blossoms" for their term of office. At the end of this term of office they undergo what van Gennep terms a "rite of separation" (1960) whereby they are returned to their original status as Dry Food People.

The *Towa é* and other officials, then, are best understood as mediators between entire vertical categories; as such they must transcend the moieties. I can further distinguish here between duties performed for the whole society and duties performed for the moiety. In the preceding chapter I noted how the latter come dramatically to the fore in life crisis rites. Here what has been most noteworthy is that the operative value of the moieties, as such, is canceled over a two-year cycle.

The quotation from an informant which opens this chapter now becomes relevant: "For you our elder, nothing is forbidden, either here in the lake or among the Dry Food People." The words were spoken by the Summer chief, replying to the expressed fears of a young Winter man who was heading the *Towa é* for the first time. The young *Towa é* felt he should not see the Summer chief's altar because he was of the opposite moiety. The broader message these words were intended to convey—by the context in which they were spoken—was that the authority of the *Towa é* extends everywhere whenever he acts in an official capacity; he may go anywhere among the Made People and Dry Food People in carrying out his duties. Not only is the *Towa é* a link and mediator between the Dry Food People and the Made People, but he is also the only check on the potentially abusive power of the latter.

In order to understand just how the *Towa é* can serve as a check on the Made People who appoint and ostensibly control them, I must again introduce the *Tsave Yoh*. These, we will recall from chapter 2, are masked supernatural whippers who dwell in the caves and labyrinths of the four sacred hills and who are impersonated by the *Towa é*.[8] The *Tsave Yoh* are impersonated only during the Turtle Dance held at the winter solstice each year. Eight days before the dance itself, a *Towa é* of the Winter moiety appears in the kiva where practice sessions are being conducted. He is dressed in buckskin leggings and shirt, and a buffalo-skin kilt, and he wears a mask which is painted *white* with *red* eye and mouth openings. He carries a whip and greets the Made People and dance participants by whipping them across the legs. The following night a *Towa é* of the Summer moiety repeats the visit. He is attired like his Winter counterpart in all respects save the mask, which is *black* with *yellow* eye and mouth openings. The color symbolism, it will be recalled, is that associated with each moiety. During the next three nights both *Tsave Yoh* appear together. In each instance, however, the Winter moiety *Tsave Yoh* enters the village from the northeast side, while the other enters from the southeast side.

During these visits anyone who has disobeyed the *Towa é* or refused to participate in rituals during the preceding year is brought to the kiva and flogged. Even Made People may be mercilessly whipped. In 1959 a *Kossa*, or sacred clown, was so treated because he had been drinking too much and ignoring his ritual duties. In the case of women and disobedient children, the *Tsave Yoh* are accompanied to the homes by the other *Towa é* and the whipping administered there.[9]

On the sixth day, or two days before the Turtle Dance, both *Tsave Yoh* appear at the same time again, but just before sundown. The purpose of this visit is to make sure the plazas of the village are swept clean. They may whip any woman of a home whose yard is unswept, giving her a hand broom after doing so. Once again, the Winter *Tsave Yoh* enters the village from the north plaza and the Summer one from the south plaza. At the "earth mother earth navel middle place" they meet, shake hands, and then proceed to the opposite plazas. In other words, the Winter moiety *Tsave Yoh* makes a sunwise circuit around the village, the Summer moiety *Tsave Yoh* an anti-sunwise one. This symbolic act of meeting and shaking hands, performed while standing atop the sacred shrine at the center of the village, is interpreted by informants as affirming the unity and partnership of the *Tsave Yoh*. It may be added, by logical extension, that the unity of the moieties is also being affirmed, for the *Tsave Yoh* represent the moieties. All six *Towa é* take turns—two by two—in impersonating the *Tsave Yoh* during these three visits, but theoretically no one in the village knows their identity or even that they are *Towa é*. This is why they can whip with impunity. There are also independent supernatural sanctions surrounding their role. It is said that a woman who once tried to resist a flogging became paralyzed from an ant bite within four days.

On the day of the Turtle Dance itself, two men who are not *Towa é* do the impersonating, and their identity is perhaps the most closely guarded secret in the village. It is most certainly never revealed to children. They police the village during the progress of the dance itself, and any native who is not participating may be placed along the line of dancers, even without ritual dress. Children who venture too close are whipped, as are any deviants who show themselves. Each *Tsave Yoh* concentrates on the people of his own moiety.

That evening, after the dance is over, the *Tsave Yoh* go from house to house to say farewell for another year. They are accompanied by the *Towa é*, and no family may deny them admission. At each home they assure the women that if their children misbehave, the *Tsave Yoh* may be summoned by a tap on the fireplace chimney, and they will return to carry the children off to their homes in the labyrinths (*tsin fo nuneh*) of the sacred hills. Particularly mischievous youngsters may be brought out and whipped, then left with the promise that they will be eaten if they misbehave again. As a parting gift to the *Tsave Yoh*, the women of each household place loaves of bread and sweetcakes in a sack which the *Towa é* carry for them. In return, the *Tsave Yoh* present small bits of meat to any member of a household who asks for it.

After every home in the village has been visited, the *Tsave Yoh* are accompanied to the homes of their respective moiety chiefs. Here they take off their masks while the moiety chief recites a long prayer of thanks to the *Tsave Yoh* who has represented his moiety. Next, the *Tsave Yoh* are accompanied to a house where the masks and other paraphernalia are kept. Here they remove the masks, and each recites a long prayer of retirement. The paraphernalia are then stored in large pottery jars for use again the following year. Two small stone bear fetishes, which the *Tsave Yoh* have been wearing around their necks in pouches, are also returned to the medicine men, who loan them each year to those who are to impersonate the *Tsave Yoh* on the day of the Turtle Dance. Thus, as suddenly and as dramatically as they appear, the *Tsave Yoh* are gone, not to return again for another year.

There is one very noteworthy difference in the prayers recited on this day, in contrast to those recited during the previous seven. On the day of the Turtle Dance, the *Tsave Yoh* mention in their prayers only the labyrinths of the northern and southern hills, while their predecessors of the previous seven days mention the labyrinths of all four sacred hills.[10] In other words, while the ritual preparations are in progress the unity, not only of the society but of the sacred physical points, is emphasized, while on this occasion the symbolic dual organization is once again reaffirmed. This is so because the *Towa é*, who impersonate the *Tsave Yoh* during the preceding seven days, are best understood not as representatives of their respective moieties; rather, they are mediators between the Made People and the Dry Food People, as the former are mediators between society and the supernatural world. There is revealed here not only a system of checks and balances in the autonomy of the *Towa é-Tsave Yoh*, but a symbolic inter-transposability of the whole (society) and its two major constituent parts (the moieties). To state it otherwise, we have here a further example of how there can be unity and division at the same time; the Tewa seem to shift easily from one perspective to the other as the situation warrants.

The *Tsave Yoh* then can best be understood as symbols par excellence of the impersonal authority of the *Towa é*. Their identity must be kept secret if they are to enforce the sanctions with which they are charged. Once they don their masks they may flog anyone with impunity, and one cannot think of revenge because one can never be certain just who is behind the mask. This applies equally to Dry Food People and Made People, and, therefore, not even the latter can completely control the *Towa é*. In fact then, the *Towa é* and the *Tsave Yoh* are one and the same, and this is why they are both of the hills in the Tewa system of classification. What the *Tsave Yoh* definitely are not, however, are "clowns" as they have been called by Parsons and Beals (1934) and by every student of the Pueblos who has ever commented on them.[11]

Admittedly not all of the points of ambiguity resulting from the interstitial character of the *Towa é* have been resolved, but I hope a fair share of the long-standing problems concerning their role in Pueblo society have now become clear.[12] Because of their mediating role between the two other major categories of Tewa society, perhaps they must always remain analytically somewhat vague, sharing some characteristics with each but being not quite either. As one *Towa é* remarked in attempting to convey some understanding of the difficult nature of his role as mediator between the two other categories: "I walk as on the edge of a knife."

5

The Made People and the Dry Food Who Never Did Become

Of the Made People ask me nothing,
for I am not of the lake.

When the Made People are discussed, "all paths come together," according to the Tewa, for I have had more than one occasion to note that they control and direct all group ritual activities and stand as the real powers behind the political officials. The term for the Made People, *Patowa*, may also be translated as "completed," "instituted," or "become." They are called such because their offices were founded and their first occupants instituted in the primordial home beneath the lake of emergence. All of the above meanings are correct, and if a bit of ambiguity is detected, it is only because none of the above terms quite conveys the full meaning. What they are not—at least not consciously—are "Fish People," as they have been so long designated in the ethnographic literature on the Tewa. Bandelier began this interesting designation (1890), and then Parsons (1929, 1939), Laski (1959), and others continued to use it without question. This despite the fact that no real rationale could be found for calling the Made People "Fish People." Although the term *pa* means "fish" as well as "made," fish are not venerated or regarded in any special way by the Tewa. On the contrary, the Tewa regard them as of no special ritual or economic significance, unlike most other land and water animals they know.

Bandelier's original argument sounded convincing because his ever-active imagination seized upon a myth in which half of the Tewa fell into a river while crossing it and turned into fish. Several decades later one of Parson's woman informants actually reiterated this myth to answer her queries on the point. Her argument sounded even more plausible than that of Bandelier because she

79

translated the name for the northern plaza in San Juan as "Fish Town Court" (Parsons 1929, Map 2). This plaza, named *Pa awe bu u* in Tewa, does indeed seem to begin with the term for fish, but the tone and vowel length are different. Moreover, the gloss has no meaning out of context. The entire phrase simply means "sloping plaza" because the northern plaza slopes dramatically at its eastern end. When I myself first asked a Made Person why they were called "Fish People," he first roared with laughter and then severely castigated me for being so ignorant as not to know they were called Made People because they were "made" beneath the lake of origin. I would suggest that the misunderstanding has endured so long because no investigator ever thought of asking a Made person to explain the term. Most Dry Food People, like Parson's informant, merely accept the more common usage of the term without questioning its logical implications when applied to the Made People.[1]

This point aside, I will first identify the eight groups which comprise the general category of Made People, in the following section, and then analyze the process by which one is recruited into them. The emphasis is upon the distinctiveness of the Made People in contrast to the two other human categories described in the preceding chapters. Next, those spirits of Category 6 that are impersonated in ritual are identified, and the nature of their linkage with the Made People examined. Then the annual ritual cycle which is planned and directed by the Made People, executed by the *Towa é*, and participated in by the Dry Food People, is examined. In the final section the full weight of evidence assembled in this work is brought to bear on the problem of Tewa subsistence. In the final two sections then, the problems of Tewa ritual, polity, and economy emerge clearly as aspects of a single integrated system. To that extent may the position be defended that this work deals with Tewa social structure as well as ritual, and to that extent also may we understand what the Tewa mean when they say that all of the paths of life join when one discusses the Made People.

The Made People have always been a subject of great interest among early students of the Tewa, although they have never been understood by their proper name. Consequently, a very impressive body of ethnographic detail has been compiled by Curtis (1926), Parsons (1929, 1939), Spinden (1933), and Laski (1959), to mention only the better accounts. But as popular as they have been, the Made People have also been extremely difficult to understand. Indeed writers such as Curtis and Parsons have focused on the

Made People to the virtual exclusion of other aspects of Tewa society and culture. The reason is simply that there are so many groups of Made People, and their duties reach into so many aspects of Tewa life, that it is difficult to avoid getting lost in the subject. Mindful of this danger and of the literature available, I emphasize in this section only their hierarchical order, process of recruitment, symbols of office, and the nature of their linkage with the deities of Category 6. Their duties are presented in more meaningful context in the following two sections.

Let us turn then to figure 7, which lists the eight groups of

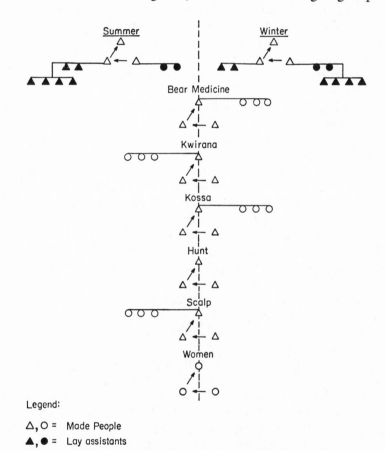

Legend:

△,○ = Made People
▲,● = Lay assistants

Fig. 7   The Made People

Made People, using conventional kinship symbols to distinguish the sexes. First, each group is conceptualized as consisting of a head and two assistants. There may be more members, of course, but each head must have a "right arm" and a "left arm" for the body to be complete. The arrows, in turn, indicate the manner in which junior members move up the hierarchy. Thus, the right arm succeeds the head, the left becomes right, and a new member is recruited to become the left arm.

In addition, four of the groups have female counterparts to assist them in some of their duties. These female assistants are not ranked, so they are presented apart from, but connected to, the male members. It will be noted that the Hunt and Women's societies have no assistants of the opposite sex. The reason in the former instance is that hunting is regarded as strictly a male activity, while the Women are already closely associated with the male members of the Scalp society. They feed and care for the scalps obtained by the latter. The Summer and Winter moiety societies, in turn, have assistants of both sexes who are not themselves Made People. These are represented by the shaded symbols. The exact nature of their relationship to the Made People is explained below.

I should like to point out, while figure 7 is still before us, that the Made People and their assistants number at least fifty-two. Occasionally, whenever a society is in danger of extinction, a person may belong to two, but in general this is not done. On the contrary, most of the eight societies usually have more than the minimally necessary number of members. What this means is that the Made People and their assistants comprise a very sizable percentage of the population. This was more true in the past, when each Tewa village numbered no more than a few hundred people. Indeed, older informants state that, until about the turn of the century, nearly every Tewa adult belonged to a group of Made People. They add that it is not good in any case for one to be a Dry Food person all of his life. I shall return to this point at the end of this section.

The dotted line running down the center represents the division by moiety. It will be noted that only the members of the moiety societies and their respective lay assistants are on opposite sides of the line; they are the only ones who must belong to one moiety or the other. The dotted line bisects each of the other six groups because their members are recruited without regard to moiety membership. The moieties are represented as equal because this is the way the Tewa conceptualize them. This equality or symmetry does not exist at any given time, but is brought about during the course of a year because each of the two moiety chiefs rules the village for one half of the year. In fact, the Summer chief rules for more than seven months and the Winter chief for less than five, but this discrepancy presents no problems to the Tewa, as we shall see below. It has, however, given rise to another long-standing misconception among previous writers on the Tewa. Most have stated that the Summer chief is more important, either because he rules for a longer period or because Summer informants stated that their chief was more important whenever the question was pressed. One Made person resolved the issue with a statement to the effect that just as males and females are both needed to maintain the village and just as the seasons must alternate, so also must the power and authority of the moiety chiefs be equal.

The remainder of the hierarchy proceeds in the order presented, except for the *Kwirana* and the *Kossa*, who may be described as "cold" and "warm" clowns, respectively. The native terms are retained on figure 7 because their etymologies are unknown, and, therefore, they cannot be translated. The point to be made here is that because of their identifications with weather, they exchange positions in the hierarchy at the same time as do the moiety societies. In other words, when the Winter chief rules the village, the *Kwirana* are fourth in the hierarchy, as presented on figure 7; during the remainder of the year, from about a month before the vernal to the autumnal equinox, the *Kossa* are fourth. This point, too, has caused some confusion in the literature when writers have attempted to determine the clowns' hierarchical rank. Since the two clown societies are the only ones besides the moiety societies that alternate in the hierarchy, there are grounds for saying that their memberships may have once been limited to the respective moieties. This must remain a hypothesis because the distinction has been a symbolic rather than a social one within the memory of the oldest Tewa informants. Both groups include members from each moiety, and neither is clearly tied to either moiety.

Now, what do I mean when I refer to the Made People as constituting a hierarchy? I mean that, with the exception of the Hunt society, this is the order in which they were "made" in the myth of origin. The four groups that alternate seasonally are reconciled in myth by the simple expedient that members of the Summer moiety almost always say the Summer chief and the *Kossa* were "made" before the Winter chief and the *Kwirana*, respectively. The reverse is, of course, true of Winter informants who relate the myth of origin. The broader implications of this tendency are explored in greater detail elsewhere (Ortiz 1966a), so I pause here only to note that it is possible to predict with re-

markable accuracy the moiety membership of a Tewa informant
by the way he relates myths. Aside from these qualifications, however, the hierarchy of myth is faithfully reproduced in ritual and
social relations; this is the order in which the Made People enter
the kiva during communal rituals, and this is the order in which
songs honoring them are sung during these same rituals. When they
participate actively in rituals, this is the order in which they line up.

The only exception to the exclusive seasonal priority of one
moiety society or the other occurs when selecting political officials,
as was explained in the preceding chapter. To recapitulate briefly,
in alternate years the Summer chief may select the head of each of
the three divisions comprising the political organization, although
the Winter chief is ruling the village at the time. We have, in effect,
two systems of time operating concurrently, each of which serves
to erase the temporary asymmetry which exists at any given time
between the moieties. The first, which is undoubtedly native, erases
the asymmetry during the course of a given year; the second, which
was probably introduced by the Spaniards and which is based on
the Western calendar, works itself out over a two-year cycle. The
two systems of time together constitute a powerful integrative
force in the society, for they make it almost impossible for either
moiety to attain a clear-cut ritual or political supremacy.

The balance is a delicate one, to be sure, but as long as the two
systems of alternation work we have a persuasive answer to the
question of how the moieties can be in a reciprocal relationship and
in a relationship of hierarchical superordination and subordination.
This issue was first defined by Lévi-Strauss (1944) and systematically confronted by him many years later (1963*a*). It has also
been raised by Maybury-Lewis (1960, p. 41), but neither he nor
Lévi-Strauss has resolved it. The answer the Tewa present is, in
a word, *time*. The asymmetrical relationship which obtains *at any
given time* between the moieties becomes symmetrical over a
period of a year or two years. The fact that the two systems of
alternation overlap also provides an answer to the question Maybury-Lewis (1960, p. 27) regards as fundamental in the study of
dual organizations: How can the society be united and divided
at the same time? The answer here is simply that since there is
temporal overlap, no clear and consistent line of division can
emerge; the moieties can never really be uniformly divided on a
major structural issue.

The recruitment of the last six groups in the hierarchy without
regard to moiety is also significant in this regard. These six may be
understood as mediators between the social and symbolic distinc-

tions represented by the two moiety societies. They represent roles that must be performed if the society is to exist as a society, just as the *Towa é* perform mediating roles of another order. Once a medicine man has been initiated, for instance, he no longer belongs primarily to his own moiety but must treat all members of the village who come to him for help. In fact, the medicine men almost always act as a unit, so it would be difficult for any one of them to perform discriminatory services on behalf of his moiety. This point emerges clearly in Laski's detailed description of the role of the medicine men (1959, pp. 93–122), and I have already described the mediating role of the Hunt chief and the *Kossa* in chapter 3. These and the other three groups are also described in detail in Parsons (1929), and Curtis (1926).

We may return now to the lay assistants of the two moiety societies. The two pairs of assistants—one pair female and the other male—who are represented on either side of the Made People in figure 7 are called *Sehshu*. The etymology of their name is unknown, but their principal function is to assist the two moiety societies whenever the chiefs hold water giving and other moiety-specific rituals. They are selected by the members of the moiety societies from among middle-aged Dry Food People of their own moiety, and they hold office for life. Their initiation rite is a simple blessing rite called "life-breath-blow," and it is performed by the chief deity of the moiety in question whenever the deities visit the village. The nominee is asked to stand before the deity, who passes his hands over him without touching him. After this he may assist the Made People in any way they request, but he may never handle their specific symbols of office. His duties are the same in each moiety, and all are selected for their general intelligence and seriousness in ritual activities. In general, these duties are not clearly defined, and the *Sehshu* are often reduced to such tasks as running errands, grinding plant medicines, and cleaning up after the Made People have been in retreat.

The four male assistants of each moiety who are represented on the outer margins of figure 7, just below the *Sehshu*, have more clearly specified duties. They are called "Keepers of the entrance to the lake"; the lake in this instance refers to the private moiety chambers that are attached to the large communal kiva. These chambers, which members of the opposite moiety may never enter, represent for each moiety the original home under the lake, as discussed in chapter 3. Each group of four assists in selecting those who are to impersonate the deities associated with each moiety. Once the selections are made, these assistants take complete charge of all preparations for the coming of the gods, on behalf of their respective moieties. As their name implies, they sit, two on each side of the door, to guard the "entrance to the lake." They are selected by the members of the respective moiety societies from among those elders who have become too old to impersonate the deities themselves. They have no initiation rite; rather, they retire into these extremely honored roles after long years of dedicated service as impersonators of the "Dry Food Who Never Did Become." [2]

I am now in a position to discuss the recruitment process of the Made People, by way of distinguishing them from the other two categories into which the Tewa classify human existence. Once again this is a subject on which much has been written (Curtis 1926, Parsons 1929, 1939, Laski 1959, and Dozier 1960). Laski's account is particularly detailed and accurate, so only a synthetic sketch applicable to all eight groups is presented, to avoid getting bogged down in the enormous detail that the subject would otherwise entail.

First, there are three methods by which one is recruited into the various societies of Made People. These have been commonly known to students of the Pueblos as dedication, trespass, and trapping, and each may be briefly illustrated. Dedication has a dual aspect in the sense that not only may a person dedicate his life to a particular society, but he may be dedicated by his parents even before he is born. To take the latter possibility, if the mother has a difficult childbirth and has to request the assistance of a medicine man, the child may be "given" to that society. If, on the other hand, a close living relative or ancestor belonged to a particular society, the child may be given to that one. A third possibility is that a child born during the period when the impersonators of the deities of his father's moiety are in retreat will be given the name of one of the deities. Later on he may officially join that moiety society because his time of birth is interpreted as a calling. A child or an adult may also dedicate himself to one of the societies for one of several reasons. He may receive a calling by dreaming of the society in question; he may discover sacred objects belonging to that society; or he may be cured of an illness by that group. In any case this self-dedication does not become official until after the child has undergone water pouring, for only then, as we will recall from chapter 3, does he become a Dry Food person; only then does he become a person of reason, capable of making up his own mind. Dedication, in any of its forms, is the most common method of recruitment. It is also the most effective because it rests either upon individual choice or upon a long process of preparation.

By trespass is meant simply that a child or adult inadvertently comes upon a particular society that is in retreat, witnesses sacred objects and activities, and hears ritual speech which "belongs" to that society. Since no Dry Food person may have this knowledge, he must join the society upon whose activities he has intruded. The *Towa é* alone are immune to this rule; they may witness these activities whenever they stand guard during retreats or otherwise act in an official capacity.

Trapping refers to one of several processes by which a society in need of new members will actively go out and recruit them by means which may be regarded as devious. During the summer of 1963, a woman from San Juan had a curing ceremony performed in her home by the medicine men. At the end of the rite the medicine men stepped into another room of the house, as if chasing a witch, and appeared with a small rag doll dressed like a *Kossa*, or "warm" clown. The woman was told that an evil *Kossa* was causing her illness, and she could only hope for permanent relief if she joined that group and learned their ways. The rationale for this action—probably recognized as such by most of the villagers— was that the *Kossa* needed a replacement for a female assistant who had passed away. The medicine men, who by the nature of their role in the society have access to a wide range of supernatural sanction, often perform this recruiting function for five of the eight societies. The moiety societies recruit by the other methods described above, and the criterion for joining the Scalp society is to take an enemy scalp. Perhaps this point helps to explain why the medicine men stand below the moiety societies but above the other five in the hierarchy; they can exert a powerful influence over the last five groups, but not over the moiety societies.

The process of becoming a Made person itself proceeds in three rather distinct phases. The first phase begins when one undergoes "Made People water giving" at the hands of the society into which he has been recruited by one of the three methods outlined above. This rite is like that outlined for the Dry Food People in chapter 3 except that it is conducted by the head of the society in question, only the members of that society may be present, and the sponsor must come from that society. Water giving removes the new member from the category of Dry Food People and gives him access to the ritual knowledge of the Made People. Henceforth, the novitiate may run errands and perform other generally menial tasks for the society as he learns its prayers, songs, and other ritual activities. This novitiate period may last many years for a youth and only a year for an adult.

The second phase begins exactly one year before the person becomes a full-fledged member of the society. It is initiated by an act called "giving a year's notice," whereby the members of the society notify the novitiate's relatives at a meeting that he will complete his novitiate in a year. This is a signal for the relatives to begin gathering food and ritual paraphernalia for the final phase. After the year's notice is given, also, the novitiate enters into a closer teacher-pupil relationship with his sponsor, and he is increasingly given more responsible duties to perform. The second phase is brought to a close twelve days before the end of the year when the members of the society go into partial seclusion to pray, meditate, and teach the novitiate what he has not yet learned, and to make a set of sacred objects symbolic of the society for his use. After eight days they go into complete seclusion. This final four-day process is called "Made People finishing," like that for the Dry Food People at large. There is, of course, no counterpart for the water pouring ritual because this is only intended to make children Dry Food People.

On the fourth or final night of the retreat, all members of the community are invited to gather in the kiva "to accept a new Made person," for on this night he enters the third phase—that of full membership in the society. He passes forever from the category Dry Food People to that of Made People. The new Made person demonstrates the skills appropriate to the society before the assembled populace. A new Summer society member may "cause" plants to sprout miraculously from the kiva floor; a Winter man may dip his arms in boiling cornmeal gruel to prove that he cannot be burned, and a new medicine man may extract foreign objects from the bodies of the spectators, by way of demonstrating his healing powers. In this way the Dry Food person passes into a completely new level of existence; one to which he must belong for the rest of his life. He, unlike the *Towa é*, can never return to the status of common Tewa.

As a grand climax to the night's activities, a group of deities may be brought to the kiva to confer their collective blessing on the initiate.[3] They welcome him as one who is now "of the lake," for he has symbolically reenacted, during the past twelve days, the mythical journey of migration back to the lake of emergence. This is why I say that the Made People and the "Dry Food Who Never Did Become" are linked; the former are the earthly representatives of the latter, and at death the former rejoin the latter in the lake.

The two categories are linked in another way, for the various objects made for the new Made person during the twelve days of preparation—objects symbolic of his office—represent the deities of Category 6. In addition to "corn mothers" representing the original mothers in the lake of origin, each Made person has other objects representing specifically named deities. Those held by the two moiety chiefs—and they have the largest number—have been enumerated in chapter 3. The junior members of the moiety societies have only their corn mothers, represented by perfect ears of white corn. As noted in chapter 4, the Medicine, Hunt, and Scalp societies have a stone figure representing the *Towa é*. The medicine men have, in addition, carved stone bears and a bear paw, and the Hunt society members have carved stone mountain lions. The *Kossa* have small figurines representing *Kossa*, in addition to their corn mothers, while the *Kwirana* have only the corn mothers.

The Women's society presents an insight of special significance. Within the group of three (or more) women who comprise the society, there are two divisions. The head, who is called "Red Bow Male Youth," has a white corn mother, but the other two, who are called "Blue Corn Women," have blue corn mothers. In other words, this is the only instance, aside from the naming ceremony, when Blue Corn Woman, the mother of the Summer moiety, is represented in tangible form. All of the other Made People have white corn mothers, and White Corn Maiden, as we may recall from the myth of origin, symbolically represents the mother of the Winter moiety. The principal duty of the Women's society is to care for the scalps in the possession of the Scalp society. The head is called "male youth" because she represents the Winter moiety and maleness, although she may be recruited from either moiety. The Blue Corn Women, in turn, represent the Summer moiety and femaleness, although they, too, may be recruited from either moiety. Several interesting lines of inquiry may be pursued with regard to these personages, but fortunately Curtis (1926) and Parsons (1929, pp. 136–42) discuss them in sufficient detail.

There are, however, three points which I should like to emphasize with regard to the Women's society. First, when one becomes a Made person his prior moiety affiliation is erased, unless he belongs to the moiety societies. Secondly, the moiety-specific symbolism is so well developed among the Tewa that they can think of a female Made person as a "male youth." Third, Blue Corn Woman, the mythical mother of the Summer moiety, is represented among the Made People only by the Blue Corn Women, but she is represented. I do not know just why White Corn Maiden is emphasized, but this is true in mythology as well as in ritual.[4]

All of the Made People also share one, and only one, common symbol which most clearly establishes them as being "of the lake." Each is presented at finishing with an elaborately decorated and terraced pottery bowl called a "lake bowl." Henceforth, whenever he acts in an official capacity, he must fill this bowl with medicinal water, place his stone figurines within, and set it before him. Dry Food People and *Towa é* who participate in rituals may be invited to drink the medicinal water for long life and general well-being, but they may never own such a bowl themselves. The bowl of water represents the primordial lake of emergence, and only the Made People are empowered to recreate it in the village.

The informant's statement which opens this chapter may now be presented again: "Of the Made People ask me nothing, for I am not of the lake." What the informant, an elderly woman, tried to communicate was that she knew little of the ways of the Made People because she was not one of them. Since they belong to another order of existence she felt it was not her place, as a "trash person," to speak of them. This view is one generally held by the Dry Food People.

Since the recruitment process has also been described by Curtis (1926), Parsons (1929), and most lucidly by Laski (1959), I need note only a few more general points, by way of summary. First, no one may be initiated as a Made person until he has undergone Dry Food People finishing, or until he is defined as an adult. Secondly, the tripartite diachronic structure of the initiation process is the same for both men and women; it differs only in intensity, due to differences in the duties the sexes perform. Female Made People serve as assistants to their male counterparts; they do not cure, clown, or go out with war parties. Rather, they feed those in retreat, grind plant medicines, and clean up after the men during ritual activities. The activities, it may be recalled, are the same ones performed by the lay assistants to the moiety societies, which do not have Made People as assistants. The principal difference between the two is that female Made People, by being initiated like males, have access to all the ritual knowledge and prerogatives appropriate to the society. The lay assistants have neither the knowledge nor the prerogatives. Perhaps the best way to underscore the distinction between Made People and Dry Food People is to reiterate the example cited in chapter 3: any female

Made person who marries a member of the opposite moiety need not join her husband's moiety, whereas conversion is normal procedure for the lay assistants and all other Dry Food People. The Made People are the only ones completely exempt from this rule.

Initiates into the moiety societies are distinguished in another way. On the morning following the kiva performance when the novitiate emerges as a Made person, his relatives must feed the entire village in their homes. If the new Made person belongs to one of the moiety societies, however, all of the members of his moiety participate in feeding the people of the opposite moiety. Initiates into the other six societies are accorded no such special treatment or general recognition. I have stated above that these six groups act as mediators within the general category of Made People; members of these six no longer belong primarily to their own moieties after initiation. Their roles are general, and they must serve the society at large. Only the two moiety societies clearly and unambiguously embody the social and symbolic distinctions represented by the moieties; they epitomize the distinctions, while the other six societies mediate them. This is why these six societies are collectively referred to as *teh pingeh in*, "those of the middle of the structure."

Turning now to the deities of Category 6 themselves, the major difference between them and the two other categories of spirits is that they are regularly impersonated in ritual. The others may be always present in the form of *xayeh* or as stone figurines in the keeping of the Made People, but the deities of Category 6 are the only ones regularly brought to life, as it were. Consequently they are especially relevant for an understanding of the way the dual organization operates in the supernatural or symbolic realm. To this end I present them in some detail, although a thorough analysis of their place in the Tewa scheme of things will also be presented in another monograph (Ortiz 1966*b*).

The "Dry Food Who Never Did Become" represent the highest order of deities in the Tewa world, as I noted in chapters 2 and 3. They derive their name from their being with the people before emergence, but unlike the people and the *Towa é* they never became *seh t'a* or "dry food." They may also be regarded as withdrawn high deities, for there is little direct use of the category in everyday conversation and conceptualization. It is rarely used because it is so abstract and overarching; it includes the sun, moon, prominent stars and constellations, trees, and those animals spoken of in the origin myth. More familiar terms for these deities are *opa pene in*, "those from beyond the world," and *opa nuneh in*, "those from within and around the earth." Here I am concerned primarily with two classes within this larger category: the variously named spirit patrons of the Made People, as described above; and the *Oxua*, or "cloud beings."

The *Oxua* are the deities that are impersonated in Tewa rituals and that are under the care and tutelage of the lay assistants who "guard the entrance to the lake." They are a class within the larger category, differentiated only in that they, rather than some other deities, are impersonated regularly. Figure 8 lists the three

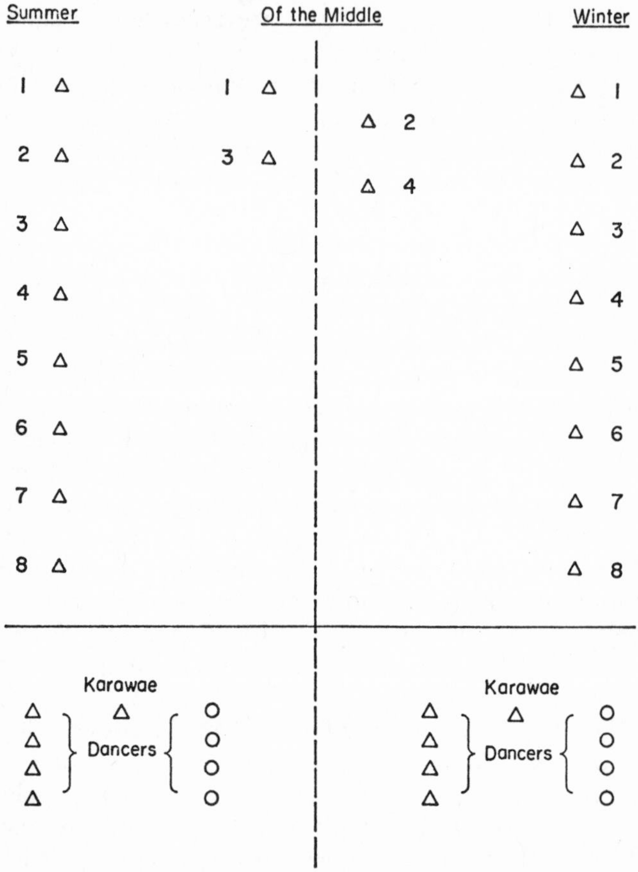

Summer	Of the Middle	Winter
1 △	1 △	△ 1
	△ 2	
2 △	3 △	△ 2
	△ 4	
3 △		△ 3
4 △		△ 4
5 △		△ 5
6 △		△ 6
7 △		△ 7
8 △		△ 8

Karawae   Karawae

△ ⎫   △ ⎰ ○
△ ⎬ Dancers ⎰ ○   △ ⎬ Dancers ⎰ ○
△ ⎭   ○   △ ⎭   ○
△   ○   △   ○

Fig. 8 The Dry Food Who Never Did Become

major groups of *Oxua* in ranked order. The names are dispensed with, for convenience, because some of them translate into phrases in English. The deities associated with the Summer moiety are listed in the left-hand column, and they are further associated with the summer season (warmth) and the growth of plants. The name of the leader is "Black mud," after the greasy black mud gathered from ponds during the summer, and which the Tewa use for body decoration. He is regarded as the most powerful force in the group for warm weather, and warm weather is always supposed to follow when he appears in the early spring. The other seven are, in order, Douglas Spruce, White Fir, Deer, Yellow Blossom, Dark Blossom, Macaw, and "Blossoms around his Temples." The *Oxua* associated with the Winter moiety are listed in the right-hand column. The leader in this instance is called simply "Cold," because cold weather in the form of snow is supposed to follow in his wake. The power of the symbolic association may be illustrated by the fact that whenever the Winter deities appear after January, the leader is left out and the remaining seven are led in by Douglas Spruce, who is also second in rank here. The fear, of course, is that it will snow if the cold leader appears, and the Tewa wish to have warm weather at this time. The other six are, in order, White Fir, Mountain Lion, Sun, Blue Spruce, "Dance of Man," and "Temples male elder." [5]

In addition to these specifically named and differentiated *Oxua*, each moiety also has another group of nine associated with it, and these appear only during the water pouring ritual described in chapter 3. Thus, the Summer group appear only once every seven years, and the Winter group every four years. This is why they are set apart by the horizontal dotted line. It will be noted that they are identically named for each moiety. The leader, called *Karawae*, is set apart from the others because he is in constant motion, running up and down between the two rows of Dancer *Oxua*. If one of the Dancers seems less than enthusiastic in his performance, the *Karawae* whips him hard across his posterior with one of the yucca leaves he carries in each hand. The *Karawae* is a small, fast bird whose identity I could never learn because it is no longer found in the Tewa area.[6] Somehow, much power is attributed to it, and it is regarded as particularly auspicious for the water pouring initiation ritual. The Dancers are not distinguished; they are the functional equivalents of the "side dancers" of the Keresan Pueblos, as described by White (1935, p. 100). There are four *Oxua* of each sex in each of the two groups, but the females are impersonated by males, as females never impersonate the *Oxua*. All eight such *Oxua* of each moiety are usually impersonated by youths who have recently undergone the finishing rite; this is where many of them begin a lifetime of impersonating the deities of their respective moieties.

Before proceeding to a discussion of the *Oxua* "of the middle," let me review the general observations made in chapter 3, by way of indicating how the dual organization operates on this level. First, only members of the moiety in question may impersonate the *Oxua* associated with that moiety, and only *Kossa* ("warm" clowns) of the same moiety may "bring" the *Oxua*, in the manner described in chapter 3. It would seem that the *Kwirana*, or "cold" clowns, would "bring" the Winter *Oxua*, but this has never been the case within the memory of living informants.[7] Secondly, those of the Summer moiety always come from the south in the spring and summer, and they are collectively associated with warm weather. Thus they emphasize yellow (for sunshine), black (for rain-laden cumulus clouds), and green (for growing crops) in their dress. The Winter *Oxua*, on the other hand, always come from the north in the fall and winter, and they are collectively associated with cold weather. They emphasize white (for winter moisture) and red (for the rouge used in warfare and hunting) in their dress. Even the feathers used reflect this color symbolism, those of the Summer *Oxua* being taken from colorful birds of the summer and those of the Winter coming from white or grey birds of winter.

The contrast emerges most strikingly when only the *Oxua* the two moieties have in common are considered; the Douglas Spruce, White Fir, *Karawae*, and the "Dancers." In each instance, the Summer *Oxua*'s mask is black, green or yellow, with one of the colors emphasized over the others, while the Winter counterpart usually has a white mask with red eye and mouth slits. Yet the dress of these *Oxua* is otherwise identical from one moiety to the other. The first two *Oxua* are common to both moieties because they are named after evergreens, which are symbolic of everlasting life to the Tewa. Spruce and fir branches are used in ritual the whole year round by both moieties, and neither is regarded as belonging exclusively to one or the other. This is true also of Blue Spruce, who is sixth in the Winter hierarchy.[8]

Two other *Oxua* are also instructive in this regard. The deer *Oxua*, who stands fourth in the Summer hierarchy, seems misplaced since hunting is associated with the Winter moiety. In fact, Winter informants insist that he once "belonged" to the Winter moiety, and that his mask was once temporarily in the care of the *Kwirana*, or "cold" clowns. In time only Summer *Kwirana* were left, so the mask passed permanently into the Summer moiety. This may or may not be true, but what is important is that Winter informants are almost apologetic about the deer *Oxua* being of the Summer moiety because they think of him as belonging to them.

The sun *Oxua*, who stands fifth in the Winter hierarchy, presents another problem. Informants of both moieties agree that he belongs with the Winter group because he is a male deity, but he also represents warm weather. Moreover, because he is believed to rise from within a lake in the east and set in a lake in the west, he actually transcends the symbolic distinctions between maleness and east for the Winter moiety, and femaleness and west for the Summer moiety. In this instance, one attribute of the deity is arbitrarily emphasized over an opposite attribute. None of the other *Oxua* associated with either moiety presents problems because each stands squarely within one cluster of symbols or the other. Nevertheless, we do not have a neat and consistent system of binary oppositions, even on this level.

We may now turn to the four *Oxua* "of the middle," who straddle the line dividing the moiety-specific *Oxua* in figure 8, and who visit the village once each year at about the vernal equinox. Their full name is actually "those of the middle of the structure," like the last six groups of Made People, but it was shortened for convenience. Their specific names, beginning with the leader, are "Bowing from side to side," Douglas Spruce, Lightning, and "Flint in hand." These deities demonstrate in every respect the principle of mediation as a principle in action. There are always two impersonators from each moiety; they "come" from a neutral direction (west); they are under the direct sponsorship of the medicine men, who are the most important group of Made People, called *teh pingeh in;* and they are "brought" to the kiva by one *Kossa* and one *Kwirana*. In other words, the "cold" and "warm" clowns work together on this one occasion because it is between seasons; it is neither hot nor cold. In addition, the name of the leader describes his graceful bowing movement from side to side (north to south, Winter to Summer) as he enters the kiva.

As is also demonstrated in figure 8, there is always an asymmetrical relationship between the moieties when they are impersonating these deities, since it is clear that only one moiety may provide the leader. But this situation, like the alternation of the political officials, becomes symmetrical over a period of two years, because the opposite moiety then gets to provide the leader (Ortiz 1965*b*). The integrity of the moieties is still preserved in the sense that the impersonators are selected equally from each moiety, but it is still clear that deities of the middle are seen as mediators between the Winter moiety, the Winter deities, and the forces of nature which they represent and the Summer moiety, the Summer deities, and the forces of nature which they, in turn, represent.

The most important point to be made with respect to the *Oxua* is that, just as there are Made People clearly associated with each moiety, so also are there *Oxua* clearly associated with each moiety; and just as there are mediating groups of Made People, so also are there mediating *Oxua*. Both the mediating *Oxua* and the mediating Made People are designated as "those of the middle of the structure." The social divisions and mediating organizations are thus reflected in the supernatural realm; in fact, they are more clearly evident there. The *Oxua*, then, present another answer to the question of how the moieties can simultaneously be in a reciprocal relationship and in a relationship of hierarchical superordination and subordination (Lévi-Strauss 1944, 1963a; Maybury-Lewis 1960). In this instance, as with the Made People, there are *Oxua* who stand in the middle and serve to bridge the symbolic gap between the moieties through time.[9]

At the end of his life every Made person may look forward to joining the *Oxua* and other deities of Category 6; this is his reward for a lifetime of service in the linked human category.[10] The Made People are first distinguished from the Dry Food People and the *Towa é* in that the survivors of the deceased's society paint the corpse in a process called "marking him to become *Oxua*." In other words, the deceased Made person is specifically marked to join the *Oxua* in the lake of emergence. Second, there is an official twelve-day period of mourning for the Made People, whereas there is only a four-day period of mourning for the Dry Food People. This means simply that the former retrace all twelve steps of the mythical migration path, while the latter go only four steps of the way. I have also noted that the Made People are the only ones who place before them large bowls of sacred medicinal water called "lakes" whenever they are engaged in ritual. The ritual objects owned by a Made person may not be used again, and these are retired to a lake or mountain shrine by the surviving members of the society.

If we look back upon Tewa death ritual as a whole—and this seems a good time to do so—some problems immediately come into focus. First, the Dry Food People and the Made People are distinguished at death, but the *Towa é* are not; in fact, they are treated just like Dry Food People. This may be because the Spaniards instituted the procedure of replacing the incumbents by rotating the office each year. Curtis (1926, p. 4) states quite categorically that the office of *Towa é* was once permanent, like that of the functionally similar Bow Priest of Zuni (Eggan 1950). If Curtis is right, the *Towa é* may once have been distinguished in some way, but unfortunately he offers no real proof in support of his statement. Second, the lay assistants of the Made People are also "marked" at death to become *Oxua*, although they are really only Dry Food People.

To complicate the issue still further, the most knowledgeable of Tewa informants are also vague about where any but the Made People go after death. Some say that even Dry Food People may eventually hope to make it all the way back to the lake of origin if they live according to tradition. Others say, with no great conviction, that one continues to be after death what one was in life. In any case all informants agree on three points. First, one should not be a Dry Food person all of his life; this is why the question of the ultimate fate of such a person's soul does not occupy them too much. Second, the soul does not go to a specific shrine but to any of them, and it may move about from one to the other. This is why offerings may be taken to any shrine during the releasing and subsequent commemorative rites. Third, while the Made People go to the original lake of origin, they may actually be present as *Oxua* at any lake, since they too may move about freely in the underworld. I have already noted in chapters 2 and 4 that the *Towa é* are both of the hills and of the mountains.

In these and other ways the elaborate spatial and conceptual distinctions illustrated in figure 2, which have proven so enlightening as a basis of analysis, become, in a sense, dissolved.[11] The three spiritual categories are brought together again in the underworld, just as the three social categories exist together in this world. Yet the physical points of reference remain to remind us that the distinctions between categories are real.

I would conclude then that when the Tewa think of their social and cultural system, including their relationship to the natural world, they think of it as a single integrated system. But when they impersonate the *Tsave Yoh* or the *Oxua*, or reenact any portion of their mythical migration, they tend to mirror the dual organization. Thus the system of thought and the system of action do not always coincide. The former is the whole which overrides the latter, but the dual organization is the basis on which most of the day-to-day life of the Tewa is structured.

One may choose to emphasize the one or the other, but the lesson I wish to derive is that both are necessary for a full understanding of how Tewa society is integrated and continues through time. Moreover, when the dual organization itself becomes potentially disruptive, "those of the middle of the structure" come into play. This is a further unifying force always operating, both socially and symbolically. In these ways the Tewa provide a further meaningful answer to the question of just how a society can be divided and integrated at the same time. I shall now consider just how this unity within division is brought about during the annual ritual cycle, by outlining the duties of the Made People.

If we can imagine, just for convenience, that the various annual cycles of Tewa ritual, social, and political activities can be peeled off layer by layer, the final layer—the one on which all of the other activities depend—would be the annual cycle of "works" of the Made People. These nine works, as illustrated on figure 9, repre-

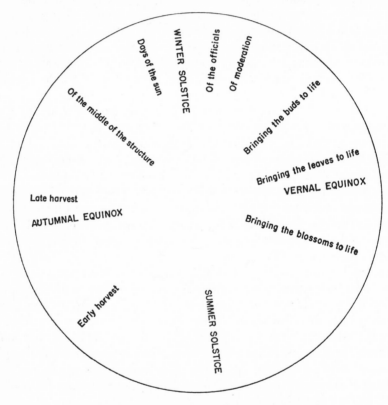

Fig. 9 The annual cycle of works of the Made People

sent the basic structure of activities in Tewa life; they consist of day-long retreats and prayer sessions by each of the Made People's societies. The intent of each work is to harmonize man's relations with the spirits, and to insure that the desired cyclical changes will continue to come about in nature. All members of a given society meet in the home of their head to pray, sing, and perform other ritual acts for a day and a night. They are followed four days later by the next society in the hierarchy, until all eight societies have worked. Thus each of the works takes thirty-two days to complete; when this is done, the whole cycle is repeated for the next work on the calendar. Each time a society works, two *Towa é*, one from each moiety, stand guard outside or in an outer room of the society head's home. This is one of their basic, recurrent duties during the year.

The two exceptions to this formula are the works called "Of the officials" and "Days of the sun." The latter is discussed below. The former always occurs on January 2, and only the moiety chiefs work, each in his own home. The purpose of this work, as discussed in the previous chapter, is to legitimize the authority of the new political officials, who are installed the previous day, by giving it supernatural sanction. This work is post-Spanish because the usual four-day interval is ignored, it does not take thirty-two days to complete, and it occurs on a convenient date which was formerly not recognized by the Tewa. Nonetheless, the Tewa have reoriented their thinking along the lines of the Western calendar to the extent that the other eight works are planned by the Made People at the time the new political officials are installed. Let me follow these through in sequence, by way of lending some credence to my claim that this is the basic structural framework on which all other communal activities during the year are organized.

The first work in the traditional cycle begins on about January 20, and it is initiated by the Winter chief, since he rules the village at the time. It is called "Of moderation" or "To lessen the cold." Its purpose is to melt the snow, if there is any, to thaw the ground, and to prevent further extreme weather. After four days, the Winter chief goes to the home of the Summer chief and asks that he now seek life for all. The Summer moiety society then has its day of work, followed by the medicine men, the *Kwirana*, the *Kossa*, the Hunt society, the Scalp society, and finally the Women. In other words, each society head notifies the next one in the hierarchy that it is his turn to work, on the fourth morning after the head's own work is completed.

The entire cycle repeats itself beginning about February 20, but this time it is the Summer chief who initiates the "Bringing the buds to life" work. This is because the Winter chief transfers primary responsibility for ruling the village to the Summer chief just before this work is initiated. The transfer ceremony itself is very simple; the Winter chief merely goes to the Summer chief's home and "gives the children back" with a ritual speech. He adds that we now "strive toward warmth" again. No tangible symbols of office change hands, but the moiety chiefs are hereafter reversed in the hierarchy of Made People. The *Kwirana* and *Kossa* are also reversed, with the latter now becoming fourth until authority is transferred back to the Winter chief in the fall. In any case, "Bringing the buds to life" is the first of the "sweet" works, called such because the two female *Sehshu* prepare a sweet drink of fermented grain for the Summer moiety society members and the *Towa é* who are standing watch. The female assistants of all the other societies do the same, in their turn.

The next two works in the cycle are also called "sweet" works, although the sweet drink is dispensed with. During this series of three works the Made People are concerned with bringing about the orderly rebirth and growth of plant life, and "sweetness" is symbolically associated with this cycle of nature. "Bringing the leaves to life" is initiated about March 20, and "Bringing the blossoms to life" about April 20. If someone in the village dies while a work is in progress, however, it is automatically postponed for four days. This is done out of respect to the soul, which is believed to wander about the village for four days. If the work is not postponed, it is believed that the spirits will become angered and the desired change in nature will not come about. Since there are usually a few deaths, the works may continue until the beginning of June.[12]

In any case, after the blossoms have been brought to life, or the entire cycle of rebirth and growth in nature is followed, there are no more works until August. One cannot help noting, however, that each of the first four works in the traditional cycle actually comes about a month before the phenomena it is supposed to bring about. In other words, snow may continue to fall and the ground may remain frozen for many weeks after the work "Of moderation." Moreover, the buds on even the earliest blooming trees in the area do not appear until late March or early April. I can only hypothesize that this may not always have been so, and I shall offer a possible explanation for this discrepancy in the following section, after presenting more of the evidence.

At any rate, a considerable period of time elapses between the end of the work for "Bringing the blossoms to life" and the "Early harvest" work, which is initiated by the Summer chief about August 15. The "Early harvest" work may also be called a first fruits festival. At this time all Dry Food People must take the products of the first harvest (sweet corn, squash, melons, water-melons, and fruits) to the home of the head of any Made People's society. The choice rests with the contributor, but he need only take it to one society. If there is a good deal, the Made People themselves may redistribute the products to other societies. The purpose of this work is to thank the spirits for the harvest, and until this is done the people may not hoard and store the first fruits. The Summer chief himself may not even eat the fruits of the current year until after his work. Only after the Summer chief has "opened the way" may the people themselves store the produce. The rule is ignored today, except by the Summer chief himself, but its purpose was to insure that drought, grasshoppers, and other insects would not endanger the crops. It is believed that if man appeared too greedy, the spirits would indeed send some disaster. In any case, if anyone violated this injunction he would be subject to a flogging by the *Towa é*. If too many did so, the *Tsave Yoh*, or masked supernatural figures, would be brought.

The festival aspect of this work begins at noon for each society, just after the first prayer and song session. The Made People invite their relatives to their respective homes for a feast, while young children are given generously of the leftovers. Later that evening the older children are given the final leftovers. On this day groups of boys wander around from the home of one Made person to another, gorging themselves on the leftovers.

The sixth work in the traditional cycle, the "Late harvest" work, is also the last one initiated by the Summer chief, because four days later the Winter chief again takes over the village. It begins, appropriately, at about the autumnal equinox, although this could not be indicated precisely on figure 9. The "Late harvest" work marks the time at which the last crops—corn and beans—may be brought into storage. Thus the Summer chief goes out into the fields to sprinkle *pose* (dew or moisture) on the mature plants, and this informs the people that it is now right and permissible for them to start moving the late crops "into the warmth." This completes the agricultural cycle; after this the poorer families of the village may scavenge what the others have left in the fields.

Early in November the Winter chief initiates his first work, and it is called "Of the middle of the structure" because, according to the Tewa, it is neither winter nor summer, hot nor cold, when it occurs. In other words, just as the last six groups in the hierarchy of Made People are called "of the middle of the structure" because they do not represent the dual organization, and just as the deities "of the middle of the structure" appear at the vernal equinox, when it is neither winter nor summer, so also is this work called "Of the middle of the structure," because it supposedly occurs when it is neither winter nor summer. But it is already well into the autumn when the work is initiated, and almost winter before it is finished. Once again we are faced with the perplexing question of whether the Tewa perceive of the seasons as changing at different times than they actually do, or whether some of the works have been shifted on the calendar. I defer the question for now, and note only that the work in question is a seasonal-transition one; its purpose is to assist in putting nature to sleep for another winter.

The final work of the year, the "Days of the sun," occurs in mid-December. It is a winter solstice and new year rite in which the whole community participates; therefore, it is worth outlining in some detail. For several days beforehand the Winter chief watches the points at which the sun rises and sets on the mountain ranges. When it is reaching its furthest point the Winter chief tells the *Towa é* to notify the people to prepare themselves for the "path of our elder the sun." The *Towa é* then go from house to house telling the people that they must prepare for a four-day period of semi-seclusion and suspended activity, beginning two days hence. There is a sudden burst of activity everywhere because the people must roast and cook all the grain that they will need for the four days, clean house and dispose of all accumulated trash, pay all debts, prepare prayer feathers to tie underneath their horses' tails, hunt, bathe, and prepare pine gum. Moreover, no one should carry burning coals or a lighted cigarette outside, and all heavy work must be avoided. Most of these expressly forbidden activities are intended to prepare the people to face the new year.

During these four days the sun reports to the other deities in the original home under the lake on all that has happened in this world during the year. At this time also, those who are to die during the coming year are marked in some way, and the semi-seclusion and pine gum are intended to aid in averting this possibility. The gum is put on the foreheads, armpits, and on all joints to enable one to attach himself, symbolically, to some part of the sun's dress. If one has to venture out of his home and encounters someone else, he quickly announces just where he is attached; for example, "I am holding onto the sash of our elder the sun." By declaring themselves to be attached to the sun and following his path, the Tewa attempt to avoid being chosen for illness or death during the coming year.

Even animals are said to be taken over by the sun for the four days, and consequently they become scarce. The Tewa declare that even if one went hunting during this period, he would find no game. Those animals that are to die during the coming year are similarly marked, like people. The game animals have their ears slit, and birds have a feather or two pulled out. Animals killed shortly after this time are found with slit ears on which the blood has not yet completely dried, and birds are found with feathers missing, This, to the Tewa, is proof that the animals were marked for their taking, and it is to avoid a similar fate that the ritual precautions are taken by people. Similarly, the prayer feathers are tied underneath the horses' tails so that they will not be marked for death; they are needed to assist man.

During the first day of this general retreat only the members of the Winter moiety society have their work, but they are followed four days later by the members of *all* of the other seven societies, who work simultaneously. This work does not take thirty-two days to complete; it must begin and end within four days for all of the Made People, since an old year is being brought to a close. At dawn on the fifth day, when the sun begins its return journey from the north, the Winter chief lights a new fire in the kiva and normal activities are once again resumed throughout the village. This then marks the real Tewa new year, not the one instituted by the Spaniards, which begins when the new political officials take office. And this brings us back once again to the work "Of the officials," which I have already outlined.

In brief review, this entire cycle of works is tied to nature's basic rhythm and to the Tewa's attempts to influence that rhythm for his well-being. In this sense it is the structure of structures in Tewa life. The one basic division in this cycle is that between the agricultural and the nonagricultural series of works. The dual organization is reflected in the preeminence of the moiety chiefs, but when we view the whole cycle as such the dual organization is over-ridden. Even the *Towa é* who stand watch at each work represent both moieties. More importantly, the entire cycle presents the Made People as being like the links in a chain; they must all act together, one society after the other, to continue nature's basic rhythm. Since this is their paramount duty the Made People cannot be seen as either Winter or Summer, or as functionally specialized and discrete organizations; they must work in unison. The works themselves have been noted before as "retreats" by a number of writers, but no one has ever indicated just how fundamental they are to understanding Tewa culture and the role of the Made People within it.

Turning now to the question of how other ritual activities relate to the cycle of works, I introduce figure 10 as representing a second layer of Tewa culture. Most of the major rituals listed have been described by the various writers on the Tewa cited in this work.

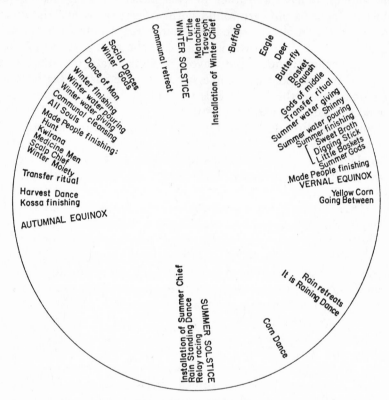

Fig. 10 The ritual calendar

What has been lacking, however, is any attempt to determine the structure of these rituals; to find the order inherent in the entire cycle, thereby deriving the structural principles operating therein. This is the task I have set for the remainder of this section.

First, despite Harrington's (1916) statements to the contrary, all four seasons are named and recognized by the Tewa. I could not make this fully apparent when discussing the cycle of works because there the emphasis is on the entire cycle. However, this four-part year is important for understanding Tewa ritual as a whole, because all activities are fitted into it, albeit sometimes loosely. This recognition is reflected in ritual primarily in the fact that new songs are composed each year for the Turtle, Basket, and Squash ceremonies because they occur at changes of season. The Turtle ceremony follows the work called "Days of the sun" at the winter solstice, and either the Basket or the Squash ceremony is held each year just before the Summer chief takes over the leadership of the village. The songs for all other Tewa rituals are unchanging. There is no set traditional ceremony for the summer solstice, but I have noted above that the first work initiated by the Winter chief in the autumn is called "Of the middle of the structure." This too is a recognition of the change in season, along with the very fact that the moiety chiefs alternate in leadership between what the Tewa now recognize as the equinoxes.

Once again, however, the basic ritual division in the year is the dual one between the summer or agricultural cycle and the winter or nonagricultural cycle. This division is reflected in many ways. Participants in rituals of the summer cycle emphasize the "warm" colors (black, yellow, and green) in their dress, for instance, in the woolen yarn traditionally worn around the knees; during the summer cycle the yarn is of the three colors named above, while during the winter cycle it is usually red or not used at all. Minerals are also classified as to whether they are "hot" or "cold." During rituals of the winter the participants may wear unlimited quantities of silver jewelry because it is "cold"; during the summer there should be little or none worn in ritual, to help prevent cold weather. Instead one should wear jet or other black beads because these are "warm" minerals. Finally, during summer rituals the songs sung are addressed principally to summer spirits, while the reverse is true during winter rituals. I have already noted in chapter 3 that the "cold" and "warm" deities appear only in their respective seasons, while in the preceding section I noted that the deities "of the middle" combine the symbolic attributes of "warm" and "cold," and appear when it is neither winter nor summer.

Another general point which impresses itself forcibly from a glance at figure 10 is that the period of intensive ritual activity is from the autumnal to the vernal equinox, rather than during the spring and summer. There is, in fact, a relative paucity of ritual activity during the rest of the year. This is in marked contrast to the situation among the Hopi, for instance, where the year is primarily marked by the solstices, and the period of intensive ritual activity proceeds from the winter to the summer solstice (Eggan 1950). It is unclear when this shift comes in the eastern Pueblos, but it represents an important difference, at least between the Tewa and the western Pueblos generally. It is, of course, also the basis on which the dual organization of Tewa ritual rests.

While the solstices are regarded by the Tewa as less basic in the operation of the year than among the Hopi or Zuni, new moiety chiefs are always installed at the solstices because these are the points in the year that epitomize the distinctions between winter and summer and "hot" and "cold." Otherwise, most Made People are initiated or "finished" during the period of relative ease that ensues after the last crops have been stored. Exceptions are the *Kossa*, who are always finished at the autumnal equinox, and Summer moiety society members and Blue Corn Women, who are finished early in the Summer chief's period of rule in the spring. The *Kossa* must be finished in broad daylight at the equinox because they are mythically rationalized as being children of the sun, while members of the latter two groups must be initiated in the spring because they represent the Summer moiety and warmth.

A final general point is that war and game rituals and communal social dances occur during the autumn and early winter, or during the reign of the Winter chief.[13] It is because of these varied ritual activities during this period that we contrast the year as agricultural versus nonagricultural. The rituals of the agricultural cycle, in contrast, are all unambiguously directed toward causing rainfall and making plants grow.

If we look back over the entire cycle presented on figure 10, what makes the Made People's duties clearer is that these are all rituals which they either perform themselves, or plan and direct. In the latter instance the *Towa é*, acting as the executive arm of the Made People, make the preparations, and the Dry Food People perform the actual rituals. Every society of Made People is responsible for planning and directing at least one mass public ritual, while most are responsible for more than one. In this way all three social or human categories share meaningfully in the annual cycle of ritual activities. The Scalp society, for instance, is responsible for planning the Butterfly and other war-associated rituals, while the Hunt society is responsible for the game and other animal rituals. The *Kossa* are responsible for the Harvest and Turtle rituals because these, occurring at changes in season, are addressed specifically to the sun. In the most important of the mass public rituals, each society of Made People has a song sung in its honor, and here their various spirit patrons vie freely for prominence. The society sponsoring the particular ritual, of course, has its song sung first. The moiety chiefs, for example, are identified in song with the two corn mothers in the mythical lake of origin, and here the forces of winter and summer themselves vie in the ritual.[14]

Turning now to the question of what all of this has to do with the works, I can state that all of the major rituals depend for their performance on the successful completion of the work after which they traditionally occur. The rituals depend on the works, and if for some reason either must be sacrificed, it must be the ritual. The two best illustrations of this, of course, are the two works associated with the transfer of authority between the moiety chiefs. Four days after the Summer chief initiates "Bringing the buds to life," he conducts the infant water giving ritual described in chapter 3; eight to twelve days after that the water pouring and finishing rituals are held, at which time the "warm" gods appear in the kiva. After this and only after this may the specifically agricultural rites follow. The analogous flurry of ritual activities follows within the Winter moiety after the Winter chief initiates the work "Of the middle of the structure." Thus, to place any specific ritual within the cycle one must know the work which it must follow, for the work is basic.

There are two other rituals in figure 10 to which I must call special attention, to suggest why there are no works before and at the summer solstice. If, by the end of the retreat for bringing the blossoms to life, the rains have not yet come, all of the Made People go on a "rain retreat" to the mountain and hill shrines west of the village. It is an overnight trip, so the *Towa é* accompany them to stand watch. Because there are not enough *Towa é* to go around, the Spanish officials and *Fiscales* are also drafted into service on this occasion. But these latter may not accompany the moiety chiefs and medicine men, who go all of the way to *Tsikomo*, the sacred mountain of the west. Only the *Towa é* may accompany these three most important groups. Their purpose is to pray, meditate, and make offerings to the spirits of the shrines and earth navels, in hopes that they will send rain. In the process they also clean the shrines and earth navels, and gather plant medicines for use in other rituals. While the *Towa é* and other officials accompany them to stand watch, they are not permitted to listen too closely to the Made People's prayers or songs, or assist in plant gathering. These are the special prerogatives of the Made People and are among the most closely guarded secrets they have. When the retreats are over and the plants are gathered, however, the guards must carry the bundles back to the village. Even then the Made People are not through, for on their return they tie their plant bundles on their backs and perform a dance peculiarly their own. It is called, appropriately, if not overconfidently, "It is raining," or "There is rain." Each society dances in the home of its head, while the *Towa é* and other officials stand watch outside. The Spanish officials and *Fiscales* may only stand watch at night, however, for reasons made clear in the preceding chapter.

While the rain retreats involve all of the Made People and *Towa é*, they are not a part of the regular cycle of works; they occur intermittently, when the rains do not come, and they occur away from the village.[15] Yet they are very much like the works, and they take the place of a regular work in occupying the Made People's time. This is one good reason why there is not another work scheduled for this period.

Turning now to the summer solstice, a ritual relay race is held at this time to "give the sun strength" for the start of its journey to its winter home. This brings me at last to the second set of moieties existing in San Juan, for the two groups competing in the relay race derive from, yet are independent of, the Winter and Summer moieties. I have described them in summary fashion elsewhere (Ortiz 1965*b*), so here I shall add some detail to that account. Long ago, according to the Tewa, the familiar relay races common throughout the Southwest were performed by the Summer and Winter moieties. One spring, however, the medicine men discovered a cache of witchcraft items buried near the center of the racetrack, and each moiety accused the other of attempting to win the race by evil means. Heretofore, according to tradition, the Winter moiety had always won, because they are symbolically identified with maleness and the male quality of endurance. Consequently, the Made People seized on this occasion to divide the men equally into a North and South division, based on existing residence patterns. Today each man automatically inherits his father's affiliation; the women are not directly affected, since they do not participate in the races. While the Winter moiety outnumbers the Summer by approximately three to two, the South moiety predominates over the North by approximately the same ratio. In fact, the South moiety includes almost as many Winter moiety members as Summer. At any rate, these moieties are at least a century old, because the genealogies of the oldest informants indicate they were already in existence during the time of their grandfathers.

There are only a few points regarding their role that need detain us here. First, the North and South moieties come into play only at this one time during the year. It is said that long ago the ceremonial shinny game at the beginning of the planting cycle (figure 10) was also conducted by this set of moieties, but no one today can remember when this was last done. Second, it may be assumed that they were derived from the Winter and Summer moieties because the spirit-patrons for each, represented by anthropomorphic figurines, are kept by the moiety chiefs. These fetishes are taken out, and perch atop long poles or standards, the day before and during the races. On the first day men and older youths of each moiety go around the dance areas of the village singing what are called "Songs of Man." Each group marches slowly and separately around the village, burying prayer-plumes in each plaza. Each moiety tries to outdo the other in numbers participating and in force of singing; in both respects the South moiety is, of course, now clearly predominant. The singing continues until about sundown, and the race itself takes place the next day, over a track running east to west, like the path of the sun. For several days beforehand, each group practices, the North moiety on the plain to the northeast of the village, and the South moiety to the southeast.

During this period the best runners of each moiety are intimidated, criticized, and gossiped about by the members of the opposite moiety. Although these are primarily men's moieties the women take part in the activities, which are intended to unnerve the opposition. Even charges and counter-charges of witchcraft are frequently made. To cite one example, many years ago the best runner of the North moiety, one who had for several years beaten the best that the South moiety could put forth, was handed an orange by a distant female relative of the opposite moiety. He did not eat it immediately, however, and when he joined the other runners of his group a medicine man asked where he had gotten the orange. The youth told who had given it to him, whereupon the medicine man fell upon the orange, tore it to pieces, and scattered it to the four directions. Then he turned to the frightened youth and severely reprimanded him for accepting *anything* from *anyone* of the opposite moiety, adding that the orange was definitely intended to weaken him so he could not run well.

On the day of the races the North moiety runners gather at the east end of the track, and the opposite moiety at the west end. The North moiety carries a red and white standard which the Winter moiety chief has decorated with fox skins, while the South moiety carries a yellow and blue standard which the Summer moiety chief has decorated with cottonwood branches. Four medicine men, two from the North and two from the South moiety, inspect the race track and bless it with eagle wing-tip feathers. The races begin right after this. Each moiety starts with its fastest runner. Since those of the North moiety are so few each good runner usually has to run several relays, while those of the South need only run once or twice. Here the symbolic attribute of endurance becomes a self-fulfilling prophecy for the North moiety; they have no choice. Throughout the races the medicine men encourage their respective charges by running alongside for a portion of the way. They also continue to police the entire length of the track throughout the proceedings. This is the one instance in the annual cycle of ritual activities in which the medicine men are set in direct competition with one another. It should also be pointed out here that the color and directional symbolism reflected is faithful to that of the original (Winter and Summer) moieties.

Those villagers not participating in the races, meanwhile, yell encouragement to their own runners and epithets to those of the opposite moiety. One receives the impression that all of the accumulated frustrations and aggressions of the community are being vented within the space of a very short time. This one time, Murdock's hypothesis (1949, 1956) that moieties provide institutionalized and, therefore, socially nondisruptive channels for expressing aggression seems to be borne out by the Tewa data. The insults and other unpleasantries are, however, supposed to be forgotten right after the race, for the Made People remind the villagers that the larger aim of the Songs of Man and the races is to give the sun strength as it begins its journey to its winter home.

As a matter of fact, the insults are sometimes not forgotten, and they emerge in various subtle ways throughout the year. An example will serve to illustrate this point. The Songs of Man sung on the day before the race differ for each moiety; those of the North mention the spirits and sacred geographical features of the north and east, while those of the South moiety mention the spirits and features of the south and west. In this sense they may be regarded as owned by one moiety or the other. Now, in 1959, two of the mainstays of the village's song corps, men who knew most of the songs sung in communal rituals, were recording some of these for me. When they sang a few Songs of Man, I noted they were all of the South moiety. I asked them next to sing those of the North, and they replied that they did not know any. This was not true, since any accomplished singer can pick up any song after hearing it sung only once or twice; they simply did not wish to sing the "songs of power" of the opposite moiety. Instead, they began to air old grudges against, and suspicions about, individual members of the *North* moiety who were also members of the *Winter* moiety, and against whom they had competed in races in the past. Yet these two men were themselves also members of the *Winter* moiety. What is obvious here is that, for the purposes of the Songs of Man and the races, they were of the *South* moiety, in direct competition with

all members of the *North* moiety, whatever other mutual ties
might be involved.

Thus, while the North and South moieties come dramatically
to the forefront only once a year—unless they also did so during
the shinny game in February long ago—the symbolic associations
and attendant attitudes can be turned on, so to speak, at any time
during the rest of the year. What is not of obvious social significance during the rest of the year is nevertheless very important in
the minds of the Tewa. Every Tewa male, at least, is capable of
doing a complete about-face in these day-to-day relations if the
situation seems to warrant it. On the other hand, we see that the
divisive influences inherent in this situation are generally canceled
by the crosscutting and overlapping moiety memberships, just as
they are among the political officials and Made People. To put it
more specifically, one may have to bear a grudge against a sister's
husband if he wishes to bear a grudge at all, and those who exchange insults on the occasion of the races may be partners in a
solemn ritual in another, common moiety a few weeks later.

To return to the earlier question of why there is not a work
here to serve as a counterpart to that of the winter solstice, I can
only say that all of the energies of the men of the village, including
Made People, are taken up with the singing, the dancing, and the
races themselves. There is no time for a work because the other
ritual activities of the summer solstice are as intense as they are
dramatic.

Now that we have some understanding of how the three social
categories of existence interrelate and interact in the ritual cycle,
let me introduce a third and final layer of Tewa culture; the subsistence cycle. This is presented as figure 11. I also return to a
theme which has been only implicit thus far; that one of the basic
tenets of Tewa dual organization is a dual subsistence system. The
Tewa do indeed see their economic activities, like their ritual
activities, as organized around an agricultural and a nonagricultural
cycle.

To explain how the social system works in economic terms I
alter the procedure followed in the two preceding sections and
begin instead with the transfer of authority from the Summer to the
Winter chief. This, it will be recalled, occurs just after the autumnal equinox, or right after the "Late harvest" work. The transfer
ceremony itself sets off a flurry of economic activities throughout
the village, and these are listed in their approximate order on
figure 11. First, all cultigens are moved into storage; what is left

may be gathered by needy families. After this all livestock may be released into the fields from their summer pastures. Next, the irrigation canals are closed, and fishing from the canals ends. To insure a nearby supply of fresh water for the village during the fall and winter, members of the Women's society direct the cleaning of two ponds on the outskirts of the village.[16]

The next act, the "sweeping of deer earth navels," brings us to the crux of the issue. At this time a small group of hunters, called the "Weasel People," undertake a pilgrimage, under the direction of the Hunt chief, to an earth navel for deer located about two miles northwest of the village. This earth navel is located at a pass which is believed to mark the zone of transition between the natural habitat of deer and antelope, and the lowlands or farming areas. Upon their arrival the Weasel People clean the earth navel and leave offerings of feathers and cornmeal, in hopes that the deer and related species will "cross over" into the lowlands, where they may be hunted more conveniently.

Now, why are these hunters called Weasel People? The weasel is a symbol of the change of seasons to the Tewa because of its ability to change its color.[17] Thus the cleaning of this particular deer earth navel by the Weasel People dramatizes not only a change in season, but a shift from an agricultural to a hunting cycle. Yet the Weasel People are a variable membership group with no permanent organization, and they have no other duties during the rest of the year. Any good hunter may volunteer to act as one of the Weasel People for this one occasion. Moreover, there are the other earth navels dedicated to game, which abound in the nearby fields and hills to the north and northwest, and these may be cleaned by anyone after the principal one at the pass has been cleaned.

At any rate, this symbolic act ushers in the period of formal, ritually sanctioned group hunting activities. After this groups of men may organize hunting expeditions to nearby mountains, for until the agricultural cycle begins again in the spring, hunting will be the principal subsistence activity. Four communal rabbit hunts are also held at this time by the village at large, one in each cardinal direction. This is also the period when geese, sandhill cranes, and ducks come through the area on their southward migratory flight. These, too, are hunted or trapped, and the remains of these and all other game animals that are not otherwise utilized must be deposited at an earth navel so that they will continue to be plentiful.[18]

There are further ramifications of this shift in subsistence activity. For instance, it is the flesh of these migratory fowl that the

Winter chief distributes to the mothers during the water giving ritual for infants. This ritual is held shortly after the work "Of the middle of the structure," which itself ritually marks the change in season. Henceforth also, boys must put away their shinny sticks and play instead with bows and arrows. Even modern games are regulated in this way. Games utilizing marbles (boys) and jacks (girls) may only be played after this time because they involve "cold" minerals and are, therefore, potentially cold-producing. In these and other ways, the shift has a chain-like effect through much of Tewa life.

Other subsistence activities which round out the cluster during this period include piñon nut and salt-gathering expeditions. Trading expeditions were also sent out to the Apaches, Utes, and Plains tribes to barter agricultural products for products of the hunt. None of these activities, however, was regulated or given ritual recognition, so I shall not go into further detail on them. What is noted simply as "redistribution of food" on figure 11 occurs whenever a Made person is finished, and whenever a major communal ritual is held. At these times the village at large contributes food to the Made People, or to those participating in the ritual. In addition, whenever the Winter moiety conducts a water pouring initiation ritual, they must feed the members of the opposite moiety, as discussed in chapter 3. The Summer moiety, of course, reciprocates whenever they hold their water pouring ritual. Similarly, when the new political officials take office on January 6 of each year, they must feed the members of the village in their homes. These several activities bear brief mention only because they provide the numerous occasions throughout the year when food is reallocated or shared within the village.

In any case, it is only hunting that is conducted regularly and intensively during the autumn and winter months, and it is only hunting which is given regular and repeated ritual recognition during this period. By ritual recognition I refer not only to the existence of a hunt society, but to the game-animal dances presented on the calendar on figure 10.[19] Thus, hunting activities continue until February, or until the beginning of the agricultural cycle. There are strong sanctions against hunting the larger game animals after this period for two reasons. First, the animals have begun to mate by this time, and the Tewa believe that even the flesh of the males no longer tastes good after they have mated. Second, and most important, the Tewa do not want to kill the females with young because this would jeopardize the future availability of game. Only rabbits are hunted until well into the spring, or until lice are found in their fur. The Tewa recognize that this makes them dangerous to one's health. But even here the rabbits are hunted only on an individual basis; there are no communal drives after the agricultural cycle has begun.

The agricultural cycle itself is initiated, as might be predicted, with the transfer of authority to the Summer chief in the latter part of February. Four days after the Summer chief takes office, each family in the village takes a basket of seed grain to him to have it blessed for planting. He takes a few grains from each basket and puts them into a hide-covered ball; this ball is used in a ceremonial shinny game which takes place the following day.[20] At this time the *Towa é* divide up the men and older youths into two groups, and they beat the ball around the village and finally into the fields. It is usually torn apart before sundown, and the person on whose field the ball spills its contents is expected to have an unusually fine harvest that year. At about this time also, the Summer chief instructs the *Towa é* to notify the people that they should put away their winter games and pastimes. Thus the order goes out during the day of the shinny game that young boys are no longer to play with marbles and tops, and girls with jacks. The belief is that since these games are cold-producing, the spirits will prolong the winter if the villagers persist in playing winter games. The games are suddenly and dramatically put away, and if anyone is caught playing them he may be flogged by the *Towa é*. A more effective sanction for bringing about conformity is that if cold weather persists the child and his family will be blamed for it. Instead then, all men and boys are urged to take up shinny, which is a warm weather pastime intended to give the sun strength for its return from its winter home.

It may be recalled from the preceding section that the Summer chief initiates the work called "Bringing the buds to life" the day after he takes office; it is this work which really initiates the agricultural cycle. When it is the medicine men's turn to perform this work, they go in a body in the dead of night to "re-seed mother earth navel," the sacred center in the village. This ritual is called "putting in squash." By their supernatural powers, the medicine men are believed to be able to reach right through the ground and place the seeds of all cultigens in the navel, thereby reawakening all of nature for the new year. These four symbolic acts, the blessing of seeds, shinny, putting away winter games, and reawakening mother earth, occur as a cluster. And just as an analogous cluster of activities follows upon the "Late harvest" work in the fall, so also do these activities follow upon the initiation of the work, "Bringing the buds to life."

By early March the three irrigation canals that tie the village into a cooperative unit with neighboring Spanish-American villages are cleaned. The principal of these is called "mother canal," and when it is opened in mid-March the moiety chiefs lead the water in from the last Spanish village. The Summer chief, who leads, scatters cornmeal along the way, while the Winter chief scatters fish scales, so there will be an abundance of fish. The fishing season, as such, begins at this time in Tewa belief, although fishing is also done in the river during the rest of the year. Henceforth also, the people obtain their water from the canals, and the springs are ritually closed until the autumn.

From April through early May, the aboriginal crops of corn, squash, and beans are planted, along with other vegetables and fruits introduced since Spanish times. This, too, is carefully controlled by the Made People, for the chiefs decide when planting may begin, and no move may be made until they tell the *Towa é* to inform the people it is permissible. Wheat, on the other hand, may be planted much earlier, and this is not regulated by the Made People. During the rest of the spring, when the storehouses from the previous year's harvest are nearly empty, the people subsist by gathering wild plants and a species of large locust which is found in the nearby foothills. Individuals may gather all wild plant and animal foods freely from anyone's land; only that which grows by individual efforts is owned, but even here one may borrow and pay back in another year. What is noted as the cessation of hunting on figure 11 refers, of course, to rabbits only.

Shortly after the solstice observance, the first berries and plums ripen, and these are gathered by women. The harvest of wheat comes between late July and early August. Since neither the planting nor the harvest of wheat is regulated by the Made People, the governor is in charge of the harvest. He does not determine the time of the harvest, but he does have charge of the machinery used. Formerly he had charge of the wild horses used in threshing the wheat.[21] The harvest period continues through the autumnal equinox, shortly after which the mother earth navel is "fed" or thanked for the harvest of the year. This is the purpose of the Harvest Dance listed on figure 10. Shortly after this the Summer chief initiates the "Late harvest" work and sprinkles dew on the mature corn plants. Then the word is sent out via the *Towa é* that the people may harvest their corn and beans, and this brings us back once again to the transfer of authority to the Winter chief. Thus we see that just as there is a complex but comprehensible dual organization in ritual, there is also a basically dual pattern of subsistence activities that ritual reflects, reinforces, and serves to perpetuate.

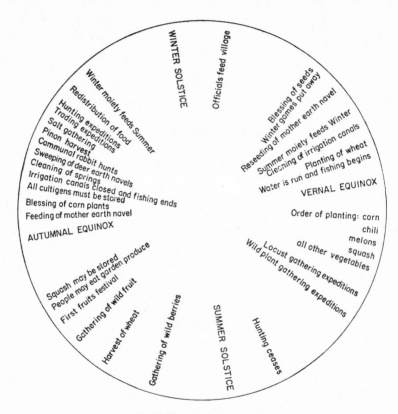

Fig. 11 The subsistence cycle

Let us return now to a question which was raised twice in the preceding section, but left unanswered; namely, why do some works occur long before or after the changes in nature they are supposed to help bring about? Why, for instance, do the three works beginning with "Bringing the buds to life" take place at least a month before the associated development in plant life? The question is worth asking because one of the consequences of the works as presently constituted is that the terms of office of the moiety chiefs are unequal. In other words, the Summer chief rules from the time he initiates the work to bring the buds to life in

February, until he initiates the "Late harvest" work in late September. He thereby rules the village for more than seven months, while the Winter chief rules for less than five. Since the Tewa really do not see them as unequal, I could dismiss the whole question as not being crucial to this work. But this would be neither meaningful nor convincing, since this is the one important instance of an enduring asymmetrical relationship between the moieties.[22] Therefore, I advance the hypothesis that the above-mentioned works did not always occur at the times they now do, and that the terms of office of the chiefs were not always unequal. The following points may be offered in support of this hypothesis.

First, note on figure 11 that while the aboriginal or pre-Spanish crops are all planted after the vernal equinox, wheat is planted much earlier. One reason for this is that while wheat withstands cold very well, it needs a long germinating and growing season. Another is that wheat must be harvested by early August in the area because this is when the insects that would endanger the crop become most numerous. Thus it is almost imperative that wheat be planted by early March if it is to be harvested before the insect scourge becomes too serious.

A second point to be made is that until recent years Spanish-American farmers have all but forced the Tewa to cooperate, by early March, in cleaning and restoring the complex system of irrigation canals they share. Work must begin at this time because it takes more than two weeks to clean out the canals. When farming was done on a larger scale, and the population was smaller than today, work had to begin in late February if the wheat fields were to have water when it was needed most. While Harrington (1916, p. 52) and others have noted that the Tewa practiced irrigation before the coming of the Spaniards, they could not have approached in complexity the present system without beasts of burden and metal tools.

A third point of relevance is that the Catholic Church formerly suppressed all native religious activities during the forty days of Lent, which begins in late February or early March. Now, the works themselves can escape detection since they occur indoors, but the mass public rituals which *must* follow "Bringing the buds to life" cannot be hidden. The Tewa were consequently faced with the choice of foregoing these rituals, or of scheduling them before or after Lent. All evidence points to the fact that they held them before Lent.

The point I am obviously leading up to is that for any or all of the above reasons the series of three works mentioned above may have been moved up a month on the calendar. This could explain why each of them begins at least a month before the development in plant life with which it is associated. Indeed, my persistent questioning on the reason for the apparent incongruity in the works once brought the response that the Summer chief must take over in February because "we are now striving toward the things of warmth again." This seemed to be no answer at the time, but now it seems that it is the only possible answer under the circumstances. In other words, with the introduction of wheat and the present system of irrigation canals, the agricultural cycle may have begun sooner, thereby shortening the period of rule of the Winter chief. In any case, if we eliminate wheat and the other obvious Spanish influences, the agricultural and nonagricultural cycles become approximately equal, and there is no longer any need for the Summer chief to take office at the time he presently does. I have already noted on several occasions that the Winter chief takes office just after the autumnal equinox, a fact more in keeping with the overall symmetry of the relations between the moieties.

I recognize, of course, that the evidence I offer is rather conjectural, but the problem is real. The solution I pose has the merit of being both plausible and possible. Moreover, it can be tested as further concrete evidence on the nature and extent of Spanish influence is compiled. I leave the problem now with the hope that such evidence will soon be forthcoming.[23]

This, then, is the social and cultural system the Made People serve, control, and perpetuate. As we have seen, the entire system is not rigorously symmetrical, but it is impressively dual and it works. Thus, a change in season (the equinoxes) leads to a change in leadership and a shift in subsistence activities. It is also a time for formalizing changes in life status, as reflected in the moiety initiations. Even then not all aspects of Tewa dual organization have been considered in detail, for within this broad natural rhythm there are other dualisms. All plants and all animals are classified as "hot," "cold," or "of the middle." Similarly, minerals are classified as "cold" (metals), or "warm" (jet). Even diseases fall into this system of symbolic classification, for a Tewa is never just ill; he has either a "hot" illness or a "cold" one, and it must be treated with the appropriate herbs. I have already mentioned the seasonally prohibited games. In essence, everything that lives and has symbolic value is so classified. In this way, what I mean by Tewa dual organization resounds not only throughout their social and spiritual existence, but into the world of nature as well. However, these findings open up large new areas of research which must wait for another time.[24] It remains now for me to summarize, and to derive some conclusions in terms of the issues set forth at the beginning of this work.

6
Summary and Conclusions

I have attempted, in this work, to clarify as many of the issues regarding the study of dual organizations as possible, while at the same time presenting the facts on the Tewa in a manner sufficiently detailed that other questions can be posed about them. I defer discussion of the specific conclusions regarding the study of dual organizations which I have drawn until the following section; here I should like to summarize my particular presentation of the data on the Tewa and their world.

I began, in chapter 2, with the Tewa myth of origin because it represents a "charter," in Malinowski's use of the term (1948), for Tewa social and ritual life. The myth not only presents the Tewa's own explanation for the existence of the Winter and Summer moieties, but defines their relations to the spiritual and natural worlds as well. In essence, the myth serves as a convenient frame of analysis for this work, and I have occasion to refer to it throughout. Yet it is not a charter in the sense of providing an explanation for all of Tewa social and ritual behavior, but a skeletal outline to which the details must be supplied by reference to ritual, prayers, and other types of symbolic action. The myth is sufficiently detailed, however, to permit me to derive meaningful insights into its content as well as its form.

Next I proceeded to define the six categories—three human and three spiritual—into which the Tewa classify all existence. While each of these categories is divided into two parts, according to the moieties, they also comprise three linked pairs. That is to say, the spiritual categories represent counterparts of the human categories, and at death the soul of each human category becomes a spirit of its linked supernatural category. Thus, a Dry Food person (Category 1) becomes a "Dry Food Who Is No Longer" (Category 4), a human *Towa é* (Category 2) becomes a supernatural *Towa é* (Category 5), and a Made person (Category 3) becomes a "Dry Food Who Never Did Become" (Category 6).

Moreover, the supernatural categories are identified with three tetrads into which the Tewa divide the natural world, in a carefully specified manner. The spirits of Category 4, who are the ancestral souls of the common Tewa, dwell at four shrines which are located just outside the village, one in each cardinal direction. The supernatural *Towa é*, who are counterparts of the Tewa political officials, dwell at earth navels which are located on top of four sacred hills and four sacred mountains, also of the cardinal directions. The mountains represent the four outer boundary points of the Tewa world, while the hills are located about midway between the mountains and the village. The spirits of Category 6, who are the highest deities recognized by the Tewa, are believed to dwell within lakes which are located near the four sacred mountains. The Made People, who dedicate their lives to serving in the demanding ritual organization of the Tewa, join these high-level deities after death.

After identifying these three pairs of linked categories and indicating their relation to the natural world, I proceeded to a more detailed discussion of their place in Tewa society and culture. Chapter 3 focuses on Categories 1 and 4. The rationale for this is that by proceeding in terms of linked categories, I can keep the relation between social and symbolic dual organization constantly in the forefront of analysis. I trace the passage of the Dry Food People through the society by analyzing six rites of passage which each Tewa normally undergoes from birth until death. At the first rite, a naming ritual performed four days after birth, the passage of the child into the society as a whole is emphasized. The linkage between the natural and supernatural categories is demonstrated by the fact that the latter are present in the home through their tangible manifestation as *xayeh*, or household fetishes, and they are invoked in giving the child his name and his identity as a member of the society.

Sometime during the first year of life another rite of passage, called water giving, is held, but this time the child begins the process of recruitment into the moiety of his father. Two other rites are held by each moiety before this process of recruitment is completed, one when the child is between the ages of six and ten, and the third when the child is in his early teens. The first rite claims the child for the moiety, while the second, water pouring, recognizes him sexually by giving him sex-specific duties and responsibilities. This rite also recognizes the child as a Dry Food person, or person of reason, by removing him forever from his heretofore carefree life as a child. At this time also, the twelve steps of migration spoken of in the myth of origin are symbolically re-enacted by the deities of Category 6. The third rite, finishing, recognizes the young Tewa as an adult member of the moiety by making him eligible to participate fully in the ritual life of his moiety. Thus, every Tewa grows up as a member of one moiety or the other.

Next, some case histories were cited to indicate certain conditions under which it is possible and even desirable to transfer from one moiety to the other. One can transfer by repeating the entire three-stage process of recruitment, but into the opposite moiety. Thus there is no exclusive rule of recruitment into the moieties. It is also suggested that, in the absence of a clear and unambiguous rule of descent, the elaborate process of recruitment itself assumes primary significance in the placement of the individual into the moiety.

The fifth rite of passage, marriage, lends support to the above points. If the bride is of the moiety opposite that of her husband, she must undergo the three rites of recruitment into her husband's moiety, regardless of her age. The process for the Summer bride is explained by informants as intended to "shake off her blossom petals and replace them with icicles, thereby pulling her over to the Winter side." The process for the Winter bride is the reverse of the above. This does not mean, however, that the moieties regulate marriage, for this ritual occurs after the fact. If the bride belongs to the Made People, on the other hand, she cannot transfer to her husband's moiety because she is no longer subject to the rules of the Dry Food People. Thus, even at marriage, other considerations come in to override what is at best a flexible rule of recruitment. Up to this point in the individual life cycle, the moieties are paramount; this is when the two parallel "paths of life" which describe the moieties in the myth of origin stand furthest apart.

At death the sixth and final rite of passage, called releasing, is held. Here, as during the naming rite, the unity and solidarity of the whole society is emphasized; the moieties are submerged in the interest of clearly drawing the line between all of the living and the dead. This point, which I did not recognize in an earlier effort (Ortiz 1965*b*), is the most important in this work, for it is the best single answer that the Tewa have to the question of how the society can be divided and integrated at the same time. The answer is that at the most important life crises, the society and not the moiety is emphasized. The soul passes, not from his moiety, but from the whole society. The underlying message of the myth of origin also becomes evident, as indicated at the end of chapter 3, for it, too, emphasizes the unity of the society at the beginning and at the end. Once again, as in the naming ritual, the linkage between the two categories is clearly drawn, for the soul goes to join its ancestors at one of the four directional shrines which surround the village, and offerings of food are taken there by the survivors.

However, most of the process of living takes place between marriage and death; this is the period of the average individual's life that must be accounted for no matter what the problem or framework of analysis. This is where the two other pairs of linked categories become relevant. After marriage a Tewa male usually becomes a *Towa é*, or political official, and these are discussed in chapter 4. The *Towa é* are mediating categories, in both the natural and the supernatural realms. In the natural realm, they are recruited, an equal number (three) from each moiety, to serve the Made People and the Dry Food People for a term of one year. They undergo a rite of transition by being given supernatural sanction as figures of authority and control. At the end of the year they undergo a rite of separation and are returned to their respective moieties and to the general category Dry Food People, although they may be asked to serve again in this capacity. Similarly, in the supernatural realm, they are regarded as not quite either, but close to both the "Dry Food Who Never Did Become," and the "Dry Food Who Are No Longer." They are of the hills and mountains, but not of the lakes and shrines, where the other spirits dwell. Their interstitial nature is thus reflected not only on both planes of existence, but in the physical world as well.

I derive three relevant conclusions regarding the role of the *Towa é* in Tewa society. First, the *Towa é* are mediators, in a vertical sense, between entire categories, between the Made People and the Dry Food People, and while they are recruited equally from both moieties, most of their duties are not moiety-specific. A second point is that because they usually act in pairs, one from each moiety, the *Towa é* represent one means by which the dual organization is mediated at a time when the society seems most divided. While only one of the moieties may provide the leader during any given year, this asymmetry is only temporary, for it is erased the following year when the opposite moiety provides the leader. A third point is that the *Towa é* represent a means by which a network of personal ties is established which transcends the dual organization. This transcendance is a logical consequence of the fact that they comprise a category related to, but discrete from, the other two. Thus, at a time when the dual organization is potentially most disruptive, the *Towa é* provide a means by which the moieties are fused into a single operational unit.

Completing the Tewa organization for social control and punishment are two groups of officials originally imposed by the Spaniards. These, whom the Tewa call "Spanish officials" and *Fiscales*, are treated by them like *Towa é*, although they perform duties which became necessary only after the advent of the Spaniards, and later the Americans. Because they are organized like, and around, the *Towa é*, and are partially fitted into the Tewa system of symbolic classification, they not only help us understand the role of the *Towa é*, but provide some understanding of how the Tewa reconciled Spanish institutions to the dual organization.

A second possible option for Tewa adult life is to join the Made People, and these are discussed in chapter 5. This category is more inclusive, for it not only includes more groups (eight), but membership in all save one is open to women. In the past this may have been the most inclusive category, for it ideally includes a minimum of fifty-two members. The *Towa é* and Spanish-introduced officials together comprise a total of only fourteen members.

The Made People stand at the apex of the Tewa social order as representatives of the deities of Category 6, who in turn stand at the apex of the spiritual world. By the process of their recruitment they are a category clearly and unambiguously set apart from the Dry Food People and the *Towa é*. Because their offices were instituted in the lake of origin—even if they had to return to this primordial home to add the last five groups—they are the most sacred of human beings. They represent the closest thing in this life to the way things were in the beginning. They are thus best understood as mediators between the planes of human and spiritual existence. The dual organization is represented by the moiety societies, which stand at the top of the hierarchical organization of Made People, but the six other groups act as mediators between the social and symbolic distinctions which the moieties represent. These six are collectively referred to by a phrase which reveals their nature: "Those of the middle of the structure."

To illustrate this concept with two examples, hunting is symbolically associated with the Winter moiety, but it is also a mediating principle because of the undeniable fact that it is an activity participated in by the males of both moieties. Thus the Hunt chief, who represents the mountain lion deity and who directs all group hunting activities, is regarded as being "of the middle of the structure" because he serves both moieties. The sun, the most ubiquitous of Pueblo deities, illustrates this concept in another way. As a male deity he is identified with the Winter moiety and impersonated by them in rituals, but because he is believed to rise from within a lake in the east and set in a lake in the west, he transcends the symbolic distinctions between maleness and east for the Winter moiety and femaleness and west for the Summer moiety. Consequently, the *Kossa*, or "warm" clowns, who are regarded as children of the sun, are also called "of the middle of the structure" because they, too, serve both moieties.

In attempting next to define the relation of the Made People to the spirits of Category 6, their linked spiritual counterpart, I find that the organization of the latter is almost an exact replica of the organization of the Made People. Since certain of the spirits of Category 6 are the only ones of the three spiritual categories regularly impersonated in ritual, they provide special insights not only into the relation between social and symbolic dual organization, but into the notion of mediation, as discussed above.

As I indicated in chapters 2 and 3, these spirits dwell beneath the sacred lakes of all four directions. The spirits of the north and east are associated with and sponsored by the Winter moiety, while those of the south are associated with and sponsored by the Summer moiety. The fourth group of spirits, on the other hand, come from the west, and they are associated with and sponsored by the Bear medicine society, the highest ranking group of Made People called "of the middle of the structure." Whereas the first three groups always visit the village in their appropriate seasons, the deities of the west visit when it is neither quite winter nor quite summer. Moreover, their "journey" is traced by the *Kossa* and *Kwirana*, acting together; this is the one occasion on which the "cold" and "warm" clowns act together in ritual. As if they were still uncertain of having succeeded in removing all possible doubt of the nature of these deities, the Tewa go one step further; the leader is called *Ká neh*, a term which describes his graceful bowing movement from side to side (north to south, winter to summer), as he enters the kiva.

To complete the picture, the Tewa also refer to them as "those of the middle of the structure." This mediating organization, sponsored by another mediating organization, "brought" to the village by two other mediating organizations, reflecting symbols and personnel taken from both moieties, and coming into being at a neutral time of the year, clarifies considerably what I mean by mediation. This fourth group represents the outstanding example of mediation found in Tewa culture; as such I could not resist detailing them once again.

While the Made People comprise a discrete hierarchical unit, they are also functionally differentiated as specialists in all major activities of human existence, and they control all of these activities. Thus the overlay technique I followed in the last two sections of chapter 5 bears out both points very clearly. The first overlay (figure 9) represents the annual cycle of works of the Made People, which I referred to as the structure of structures in Tewa life. This cycle establishes the eight groups of Made People as collectively constituting a segmentary organization which must act together in their hierarchical order to maintain harmonious relations between man and the spirit world. Their paramount duty— and it is a collective duty—is that of assuring the continuity of nature's basic rhythms so that the Tewa may continue to survive and thrive within their world. The dual organization is submerged in the interest of this larger collective concern.

The second overlay (figure 10) represents the annual cycle of ritual activities planned and directed by the Made People, administered by the *Towa é*, and participated in by the Dry Food People. Here we see in operation the more discrete ritual functions with which individual groups of Made People are charged. More importantly, however, we see the relations of the three categories of existence in carrying out this annual cycle of ritual activities. Thus the *Towa é* are seen as the visible means of applying and enforcing, among the Dry Food People, decisions made by the Made People. The final overlay (figure 11) presents the annual cycle of subsistence activities, which is directed by the Made People through the *Towa é*. This final overlay also establishes most convincingly the fundamental basis of the dual organization of Tewa ritual and society, for we note that there is a basically dual pattern of subsistence activities; the year is divided into an agricultural and a nonagricultural cycle, with hunting emphasized during the latter cycle.

Indeed, the dual organization has been in the foreground even while I have been discussing the two other cycles of ritual activities, but this final section indicates most clearly the basis on which it rests. Thus I note why not only the annual cycle of works, but the larger cycle of communal ritual activities is divided between an agricultural and a nonagricultural group. All of these activities, including even the moiety initiation rites and the transfer of au-

128

thority between the moiety chiefs, reflect this dual pattern of subsistence. I note in passing, moreover, that everything else which
has symbolic significance to the Tewa—games, plants, and diseases
—is classified according to whether it is hot or cold, winter or
summer, or of the middle. This system of symbolic classification
thus serves to reflect, reinforce, and perpetuate the social order on
which it is based.

   While I have attempted to present faithfully the facts on Tewa
ritual and social behavior, I have also attempted not to lose sight
of the issues discussed in chapter 1. I have systematically taken these
up in approximately the same order they were presented in the
first chapter. It remains now for me to draw together my conclusions on these issues.
   Returning to the first point raised in connection with Lévi-
Strauss's analysis, it may be seen that he places too heavy a reliance
on his triadic structure. Figure 1 in chapter 2 indicates that the
Tewa view existence as constituting a hexamerous structure; they
divide the entire human and spiritual world into six categories. If
we were to concern ourselves only with the human categories,
however, we would see them as a triad which is replicated in the
supernatural realm. Yet an analysis based on only one triad would
result in only a partial understanding of Tewa society and culture,
because it would result in a blocking out of the many implications
which each triad has for the other when all six levels are on the
ground, as it were. I have attempted to indicate in the preceding
three chapters that this is precisely the case. Thus Lévi-Strauss's
triadic structure, the maximal structure he considered, which he
regards as a "formula" (1960, p. 47) to explain away the dual
organization, would only have imposed an arbitrary limitation on
the Tewa data.
   Lévi-Strauss's notion of "concentric dualism" also figures prominently in his general thesis. By this notion he refers to one or
another type of opposition between the center and the periphery
which he finds reflected in each of his ethnographic examples. In
each instance his argument is buttressed by a circular village structure; this is what is used to justify the designation of the phenomena
as concentric. The Tewa data, as figure 2 and the discussion at the
end of chapter 2 indicate, reveal not a circular village structure but
one of four parts in which the corners are always kept open. So
pervasive is this tetramerous aspect of Tewa symbolic classification
that it reaches from the distant sacred mountains, hills, shrines,
and plazas right into the home itself, where sacred objects are

buried in the four corners of at least one room. From here it flows out again into the dance plazas, where it is danced out, sung out, and prayed out. Quite simply, it reaches into the Tewa mind itself, from which it all emanated in the first place.

Nor is there a simple spatial opposition between the center and the periphery reflected anywhere in the Tewa system of classification. I noted, on figure 3, that both the "earth mother earth navel middle place" at the center of the village and the four earth navels on top of the four sacred mountains are realities of the same order; both are points at which one may communicate with spirits. Both are sacred, and it would be fruitless to argue about which is the more so. Moreover, since the world enclosed by these mountains is a large one—all meaningful, purposeful activities usually took place within it—it would be pointless to oppose this world with what is outside of it. Even the trash dumps surrounding the village will not do, because this is where the Tewa buried their dead, whom they worship, and this is where the four sacred shrines are located. If one wished to limit his perspective to the village itself, one could find various limited-range oppositions between the sacred and the profane, the center and the periphery, but one would have to ignore the larger world which I have found to be so necessary for the most general, most complete kind of understanding.

The notion of concentric dualism happens to be crucial to the development of Lévi-Strauss's general thesis because, he argues, it is the agency through which the transition takes place between diametric dualism and triadism. But the notions of the central circle and the outer circle depend for their definition upon a third concept, in this case "brush," "forest," or "nature." This is precisely where the Tewa data present problems, for, ultimately, we have only the Tewa world and the non-world. We may choose to read some formal significance into this opposition, but the Tewa—and they are by no means alone, even in the Southwest, in defining the outer limits of their world by four sacred mountains—do not worry very much about what is outside their world. The highest deities may dwell there, as they indeed do, but this is recognized only during the water pouring rituals. This reflects the Tewa belief that the further away from the village one goes, the less *seh t'a* the world is, and the deities must have the aura of mystery provided by distance; otherwise their omnipotence would have much less plausibility. The living themselves may not venture there without fear of pollution or harm. And they certainly may not do so without taking special ritual precautions, both before departing and upon returning.

The questions raised regarding Lévi-Strauss's exclusive reliance on societies with unilineal descent, and his apparent equation of social structure with marriage systems, may be taken together. This second point has also been made by Maybury-Lewis (1960) and Schneider (1965). The Tewa have been getting along successfully for at least a century without unilineal descent, and the Tewa moieties are not exogamous. Moreover, this situation may be far older, for nowhere in the available historical and ethnographic literature have I found concrete evidence for either unilineal descent or moiety exogamy. It is recognized that the weight of the evidence from around the world argues against reading too much into the data, but there is evidence—provided by Maybury-Lewis —that the Tewa situation is by no means unique: "I had set out to study a moiety system and discovered that the Shavante saw their own society as a thorough-going system of opposites, yet dispensed with the institution of intermarrying moieties" (1965, p. 265). Elsie Clews Parsons made a similar observation of the Tewa more than four decades earlier (1924, pp. 336–38). Thus the five binary oppositions to which Lévi-Strauss finally reduces all of his ethnographic examples (1963a, pp. 154–60) cannot apply to the Tewa data at all, because they are based on societies with unilineal descent and unambiguous marriage rules. I would conclude that neither should be taken as defining criteria for dual organization.

I suggest this is so because I have also asked here the same grand questions that students of kinship and marriage ask: What are the relevant groups in the society? How do they recruit their members? How do they achieve continuity? What is the total framework of integration for the society? Consequently, while this work has had less to do with kinship and marriage—and, therefore, with social structure, insofar as it is defined in these terms—than with religious ideas and practices, it is because ritual shapes social relations to such a tremendous extent. Thus, we have not descent but ritual, not exogamy but ritual again. If the suspicion lingers that I have substituted one kind of reductionism for another, I can only point out that I have attempted to keep in mind throughout this work not only man as a member of society, but man in nature; not only ritual man, but myth making man. I have, in other words, attempted to actualize, in this one case study, the challenge foreseen for social anthropology by Eggan more than a decade ago: "The interrelationship between ritual and social structure and the mediating role of myth represent the new frontiers of social anthropological research" (1955, p. 502). Taking this broad view will mean no loss for the kind of general understanding anthropology seeks. Nor can the Tewa, finally, be dismissed as an aberrant case; as Lévi-Strauss himself recognizes, the intensive analysis of the single case is still the best method anthropology has for raising issues and for solving problems (1963*b*). Or, as Geertz (1965) points out, on a different dimension of argument, if Becquerel had not been so interested in the peculiar behavior of uranium modern physics might be in rather a different state than it is today.

I come now to Lévi-Strauss's denial of the existence of the dual organization. The dotted line dividing north and east from south and west on figure 2 has been found to have a reality of its own, for the Tewa structure the greater part of their everyday thought and behavior in terms of the Winter and Summer moieties. The several tetramerous structures are resolved, for purposes of ritual and social behavior, into the moieties, which also neatly bisect each level of the hexad. The one thing all six categories of existence have in common is the dual organization. I have, therefore, used dual organization, as defined early in the first chapter, as an analytic concept to deal meaningfully with the widest possible range of phenomena reflected in the Tewa world. Nothing else would have taken in as much. In the end, the question must be whether the concept of dual organization explains the data in a more meaningful way, and whether by using such a concept we better understand how Tewa society works. The fundamental test of a problem-oriented monograph, I feel, is that it meaningfully alters our perception of the phenomena dealt with. In this case I hope it is in the direction of deepening and expanding our understanding of the complexities of dual organization.

Turning now to Maybury-Lewis, I find the difficulties inherent in his position to be more fundamental. In his persistent concern with the dual organization as such—with the actual social segments comprising the dual organization—he offers no alternative method by which we might better understand what the total framework of integration is in a given society with dual organization. Although he recognizes that "the simultaneous awareness of the division and the unity of society is common enough in conjunction with dual organizations and might be said to be the fundamental problem in their analysis" (1960, p. 27), he does not indicate how we are to go about resolving the issue. Instead he takes the point of view that social dualism, of which exogamous moieties may be one expression, results from a universal tendency to think in opposites. The dual organization, in his view, is merely the social expression of this universal tendency. I propose to reject a portion of this argument on the grounds that to talk about a "universal tendency" is to say little that is analytically useful. The question of why this is so for some societies and not for others still remains.

The issue is then rephrased in terms of "how and why conceptual antitheses receive institutional expression in dual organization, and why dual organization is mainly found in more 'primitive' societies" (1960, p. 42). My answer to the first portion of this statement has been a major theme throughout this work, while the second portion presents a curious paradox. The Tewa have dual organization in Maybury-Lewis's terms, but they are not among the more primitive of societies in the world. Moreover, unlike most societies with dual organization, Tewa social structure did not disintegrate upon contact with European culture. Rather, the Tewa and the other eastern Pueblos with dual organization have been among the most enduring primitive societies in the world, considering the serious and sustained pressures toward change to which they have been subjected. Consequently, either the Tewa have little in common with primitive dual organizations, or we must disregard the degree of primitiveness as not crucial to the larger issues of why dual organization, and how does it work.

There is yet another dimension to the question. Although Maybury-Lewis, in the statement quoted above, is primarily concerned with the question of how and why the dualisms of thought are reflected in the dual organization of society, we might also ask how and why certain basic dualisms of nature find their expression in human thought and action. In other words, why are dual organizations, wherever they are found in the world, usually associated with at least two of the following conditions in nature: first, a pronounced and often dramatic change in climatic conditions from one half of the year to another, usually accompanied by (2) a dual subsistence system for the people living there, and/or (3) population movement from one place to another during each half of the year? Wherever we have dual organizations we seem always to have also, by my present understanding of the comparative evidence, some combination of, or variations on, the above factors operating. And it is these broader, more basic antitheses that find their reflection and reinforcement in social and symbolic dual organization.

A consideration of these factors would put us on a more solid footing for comparative studies because they represent something all dual organizations seem to have in common, rather than something all men seem to have in common. One cannot, after all, explain a variable by a constant. The question can then be rephrased, not by exclusive reference to a pan-human "tendency to think in antitheses" (Maybury-Lewis 1960, pp. 41–42), but in the more modest and analytically more attainable terms of why some combination of these same factors occasionally obtains without the kind of dual organization I have discussed in this work. This is, of course, a problem for cross-cultural research, and beyond the scope of my present effort; but it does represent one of the directions in which the study of dual organizations should go in the future. And if we can explain these negative instances, especially those in Africa, without exclusive recourse to the human mind, then we are well on our way to answering the larger question of how dual organizations come about, how they work, and why they persist.

Perhaps the most serious difficulty of the position Maybury-Lewis is trying to maintain is exemplified in the following statement:

> One of the purposes of his [Lévi-Strauss's] paper was to suggest a way in which the reciprocity characteristic of dual organization could be reconciled with the hierarchical superordination and subordination so often found associated with it. It would seem, however, that the problem itself is created by Lévi-Strauss' formulation of the apparent paradox and that an alternative approach to the analysis of dual organization would automatically resolve the contradiction or would avoid it altogether [1960, p. 41].

Yet the problem is real, and Maybury-Lewis's position seems to be to ignore both the contradiction and a beginning to the solution by minimizing the role of symbolism—which is, in large measure, culture. For even when he admits the relevance of symbolism he means that "one of the fundamental analytic problems in the study of dual organizations is that of the relation between social and symbolic dualism" (1960, p. 41).

I need only briefly recapitulate the implications of the Tewa data in the light of this argument. If I accepted it, I would be left with the moieties and that area of symbolism which happens to be dyadic—which happens to reflect the dual organization. The deities and the Made People who are called "of the middle of the structure" would have no place in this formulation. Neither would the several tetrads and the hexamerous structure of Tewa existence. To become too preoccupied with determining the relationship between social and symbolic dualism would be to follow something of a false scent, for, in addition to the above examples, we have seen that there are general, transcendental symbols that most clearly come into play for the Tewa at birth and at death. And it is in determining the nature of the relationship between these transcendental symbols and the activities in which they come into play, on the one hand, and the more specifically dual symbols and activities on the other, that we begin to see not only what the dual organization means and does not mean in the Tewa world, but what their own most general conceptions of order are.

A more meaningful approach to the problems Maybury-Lewis raises is to introduce the time dimension. To take, for example, just the reciprocity and hierarchy issue defined above, about which much has been made, I might formulate a solution as follows. The asymmetrical relationships which obtain *at any one time* between the Tewa moieties become symmetrical when viewed in terms of annual or biennial cycles. Thus the asymmetry reflected in the hierarchical organization of the *Towa é* and the deities "of the middle" is erased over a two-year period, while the asymmetry reflected in the hierarchical organization of the Made People is erased during the course of a single year. An important point to be made is that in attempting to resolve this issue for the Tewa, I have taken the broadest possible time perspective. In chapter 3 I considered the entire life cycle, while in chapters 4 and 5 I considered the annual and biennial cycles. Time then helps me to resolve the reciprocity and hierarchy issue, at least for the Tewa.

The issue happens to be crucial also in the light of Lévi-Strauss's observation:

> Diametric dualism is static, that is it cannot transcend its own limitations; its transformations merely give rise to the same sort of dualism as that from which they arose. But concentric dualism is dynamic and contains an implicit triadism. Or, strictly speaking, any attempt to move from an asymmetric triad to a symmetric dyad presupposes concentric dualism, which is dyadic like the latter but asymmetric like the former [1963*a*, p. 151].

I would deny that diametric dualism, at least as the Tewa practice it, is static. If I have demonstrated anything in this work I hope it is that, through the various ways they use their notion "of the middle of the structure," the Tewa provide a dynamic and flexible response to the challenges presented by their rigorous dualism. And they do this without sacrificing the essential integrity of the dual organization, which is what, in each instance, gives rise to the various ideas and institutions "of the middle of the structure." They do this, in other words, without the benefit of concentric dualism and triadism, in Lévi-Strauss's use of the terms.

Just how dynamic and flexible Tewa dual organization is can be best illustrated by events which took place shortly after the turn of the century in the little Tewa Pueblo of San Ildefonso, located just fifteen miles to the south of San Juan. The account is summarized from Whitman's (1940) report, supplemented by my own field work. At this time, due to a variety of misfortunes which befell the Pueblo over a period of years, the already small Winter moiety was reduced to two families. As a result the people were confronted with the unalterable fact that they could no longer operate on the basis of the traditional Winter and Summer moieties. Consequently, the Summer moiety divided into a north and south division, on the basis of residence, with the north side absorbing the two Winter families. On this basis they attempted to reconstitute the dual organization much as it had existed in the past. Some other factors, including antagonism between members of the two groups, were involved in this split, but the lesson I wish to derive from this brief sketch is that the people of San Ildefonso regarded the dual organization as the only way they could operate meaningfully in social relations, and the only way they could impose order on their world. And they are still attempting to sort out the many problems necessitated by this shift. They may not succeed in doing so, due to other, external influences operating today, but it certainly will not be because they have not tried. Consequently, I cannot accept any suggestion that the dual organization is a logical subterfuge perpetrated on the anthropologist by the Tewa, and that it masks a more fundamental underlying ternary structure.

Curiously enough, Lévi-Strauss himself, in one of his earlier papers, pointed a way out of the reciprocity and hierarchy problem, but he failed to follow it up:

> A perhaps one-sided analysis of the dual organization has too often put the emphasis on the principle of reciprocity as its main cause and result. It is well to remember that the moiety system can express, not only mechanisms of reciprocity, but also relations of subordination. But even in these relations of subordination, the principle of reciprocity is at work; for the subordination itself is reciprocal: *the priority which is gained by one moiety on one level is lost to the opposite moiety on the other* [1944, pp. 267–68, italics mine].

If we but add the word "time" to that of "level" above, we have a good statement of how the Tewa solve the problem. In terms of levels alone, we have seen how the reciprocal advantage gained by the Summer moiety through having its water pouring ritual occur less frequently is offset by the more severe dietary restrictions imposed on those undergoing the rite, and by the regular beating it sustains at the relay races of the summer solstice; how the advantage gained by the Winter moiety through the asymmetry of the sexes is offset by its numerically subordinate place in the village; and even how the advantage gained by the Summer moiety through the fact that their chief rules for a longer period of the year is offset, on another level, by the fact that the people of the Winter moiety may bring their gods from two directions. I could go on and on in this vein, but I have already shown how, at each level and time, the asymmetry is of the moment, to be wiped out at another level or in another time.

A further, complementary approach which I have found useful is to look for mediators. There are several Tewa examples of attempts to mediate and override the social division when it threatens to be most disruptive. When the moieties seem to stand furthest apart, during adult life, the Tewa have not only Made People who are "of the middle of the structure," but deities who are sponsored by these Made People, and who are also called "of the middle of the structure." This may be called horizontal mediation, although it is found on two discrete levels of existence. In addition, there is also vertical mediation, as represented by the *Towa é*, who mediate between the other two categories as well as within them.

Symbolically, the attempt is more often made to override the dual organization completely, as in combining the dyadic structures of spiritual existence into three tetramerous structures, and in having transcendental symbols such as the sun. The *Tsave Yoh*, as discussed in chapter 4, are particularly instructive in this regard, for they show how the Tewa can shift from one perspective to another, from one day to another. Thus, when the *Towa é* themselves impersonate the *Tsave Yoh*, all four sacred hills are prayed to, but on the day of the Turtle Dance itself, when non-*Towa é* impersonate them, only the hills of the north and south, which epitomize the moieties, are prayed to. Thus, my conclusion is not that "dualism does not exist per se, it entails and implies a triadic way of thinking" (Lévi-Strauss 1960, p. 47), but that "dualism" does exist, and it implies mediation. Nor are the Tewa alone, among societies with dual organization, in devising mediating ideas and institutions by combining ideas and personnel from each half of the existing dual organization. To cite just one North American example, D'Azevedo and his collaborators point out, in their studies of the Washo of Nevada (1963), that they divide into a west and east moiety each year for the pine nut harvest. Each moiety is designated by the direction in which it goes to camp. But there is also a third "moiety" which camps between the other two, and which includes members from each of the others. This third "moiety" of the middle bears striking resemblence, both socially and symbolically, to the various Tewa organizations "of the middle of the structure." Perhaps we have not, in the past, known how to interpret phenomena such as these, but we should now.

To be sure, the Tewa never completely succeed in doing away with the asymmetry found in their system at any given time, but time, the notion of levels, and the several kinds of mediation provide an answer to the fundamental problem of how a society can be united and divided at the same time. What remains, it is hoped, is an understanding of how a society with dual organization achieves integration and continuity by (1) overriding the division at crucial points in the life cycle, (2) devising systems of mediation, (3) making possible a network of crosscutting ties which transcend the division, and (4) equalizing the asymmetry within the division over a period of time.

I shall conclude by noting that the problem for this work has been dictated not only by interest and relevance, but by urgency, for the Tewa in particular and the eastern Pueblos in general may well be among the last societies with dual organization surviving under something approximating ideal conditions. Lévi-Strauss states the case for the problem well, if dramatically:

> We can only hope that in the world of men, often as indifferent as the infinite universe whose silence terrified Pascal, the rare so-called dual organizations still functioning may find their Einstein before they—less enduring than the planets—disintegrate [1963a, p. 162].

Notes

IN THE BEGINNING

1. In some other versions of the myth the Summer People are said to have subsisted on wild plant foods alone. Sometimes these plants are named and divided into "hot" and "cold" categories, a point which becomes relevant in chapter 5.

2. In Tewa mythology, and in all thinking about distant events, there is the tendency, clearly indicated here, of reducing time and space into minimally meaningful units. The number twelve is used as a formula in ritual speech and behavior to dramatize this first migration. Thus, in prayer and speech sacred objects and events are named in groups of twelve, sacred distances are measured in terms of twelve steps, and rituals often take twelve steps to perform. Four is not used as extensively in the most sacred contexts, but it is far more common in everyday life. The reason for this becomes clear in chapter 3, but one example will serve to illustrate the point here. One famous battle with the Navajo was said to have occurred at a distance of four days' march from the Tewa villages, and the battle was said to have lasted four days. Neither is true, but the number four does serve as a formula to preserve the record of a distant event which might otherwise be lost from memory entirely. The further back in time an event occurs, the more likely it is to be "preserved" by one of these numerical formulas. If it is an unusually sacred event twelve is most likely to be used; if the event is more in the realm of ordinary existence, four is likely to be chosen.

3. The myth has obviously been brought into line with present-day

reality because, when a party of Coronado's men first came through the Tewa area in 1540–1541, there appeared to be several more Tewa-speaking villages (Winship 1896). There were eight at least until the aftermath of the Pueblo Revolt of 1680. In any case, I am not claiming here that the myth accurately mirrors even recent Tewa history.

4. There is a seventh category of existence which the Tewa try not to think about, the *chuge ing*, or witches. The reader will recall that the Tewa brought with them the knowledge of witchcraft from the underworld, and have, therefore, had to contend with witches ever since. Witches constitute a cultural category of being because the Tewa believe in them in the same sense that they believe in the other three categories of spirits. But witches do not exist, even in the Tewa mind, independently of the three living categories of being, because they recruit their members from the living and lead a parallel existence with them in this life. Because witches live on the unexpired lives of their victims, it is believed that they must continually kill or perish themselves. Thus, witchcraft is a shadowy but parallel partner in this life; it is a spectre which stands ever ready to invade the other three human categories.

If and when a witch dies, however, he becomes *nang opah*, "dust of the earth." The Tewa explain this interesting concept as follows. When a suspected witch dies there is usually a severe dust storm within four days, which is the normal length of time it takes a soul to get into the underworld. This shows that the soul was rejected in the underworld, and it consequently becomes *nang opah*. That is to say, it ends its existence as dust and is completely forgotten.

I can now make a fine analytic distinction between the terms category and level as used here. Witches constitute a *category* of being but not a *level* of being, because they are not believed to have an existence independent of the three human levels. They constitute a seventh category but not a seventh level, so I exclude them from figure 1.

5. Harrington (1916), Hewett (1930, p. 97) and others give San Antonio Peak, which is on the New Mexico-Colorado line, as the sacred mountain of the north. This, obviously, is much further north than Conjilon Peak, and extends the conceptual range of the Tewa world to the north by about 50 miles. San Juan elders indicate that San Antonio is an important mountain, but not one of the sacred mountains of the directions. All of these latter can be seen from some reasonably high elevation anywhere in the Tewa country, but this is not true of San Antonio Peak. The point is, of course, not crucial here, but it could be that the northern conceptual boundary of the Tewa world has receded since Harrington's time. But the question might then be raised why this shrinking world image, so to speak,

has not affected the other sacred mountains. This is an interesting question, but one for which an answer which would reconcile all of the discrepancies in the literature cannot be offered here.

Of these four sacred mountains, the one closest to the particular Tewa Pueblo under consideration is most important, in the sense that pilgrimages are made to it more frequently and it plays a disproportionately larger role in their religious life. For the Pueblos on the west side of the Rio Grande (San Juan, Santa Clara and San Ildefonso), *Tsikomo* is obviously the most important in these respects. For Tesuque and Nambe, both of which are located on the east side of the Rio Grande, Lake Peak in the Sangre de Cristos range seems to be the most important, although the situation for Nambe is not entirely clear. One Nambe resident insisted it should be Truchas Peak, rather than neighboring Lake Peak, although Harrington (1916) lists the latter. In any case we have, in Lake Peak, the only exception to an otherwise pan-Tewa group of sacred mountains of the directions.

6. The earth navel is a keyhole-shaped arrangement of stones in which the bottom end is always kept open and pointed toward one or more of the Tewa villages. It functions as a sacred center in two respects. First, it is a point at which one may communicate with the spiritual underworld, and second, it serves to gather in blessings from the three world levels and directs them, through the open end, to the Tewa villages. The latter is the most important meaning attached to it. Of the earth navels under consideration here, the one on *Tsikomo* has been extensively reported upon by Douglass (1912, 1915), Stevenson (1913), Curtis (1926), Parsons (1929), and others. All of them present sketches of the earth navel, although all refer to it simply as a shrine. Of these, only Douglass visited it, and only he labeled it a "world quarter shrine," thereby coming much closer to the truth than the other investigators. *Tsikomo* has received considerable attention, whereas the others have received almost none at all, because most investigators among the Tewa have worked in San Juan, San Idlefonso, or Santa Clara (see footnote 5).

7. Unlike the mountains, most of the *Tsin* are too close to particular Pueblos to provide even a partial system common to all. The four listed here for San Juan could hold true for Santa Clara as well, but not for any of the other Tewa Pueblos. To take an obvious example, *Tun Yoh* cannot be the southern *Tsin* for any of the others because all are located to the south or southeast of *Tun Yoh*. Thus Harrington (1916, pp. 295, 321, passim) lists three *Tsin* for San Ildefonso that are not shared by San Juan, although they and Santa Clara have *Tun Yoh* in common. Harrington presents only partial data for Nambe and Tesuque, the least known of the Tewa Pueblos.

8. Unlike the mountains again, the *Tsin* are regarded as very dangerous places for anyone but the *Towa é* to be, not only because of the labyrinths, tunnels, and/or caves found there, but because the *Tsave Yoh* live there. San Juan elders frequently relate stories about people who have actually been drawn into the tunnel at *Tun Yoh* by a strong wind which is believed to be always present there; they were never seen again. Harrington (1916, p. 295) records a story in San Ildefonso to the effect that *Tun Yoh* was once inhabited by a family of giant *Tsave Yoh*, the father of whom made periodic forays ("in four steps") into San Ildefonso to capture children whom he would feed to his family. In time the *Towa é* killed the family. Harrington (1916, pp. 295, 342, passim) also records information from San Ildefonso and Santa Clara to the effect that *Tun Yoh* and *Tsi Mayoh* were places from which smoke and fire belched forth in ancient times. Like the mountains, however, as these brief accounts indicate, the *Tsin* most convenient of access figures more prominently in mythology and religious thought than the other three. For San Juan, Santa Clara, and San Ildefonso this one seems to be *Tun Yoh*.

9. Gertrude Kurath, in an interesting analysis of Tewa plaza dance circuits (1958), called attention to the puzzling fact that only three plazas seem to be in use in San Juan today. In other words, what is presented here as the west plaza (N) is not used at all in *most* dances. Rather, the dancers proceed from plaza M to O to P and then perform a fourth time inside the kiva, which is located alongside plaza P. All of this is true enough, but the two regular exceptions to this complicated circuit help to resolve the issue. First, let me present some background to this interesting problem.

Plaza N is today bisected by a paved road which leads to several Spanish-American villages located west of San Juan, and to village farmlands on the west side of the Rio Grande (see Laski 1959, p. 6, for a sketch of the village which shows this road). The road has not always been paved, of course, but it has always been there within the memory of the oldest living villagers. Now, since most Tewa plaza dances are performed by one or two long lines of dancers, Plaza N cannot be used without obstructing traffic. Because a church has been in existence on the edge of the plaza at least since 1726 (Aberle, Watkins, and Pitney 1940; Adams and Chavez 1956), and a general store nearby since 1863, the traffic has long been considerable; both the store and the church serve several communities beside San Juan. This plaza has not been used regularly for so long that many, if not most, villagers do not recognize it as such. This is where the two exceptions, the Harvest Dance and the Spanish-introduced Matachines, become relevant.

The Harvest Dance is performed at about the autumnal equinox every other year. It is one of the key public religious dances of the Tewa because it is regular and because it is the one occasion during which all of the Made People, the *Towa é*, and some Dry Food People dance together. The purpose of the Harvest Dance is to thank mother earth for the agricultural harvest of the year; thus its name. But, unlike all other native dances, the dance formation is *circular*. Consequently it is possible to use Plaza N without blocking off the road, and this is done; here the circuit does indeed proceed from M to N to O to P, with no performance inside the kiva.

The Matachines Dance adds further confirmation of the general dance circuit presented on figure 2. Here only a prescribed number of dancers may participate, and they form two parallel rows of five dancers each, with a few other performers within these two short rows. Again, only a small portion of the plaza is necessary for the performance, and so it can be utilized.

On the basis of these examples, then, I can justify the existence of four plazas even if most villagers might not recognize one of them as such. In any case, the pattern of performing dances four times continues, since the fourth performance for other dances occurs inside the kiva.

10. One still wonders, of course, despite these perfectly rational historical explanations, whether there is not something else at work here of which the Tewa are no longer consciously aware, for the resultant dance circuit is an anti-sunwise one, a not infrequent occurrence in Tewa ritual. For instance, in discussing the naming ceremony for infants in the following chapter, I have occasion to note that *two* circuits are in operation, a sunwise one (NWSE) for the winter half of the year, and an anti-sunwise one (SWNE) for the summer half, excluding up and down, which always occur in that order. Kurath again provides an insight of relevance here. While observing a dance at Tesuque she notes that during the morning performance the circuit was sunwise, while during the afternoon performance the dancers shifted into an anti-sunwise circuit (1958, p. 21). Here both circuits are in operation simultaneously during a single dance, while the San Juan Tewa adhere relentlessly to the anti-sunwise circuit in dances.

This question merits further examination because the Tewa are given to reversals or symbolic transformations of this kind. They do it with colors, as when, in some rituals, the colors for north and south are reversed. They also sometimes do it with ideas and institutions they share with neighboring tribes. For instance, among the Keresans of Cochiti the two sacred clown societies, *Quirana* and *Koshare*, are associated with summer and winter respectively (Lange 1959), while among the Tewa the analogous *Kwirana* and *Kossa* are symbolically associated with the winter and summer respectively. The questions here obviously are, first, what are the rules for these transformations, and who borrowed what from whom? I do not have detailed answers in hand now, but I can at least point out that the Tewa seem to shift easily from one perspective (or transformation) to another in accordance with some consistent set of rules.

I might cite just one final example to illustrate this last point. Among the Tewa the right hand is associated with the living and the left with the dead. Thus one feeds oneself with the right hand, but when one "feeds" or makes offerings to the "Dry Food Who Are No Longer" (ancestral souls) one uses his left hand. *However*, when one feeds or makes offerings to the "Dry Food Who Never Did Become" (deities), one uses his right hand again. The reason here is that the latter cannot be treated like the dead, because they are ancestors, of sorts, who *never* became dead. Some similar process may be at work in Zuni, for instance, because they presented a discrepancy which Hertz (1960) could not explain away in his comparative analysis of the symbolism of the right hand.

11. It is suggested that a lack of awareness of all of these categories is what has hampered our understanding of the Tewa, and perhaps other Pueblo groups as well, in the past. The focus has usually been on the Dry Food People alone, but by some other name, or on unsystematized relations among only the three living categories, with the spirits lumped together into a general and vague category somehow relevant for social well-being. Other investigators, notably Parsons (1929) and Curtis (1926), got themselves almost completely lost in the rich ceremonial life of the Tewa, much to the detriment of our understanding of other aspects of culture. My intent here is not high-handedly to fault these earlier investigators among the Tewa, for even the modest contribution attempted here would not have been possible had they not defined problems and provided a solid base of ethnographic knowledge upon which to build. Rather, I am only trying to make clear the point that whatever novelty may lie in this work derives entirely from the discovery and ordering of the data in terms of these six categories of existence.

The question may then be asked, if these categories are so fundamental why has someone else not discovered them before? The answer may be summarized as follows. Until the very end of my field work I too operated with a simple distinction between people and spirits; I believed that by studying closely the activities of the living everything else would somehow fall into place. But then I recorded a large number of prayers and speeches by Made People and noted the term *seh t'a di popí* (Dry Food Who Never Did Become) occurring now and again when they referred to spirits. Clearly this was different from *seh t'a di mupí* (Dry Food Who Are No Longer), which occurred much more frequently. Category 6 came into being and the whole system then began to emerge. This term has never been noted before because it is primarily a subconscious concept; even when Made People are asked about spirits they usually specify individual ones exactly or lump them all together under the more common term. Here then is what may be characterized as a borderline area between conscious and unconscious categories of thought, for no amount of direct questioning or probing ever elicited this concept; it had to be filtered out, so to speak, from the several hours of taped prayers and speeches. Once individual elders could be confronted with the question of why two terms if the only distinction they were aware of was that between spirits and different groups of the living, then we could begin to work the system out together. And some of the implications of the system surprised even the one elder who worked most closely with me; but he found it all perfectly reasonable, although he could not really grasp it in its entirety.

The place of the two categories of *Towa é* in the whole system was arrived at equally laboriously, because I had accepted the usual view of them as being Spanish-derived. But the discovery of Category 6 was the critical turning point. This lengthy discourse on the role of chance —and good fortune—in field work is recorded here so that the reader might sympathize with the titles of the next three chapters, as well as to provide the student of the Pueblos with some leads for research elsewhere.

12. I might also record here that my findings corroborate the broader observations made by Reed (1956) that the Tewa villages alone among modern Pueblos retain an unambiguous spatial orientation of house-blocks facing inward unilaterally to a central plaza, or multiple plazas. This pattern was much more widespread in recent Pueblo prehistory. I must, however, register disagreement with Reed's interpretation of San Juan as being more disrupted, "presumably by closer contacts with the Spanish" (1956, p. 15), than the other Tewa villages. In the view outlined here, the San Juan village plan should be seen as an enlargement or explosion of the earlier widespread pattern of houses facing inward toward a central plaza. Thus I can, with greater plausibility, interpret the San Juan pattern as beginning with a single plaza—a point so explicitly made by Villagrá—then, with the growth of population

(Aberle, Watkins, and Pitney 1940) and the easing of the need for defensive fortifications, expanding gradually into the present four-plaza pattern.

The reason this point is important is that it may well be the solution to one of the central problems Reed points up in interpreting recent Rio Grande prehistory; namely, why did everyone else but the Tewa have villages consisting of parallel alignments of houseblocks, or a combination of the alignment and plaza type after about 1300? If the gradual development of the San Juan pattern can be taken as a model, then population size seems to be the answer to the problem. This solution becomes more plausible if I point out that Santa Clara, which has long been second only to San Juan in population size, is also tending toward the San Juan model, as Kurath's analysis of the dance circuit indicates (1958). Armed with this hypothesis one might then attempt to determine the relative population sizes of representative villages reflecting the two types of village pattern. This comparison might also be carried through into recent centuries, insofar as population figures are available in the Spanish documents.

As an alternative, though not necessarily contradictory, hypothesis, one might also say that the Tewa represent some of the original inhabitants of the upper Rio Grande, and that they therefore retained the earlier inward-facing village pattern. Since there was a sizable influx of population into the general area about 1300, the two hypotheses might actually come together to help clarify the problem. The larger question, as before, is who was already in the area and who moved in? Whatever the answer, the Tewa cannot easily be dismissed as latecomers now.

3
THE DRY FOOD PEOPLE AND THE DRY FOOD WHO ARE NO LONGER

1. Tewa color symbolism is actually much more complex, of course, but these are the primary referents of these five colors when they are specifically identified with the respective moieties and used by them in ritual.

2. A useful way of viewing the problem is to regard "man" as the unmarked category and "woman" as the marked category in Tewa, following Greenberg's discussion of the notion of marked and un-

marked (1966, pp. 25–55). To quote Greenberg on the distinction: "The general meaning of a marked category states the presence of a certain property A; the general meaning of the corresponding unmarked category states nothing about the presence of A and is used chiefly but not exclusively to indicate the absence of A" (1966, p. 25). He goes on to demonstrate that the sexes in English are also distinguished in this way, not too dissimilar to the Tewa, and points out that in general the unmarked category in any such pair is ambiguous, in the sense that it indicates both the marked category and its specific opposite. The marked category in such a pair of course indicates only that, as demonstrated in my Tewa example by the category "woman."

While this is not the place to go into a detailed discussion of the implications of the notion of marked and unmarked categories for the Tewa data, I might point out that, in general, the symbols and attributes of the Winter moiety are unmarked. But where this is true on a symbolic level, the Summer moiety attains preeminence on another level. So the situation implies no enduring relationship of asymmetry between the moieties. The picture for the Tewa is complicated further by the fact that, in some lexical domains—plants and animals for instance—the distinctions either do not apply or are obscured by an equivocal or "neutral" category the Tewa refer to as "of the middle of the structure." Nonetheless, the notion of marked and unmarked categories is a potentially very useful one for understanding much of the data presented in this work, and relevant aspects of it should be re-analyzed in these terms.

3. The question has been raised by one colleague that perhaps this rite arose from an attempt to emulate the Spanish Catholic baptismal rite. Now, it is true that all Tewa are baptized, confirmed, and receive their first holy communion, but this is a parallel series of rites, existing completely independently of water giving and the other early life crises rites described in this section. Yet the question is worth exploring because Edward Dozier has recently informed me (personal communication) that the water giving rite has either lapsed or it never existed in Santa Clara. This is one instance in which the Spanish historical record, which is ethnographically disappointing save in accounts of witchcraft, has proven illuminating, at least for resolving the first question. The following eyewitness account of what is very likely the water giving rite, observed in San Juan in 1631 or 1632, is reproduced by Scholes:

"Pedro de la Crus soldado y vesino de la villa de Santa Fee . . . dixo que abra ocho meses que yendo en compañia de Geronimo Pacheco mestizo y soldado a recojer yeguas, de buelta entraron en

una estufa del pueblo de San Juan a calentarse y que estando
los indios jugando a los patoles, estando este dicho declarante
recostado, dice que una india traxo una criatura y que se lebanto
un indio de los que estaban jugando que era fiscal llamado pindas
i tomo la criatura y se sento con ella teniendola en los brasos
mientras truxeron un cajete de agua, en el qual hecharon los patoles
i los lavaron i labados los sacaron i poniendo la criatura en un petate
tomando cada uno su cañuela o patole todos juntos a la par tiraron
asia arriba los patoles como quando juegan y caieron algunos sobre
la criatura y tomando cada uno en la boca una poca de agua se la
hechaban a la criatura en la boca i despues soplaban todos a la
criatura la cabesa manos i pies y que pregundando este dicho
declarante a los indios que por que asian aquello respondieron que
era para ponelle nombre en su lengua y que asi lo solian aser en la
jentilidad i que con esto se salieron el dicho declarante i el dicho
Geronimo Pacheco." (Declaration of Pedro de la Cruz, September
14, 1632; quoted in Scholes, 1935, pp. 240–41)

This account, recorded just 34 years after the first permanent Spanish
settlement was established in New Mexico, of a ceremony not recognized as Spanish by the eyewitness, and certainly not sanctioned by
the Church, indicates considerable antiquity for the rite, at least in
San Juan. Two other versions of this deposition are presented by
Scholes, but they agree substantially with the above. Together they
constitute the only eyewitness account of a key Tewa ritual known
to us from the Spanish historical record. The principal differences
between the rite as conducted then and today seem to be that the
game with beans is now absent, and the abalone shell is today substituted for the mouth-to-mouth administering of medicinal water.
The time cannot be fixed with any certainty because the three accounts
do not agree.

4. Many Tewa elders show a very detailed knowledge of the region
north and northwest of San Juan into what is now southwestern
Colorado. This is true even if they have never been there themselves.
There are Tewa names for ruins, lakes, ponds, springs, and other
prominent topographic features in this area, especially those in the
Chama Valley. To cite a few brief examples, Pagosa Springs in Colorado
is mentioned as the place to which members of the Winter moiety
society used to journey, until a few decades ago, to gather sand for use
during winter solstice observances. Secondly, a lake behind the water-
fall at the head of the Brazos River in northwestern New Mexico is
one of the places from which the winter deities of Category 6 are said

to come. Third, the names of three of the four prominent lakes on the present-day Jicarilla Apache Reservation, Stinking Lake, Stone Lake, and Horse Lake, are translations of Tewa names for them. We may assume the Tewa did not adopt these names from the Apaches for two reasons. First, the latter were not permanently settled in the area until after their reservation was set aside in 1887, and, secondly, the Tewa regard them as sacred lakes in which the deities of Category 6 dwell. Moreover, their names are surrounded by a considerable body of mythology, and the entire area is associated with other ritual uses.

The point to all of this is that such detailed knowledge does lend credence to the Tewa's migration traditions and claims that they once occupied an area considerably to the north and northwest of where they are now. Their knowledge of these distant areas, when contrasted with their knowledge of areas in any other direction, is so detailed that we must regard this as independent evidence of what many southwestern archaeologists have long suspected. In any case, much more research needs to be done on the question of Tewa prehistory.

5. Edward Dozier, in the same personal communication cited in note 3 above, stated that Santa Clara deities today come from only two directions, north and west. San Juan deities, on the other hand, are "brought" to the village from all four directions. I shall have occasion to note the instances in which they come from the west in chapter 5, but I might mention here that they do not come as frequently from the west as from the north or south. By contrast, they are brought from the east on only one, infrequent, occasion; whenever a new member is being initiated into the Winter moiety society. The directional symbolism works out on this level, therefore, as follows. North and east belong exclusively to the Winter moiety, west is shared, and only south belongs exclusively to the Summer moiety, as far as tracing the journey of the deities is concerned. Thus, whatever economic advantage the Summer moiety gains by having the water pouring ritual less frequently is offset by its subordinate position on this symbolic level.

It might also be noted in passing that, during the water pouring rituals for both moieties, the deities are brought from lakes well outside of the boundaries of the Tewa world as defined by the sacred mountains. The winter deities are brought from Sandy Place Lake, the primordial home, which all informants locate even further to the north than San Antonio Peak on the New Mexico-Colorado state line. The Summer moiety brings its deities from a lake which has dried up, but which was formerly located near the present Pueblo of Laguna. This is about 40 miles to the southwest of Sandia Peak, the sacred mountain of the south. This is true, however, only for the two water pouring rituals; for every other ritual the deities are always brought from the lakes at or within the boundaries of the Tewa world.

6. Pride on the part of the old man is involved here to some extent, since he could not pass his office or other ritual prerogatives on to his grandson. But there is more to this kind of adoption than that. In the Tewa Pueblos, as in all others, religious responsibility is overwhelmingly in the hands of the men, and participation in rituals tends to run along family lines. A man who does not, therefore, have at least one son to participate with him is, relatively speaking, a weak man. This is all the more so if a man is a member of the permanent religious hierarchy and therefore cannot participate directly in many rituals himself.

7. One might also argue here, on the contrary, that it is precisely those in key positions in the society—members of the formal religious hierarchy—who have an interest in these transfers of identity because such formal transfers reinforce the symbolic distinctions between the moieties. Logically, the argument is sound, and there might well be something to it. But, empirically, these transfers are caused by unusual circumstances, and they also occur among people who have no vested interest in the matter. I am indebted to Nicholas S. Hopkins for pointing out this possibility.

8. There is one long-standing problem—perhaps the most important in terms of the confusion it has engendered in the literature—in Tewa kinship which I can resolve through the data and method of analysis presented in this chapter. This is the problem pointed up by the seemingly contradictory evidence when scholars, to mention only Murdock (1949) as the most recent example, have attempted to classify the Tewa kinship system into one or another type on the basis of its terminology. Let me first note what earlier scholars have written about Tewa kinship terminology for siblings and cousins, by way of defining the problem.

Harrington, in the first systematic article written on Tewa kinship (1912), notes that two of the several terms of address for aunt and uncle, *ko'o* and *mae mae*, respectively, are extended to cross and parallel cousins of whatever age. On the other hand, sibling terms of address are extended to all other cousins, according to Harrington. In a short article published just a dozen years later, Parsons takes Harrington to task for not recording all of the terms found in the various Tewa Pueblos, for not noting variations thereof, and for not conceding that kin terms were, after all, only linguistic phenomena, having no profound implications for social life. To support her view that there is a lack of systematization in the use of kinship terms, Parsons offers the view, contradictory to Harrington's findings, that in the speaker's generation Tewa parallel cousins may be addressed by sibling terms, while cross cousins may use the same aunt-uncle terms given above (Parsons 1924). This is obviously very different from Harrington's observations, and it is perplexing in view of the fact that these two scholars worked for many years among the Tewa.

There is yet a third view. Whitman, who did field work in San Ildefonso during 1936 and 1937, came to the honest but equally perplexing conclusion that some of his informants applied the two sibling terms to cross and parallel cousins, while others applied the terms for uncle and aunt. He further noted that both groups of informants insisted they were right, and that they used the terms systematically. Unfortunately, Whitman failed to pursue this last point, dismissing the differences as confusion caused by breakdown within the system (1940). Obviously then, this is one of the problems anyone attempting to classify the Tewa kinship system has to resolve. Since cousin terminology has been one of the important bases for such classifications for several decades now, many people have been led astray. Thus Murdock (1949), by deciding to follow Harrington, classified the Tewa as Normal Eskimo, with a probable former Omaha type of patrilineal structure. He really did not know what to do with the Tewa, because he recognized that the evidence is contradictory.

Let us return now to the Tewa life cycle. The reader will recall that, instead of descent, each Tewa becomes a member of his moiety through a three-stage process of initiation, with the last being the most important. This third, called finishing, comes between the ages of 10 and 15 for most Tewa, and establishes them as full adult members of the society. It is here that I find the answer to the problem of conflicting evidence on terminology. Those Tewa cross and parallel cousins who are approximately the same age address one another by sibling terms, but if there is a great disparity in their ages, the elder is addressed by the term for uncle or aunt, depending on his sex of course. He, in turn, uses the appropriate reciprocal in addressing his younger cousin. Now, relative age is obviously important in terms of address, but this is not all. The crucial distinction is whether the person addressed has undergone the finishing rite or not. If a 9-year-old child who has not been finished is addressing a 15-year-old cousin who has been, he will use the term for uncle or aunt. If both have been finished, they will use sibling terms for one another. Yet, if the age disparity were too great, they would continue to use the more respectful uncle-aunt terms until well into their adult years. The point, then, is that the terms may shift between any given pair of speakers, and the only reliably fixed point of reference we have for predicting what terms will be employed is the finishing rite. And the Tewa kinship system will continue to defy classification on the basis of any *a priori* assumptions that the same terms of address will be used throughout their lifetimes by any given pair of speakers.

To summarize briefly, it is clear that Harrington, Parsons, and Whitman were all partially right, with Whitman coming closer to the truth than the others. There is neither confusion nor breakdown, nor is there a single pattern of usage. Several alternatives are possible in the total terminological system, and these are determined by the relative age and social status of the people concerned. In this way we see how important an understanding of the elaborate cycle of rites of passage is to clarifying even problems of a nonritual nature.

9. In the Tewa's continuing association of the dead with the shrines located at the trash mounds near the village, we have what we might term an instance of cultural lag. In other words, despite the now centuries-old practice of burying all dead in a consecrated Church cemetery east of San Juan, the Tewa still persist in the more ancient belief that the dead are really at the shrines surrounding the village. Thus, all ritual offerings are taken there, rather than to the cemetery.

10. That this commemorative date has taken hold is not as unusual as it might seem, aside from the fact that it is observed with a purely native ritual. The last chief of the Summer moiety, who passed away in 1963, used to have a feast for his relatives in his home on the eve of Good Friday every year. Sometime during the course of the meal, which was always served in the traditional manner on the floor, all lights would go out. Those within would hear light footsteps in the dark, and, when the lights were restored, would find most of the food gone. The Summer chief always assured the people that the spirits had come to avail themselves of the food. All of this was just his way of competing with the Catholic Church during its week of intensified ritual, and in this way reinforcing the faith of at least a few members of his moiety in the efficacy of the traditional religion. He would also point out that, since the Spanish *penitentes* had meetings during Holy Week, the Tewa too should have a native ritual observance of some kind. The annual feast was never institutionalized by other groups in the village, and therefore has not been held again.

All this discussion is intended to communicate is that there is nothing at all unusual about celebrating a date on the Church calendar with an observance which may be oriented toward a completely different end. The difference in the All Souls' Day ritual is that it was generally accepted and institutionalized.

11. Let me hasten to emphasize again that my intent is not to read marriage out of the picture completely, for documentary evidence from the early Spanish period may still one day turn up to indicate a prior

state of moiety exogamy, or anthropology may still develop the means to infer it reliably from evidence presently available to us. It is a well-known fact that the Catholic Church has never been able to tolerate dissent in life crisis rituals, but it is in marriage and death practices that the Church seems to have clashed especially seriously with the Tewa. And these are precisely the rites, as I have demonstrated, in which there is the greatest amount of Spanish influence reflected. To speculate just a bit, a situation of prescriptive or preferential cross-cousin marriage would simply not have been tolerable to the early Spanish friars, given Catholic rules of exogamy, if they had encountered it in the Pueblos. Nor would, for instance, any elaborate reciprocal services and rituals at death, such as are frequently found associated with dual organizations, if they were felt to conflict with the Church's prerogatives. And in New Mexico during the 17th century almost everything Indian was regarded as an ecclesiastical prerogative at one time or another; this much seems reasonably clear from Dozier's admirable synthesis of the historical records of that period (1961). Situations such as that reported by Chapman (1962) for the Jicaques of Honduras, such as the survival of some dual notions about death—a portion of the cemetery is still reserved for each moiety—appear to be rare wherever there has been serious and sustained missionary activity. Speculation and reflection aside, the point to be reiterated here is that by being forced to look beyond marriage relations I find I am still able to formulate meaningful conclusions about the operation, continuity, and integration of Tewa society.

12. Actually, however, one shrine, Sun-Water-Wind of the north, is visited far more frequently than the others, and there is much more personal identification with it. As one informant termed it, "Where the Sun-Water-Wind are is where one should go if he has a problem; it is the most kind of souls-dwelling middle-places. Whenever I need something I place offerings there and have always gotten my wish." In group ritual also, this shrine seems to be the most prominent of the four. Late on the night those who are to impersonate the deities of Category 6 are chosen, the "Keepers of the entrance to the lake" take them to this shrine to make offerings, to pray for the success of their joint effort, and to swear that they will see their four-day period of confinement through to the end.

As with the mountains and sacred hills, then, one shrine seems to figure more prominently in religious belief and action. Let me review the evidence thus far for the three sets of sacred tetrads. The most prominent mountain is to the west, the most prominent hill is to the south, and the most prominent shrine is to the north. Since we have run out of sacred tetrads, what is left for the east? In a very real sense the east is the most important direction in daily life because of its identification with the sun, which is believed to be the source of all life, as the primary fertilizing agent in nature. Thus the first act a Tewa male performs when he gets up in the morning is to take a pinch of white cornmeal, throw it to the sun as an offering, and ask for long life. I have already described above how, at the naming ceremony, the infant is presented to the sun. On a group level, after most ritual dances, those articles which cannot be used again are deposited east of the village; when a Made person dies, those of his sacred objects which cannot be used by his successor are deposited in the foothills to the east. Ten of the twelve kivas in use in the Tewa villages today, including both of those at San Juan, have doors facing to the east or southeast. What all of this is intended to demonstrate is that on one level or another, each of the directions is emphasized in turn, and the direction which seems to get short shrift in a specific, formal sense has preeminence in a general sense. The implications of all of this for cultural integration should be obvious.

4
THE TOWA É

1. Yet they are also one with what the Spaniards call *capitanes de la guerra*, or "war captains." This is part of the reason for the confusion in the literature. I shall attempt to indicate presently just how this integration of the two might have come about.

The head of the group is also referred to as *Towa é sehn*, "person man," to set him off as the elder brother when he and his second-in-command act together in an official capacity, and when a decision for the whole group has to be rendered by someone. This distinction is analogous to the distinction between elder and younger brother war gods in other Pueblos. The group is also referred to collectively as *akon gein*, "those of the plain." This derives from the fact that they formerly often stood watch on the plain outside the village during important ritual occasions. By this usage, the head is referred to as *akono tuyoh*, "chief of the plain," or "outside chief," as in the literature (Parsons 1929). Sometimes, when only two are acting as *Towa é* and the others as guards on the plain, only the latter are referred to as *akon gein*. One can begin to understand the reason for some of the confusion in the literature. The point to be reiterated here is that the entire group is most often referred to as *Towa é*, and, as we shall see presently, any pair within it can be designated as representatives for the whole group.

2. Until about 20 years ago there were two other functionaries, one native and the other Spanish-imposed, who were related to these three groups of officials. The town crier, who was native, formerly announced news of important events which had taken place, or were about to take place, on behalf of the Made People and the political officials. He was an old man with a strong and clear voice, who was appointed to this position for life by the moiety chiefs. In return for his services he was excused from serving as a political official, and from other communal work responsibilities.

The *Sacristan*, who was Spanish-introduced, served as an assistant, altar boy, and general errand boy for the resident priest. He was an adult man who, of course, knew the details of the Catholic mass, and could read prayer books in Spanish. This man was chosen from among the more devout of the village by the priest, and he, too, served for life. The *Sacristan* was also relieved from many communal work obligations, and sometimes received a very modest weekly honorarium from the priest. Both officials have been replaced; the *Sacristan* by a stable of altar boys and a parish council, and the town crier by radio, television, pickup trucks, and now the telephone.

3. The four *Fiscales* are referred to in everyday discourse as the "Keepers of the entrance to the church." An analogy is perceived in Tewa thought between these four and the four lay assistants to each moiety society, who are in charge of rituals involving the deities of Category 6, and who are referred to as the "Keepers of the entrance to the lake." These lay assistants are presented on figure 7, and discussed in the following chapter. To the Tewa mind, in other words, the *Fiscales* are to Catholic ritual and to the Church what the "Keepers of the entrance to the lake" are to native ritual and to the earthly representation of the primordial home.

Another analogy can be drawn between the way the Tewa perceive the governor and his two lieutenants (figure 4), and the way they perceive a society of Made People. Both organizations are perceived to consist, in operational terms, of a head and a right and left arm. This fact is not obvious for the Spanish officials presented on figure 4, because the *Aguacil* is also included.

4. The *punan* are the functional equivalents of the *principales* in other Pueblos (Parsons 1939, I:146); they serve as advisers to the governor. The folk etymology of the term helps to clarify the role these men play in Tewa political affairs. *Punan* refers to the process of building up earth around young corn plants when they grow tall

enough to be endangered by stiff winds; in other words, "to support" the cornstalks. Similarly, the *punan* are regarded as "supporters" of the governor because each has held the office and may hold it again.

5. Although this is neither the time nor the place to go into a detailed exposition on the significance of Catholic saints in Tewa belief, one more point of clarification may be added. Of the saints, the ones most venerated by the Tewa are those who are not only "good to think," but who are compatible with native belief; those, in other words, who represent new and useful concepts introduced by the Spaniards. Two of these are Saint James, the patron saint of horsemen, and Saint Raphael, the patron saint of fishermen. Both are venerated because the Tewa, while weaving the horse and new fishing techniques completely into their culture and becoming heavily dependent on both, really had no native spirits for either. These two saints have therefore been taken out of the Church and into the mind, so to speak, to the extent that native offerings of white cornmeal and prayer feathers are presented to them at various times during the year.

I believe that the entire literature on Spanish-Indian acculturation in the Pueblos should be reviewed, insofar as it is possible to do so, as a problem in the interplay of ideas and symbols. Much new light can be shed on the points, such as those touched on in this chapter, at which the two cultures merged.

6. The governor and his two lieutenants, together with all previous governors and the seven male heads of the Made People's societies, also form a village council. It meets frequently but irregularly to formulate village policy on all dealings with the outside word. In reality, however, the council traditionally served only as a forum where the Made People —especially the two moiety chiefs—could impose their will on the governor and his advisory staff of *punan* on all important decisions. In terms of the maintenance of the society the council traditionally meant very little; most relevant decisions in this area were made on the other levels and in the other ways discussed in this work. This point is worth making because most writers, notably Aberle (1948), have exaggerated the importance of the council as the governing body of the Pueblo.

Social control may be taken as a case in point. The council serves as a court of law for cases of what may be loosely termed civil disobedience (failure to participate in work connected with the irrigation canals, permitting one's livestock to damage a neighbor's property, stealing, acts of violence, etc.) and wrongs committed against Spanish-American neighbors, where these are not covered by state or federal law. For these and other violations the *Aguacil* is charged with the duty of bringing the transgressors to court in the governor's home. However, the moiety chiefs do not even attend, since they, ideally speaking, should not listen to harsh words, and they should not arbitrate in the quarrels of the Dry Food People. The other Made People may attend or not, as they wish, and this usually depends on the importance of the individual case and their interest in it. These cases are, then, usually settled by the Spanish officials and *punan* alone. The Made People are quite often not involved, and the *Towa é* never, since they do not even belong to the council.

However, the majority of antisocial acts for which some form of punishment was prescribed traditionally fell under the direct purview of the *Towa é*. These, which I might term breaches of custom, range from failure to participate in ritual activities to charges of witchcraft. In exacting retribution or administering punishment for these breaches, the *Towa é* and, as we shall see presently, the *Tsave Yoh*, are in complete charge. And in this they merely act as the executive arm of the Made People, unless it is a Made person himself who must be punished.

I have qualified these several statements on the role of the council with the word "traditionally" because the situation has been slowly but surely changing during recent decades. As the number of outside matters which can be clearly dissociated from the daily life of all villagers has dwindled, the council has, almost in spite of itself, had more and more power thrust upon it; as the number, nature and complexity of the Pueblo's dealings with the outside world have increased, the Made People have felt less and less adequate to the task of rendering decisions, and entrusted them more and more to increasingly younger and better educated governors. Conversely, as the hold of tradition on the villagers lessens, the *Towa é* are finding it increasingly difficult to enforce the sanctions with which they are charged, with the result that today even witchcraft accusations are debated by the council-court.

What we have, then, is a slow process whereby the council has appropriated more and more duties for itself and assumed more and more power at the expense of the *Towa é*, as the village has become more secularized. Yet the whole process is proceeding rather more by unavoidable accretion than by design. And the changes have arisen from conditions which certainly did not exist until a few decades ago.

The lessons to be drawn from this brief sketch of the role of the council are, first, that the Spaniards unwittingly gave the Tewa a means of coping with change by providing them with a non-tradition-bound institution to serve as a receiver for decision-making power. Secondly, we should not assume the present importance of the council as something which always existed, as most writers have done; rather, it is only against the background of the traditional system as outlined here in this work that the changes can be understood, for the underlying native models still serve to guide the changes in clearly discernible ways.

7. An incident which occurred several years ago in San Juan will serve to underscore the operational distinction between the Spanish officials and the *Towa é*. In recent years the people of San Juan have permitted the taking of photographs of native dances by tourists. A fee is charged for this privilege by the *Towa é*, who patrol the plazas while the dance is in progress, and an identifying tag is issued to each photographer so he shall not be charged twice. During three successive days at Christmas, however, both the Matachines, a dance introduced by the Spaniards, and the Turtle Dance, a native solstice ceremony, are performed; the former on Christmas eve and Christmas day, and the latter on December 26. Because the Matachines is clearly recognized as Spanish-derived and associated with the Catholic Church the Spanish officials are in charge of organizing the dance and patrolling the plazas while it is in progress. Accordingly, they also collect the photography fees from the tourists. The *Towa é* have absolutely nothing to do with this dance, just as the Spanish officials have nothing whatsoever to do with the ensuing Turtle Dance.

The incident occurred as follows. A group of tourists who stayed for all three days of dancing, unmindful of the functional division between the two groups, approached the governor for a permit to take photographs during the Turtle Dance. The governor, thinking he would get away with a few extra dollars, went ahead and sold the tourists a permit. Somehow a *Towa é* found out and reported the incident to the leader of the group. The latter confronted the governor on the plaza and gave him a tongue-lashing for selling the permit, ending with the words: "You have absolutely no part in this dance, and you have no right selling permits, just as I have no right to interfere in the performance of the Matachines." This was an extraordinary incident, but it serves to make the point.

Only during periods of intensive ritual activity, when the *Towa é* sometimes find themselves understaffed, is the operational distinction blurred. On these occasions the Spanish officials may stand watch as replacements for the *Towa é*, but they may do so only at night. During these periods the Spanish officials are referred to as "those of the night." Here a symbolic duality is substituted for the functional one, with the result being that both groups still retain their distinctiveness in the minds of the Tewa.

8. Six different kinds of *Tsave Yoh* are recognized by the Tewa, the *Kunye* (Turquoise), *Po tsunu* (White Shell), *Pi t'i* (Red Shell), *Towa Yoh* (Giant Person), *Po ka* (Water Plant), and the *Po eh Tsave Yoh*

(Sacred, or Traditional). Of these only the last are impersonated today, although it is said that in times past, whenever the children misbehaved too much, the Water Plant *Tsave Yoh* was brought to the village to punish them. He is called such because, when he appears, he is covered with a stringy green plant with broad leaves which grows in shallow ponds in the area. He might be compared to the "River Man" of Cochiti Pueblo because, like the latter, he formerly appeared in the spring. The rest of the *Tsave Yoh* are known only in sacred traditions, as inhabiting the labyrinths of the four sacred hills, but they are so fundamentally rooted in these traditions that it is difficult to believe, as some writers do, that they are Spanish-derived.

I should also note here, in passing, that while all of the basic colors of the cardinal directions are represented among the *Tsave Yoh*, none of them is unambiguously associated with a single direction. In this regard they contrast sharply with the deities of Category 6, who are unambiguously identified with particular directions by color. In general I might say that whenever Tewa color directional symbolism is applied to the spirits, it tends to break down the closer we get to the village. Thus the *Tsave Yoh* are colored but not associated with particular directions, while the souls dwelling in the shrines surrounding the village are not colored at all.

9. The *Tsave Yoh* also perform a therapeutic function. During their visits to various homes the sick of each household may be brought out so the *Tsave Yoh* may minister to them. This is done by giving the patient four light strokes with the whip on his wound, sore, or painful area. After this the *Tsave Yoh* takes a small portion of spruce from his collar and gives it to the senior woman of the household. She is asked to chew this, along with white cornmeal, and spit the solution on the patient's afflicted area each day for four days. This treatment is believed to be effective when others fail.

This therapeutic function also serves to distinguish the *Tsave Yoh* from the deities of Category 6. Their curing rite or blessing, called *e'te tanweh fere* (children illness blow away), is distinguished from the blessing that the "Dry Food Who Never Did Become" give, which is called *woa ha sifen* (life breath blow). It is different in the sense that, while the *Tsave Yoh* may cure bodily ailments, only the deities of Category 6 can offer life; while the *Tsave Yoh* can offer only temporary relief from sickness, the deities of Category 6 can bestow life itself, and this they do only to the Made People and their assistants when they are initiated. Thus, the *Tsave Yoh* are concerned with and accessible to the Dry Food People, while the "Dry Food Who Never Did Become" are not accessible to the Dry Food People as such, since they never bestow their blessing directly on them or visit them in their homes. The power of the deities of Category 6, while greater, is also more generalized and diffuse, while that of the *Tsave Yoh* can have immediate and practical implications for the individual Dry Food person. This is a fundamental axis of differentiation between the two kinds of masked beings who visit the Tewa, despite their formal similarities in dress.

10. I can now summarize what I believe to be the meaning of the labyrinths of the sacred hills in Tewa religious thought, for clearly they are as distinct from the earth navels as the *Tsin* are from the sacred mountains. Here the basic insight is that of Eliade, who, working within a broad comparative framework, summarizes the evidence on the religious significance of labyrinths generally as follows: "Without being over-hasty in deciding the original meaning and function of labyrinths, there is no doubt that they included the notion of defending a 'centre.' Not everyone might try to enter a labyrinth or return unharmed from one; to enter it was equivalent to an initiation. The 'centre' might be one of a variety of things. The labyrinth could be defending a city, a tomb or a sanctuary but, in every case, it was defending some magico-religious space that must be made safe from the uncalled, the uninitiated. The military function of the labyrinth was simply a variant on its essential work of defending against 'evil,' hostile spirits and death. Militarily, a labyrinth prevented the enemy's getting in, or at least made it very difficult, while it admitted those who knew the plan of the defences. Religiously, it barred the way to the city for spirits from without, for the demons of the desert, for death. The 'centre' here includes the whole of the city which is made, as we have seen, to reproduce the universe itself.

"But often the object of the labyrinth was to defend a 'centre' in the first and strictest sense of the word; it represented, in other words, access to the sacred, to immortality, to absolute reality, by means of initiation" (Eliade 1958, p. 381). The reader is referred also to the discussion of the Tewa labyrinths presented in chapter 2, and particularly to notes 6 and 8 of that chapter. Viewing the accumulated evidence in retrospect, we can see that if but a few words were changed in the above quotation, Eliade could well be talking specifically about the labyrinths of the sacred *Tsin*. Thus the *Towa é* and *Tsave Yoh* both defend the center or village, the former by standing watch on the *Tsin* to keep enemies from entering the center, and the latter by preventing the uninitiated within from venturing too close, and perhaps, in former times, from attempting to leave the center. Indeed, there is firmly grounded in Tewa thought the belief that women and children should never venture beyond that area of the Tewa world bounded by the *Tsin* anyway. Ecologically this works out quite well, for the types of subsistence activities in which women and children are permitted to participate are almost entirely limited to the river valley and foothills—well within this boundary.

In addition to defending the center, the labyrinths also include some idea of purifying or consecrating it anew at critical points during the year. This point is borne out by the *Tsave Yoh*'s appearances at about the winter solstice to punish deviants, reaffirm the solidarity of the moieties (society) through the ritual handshake at the mother earth navel, enforce participation in the Turtle Dance, and to insure that the village is swept clean for the ritual. Inasmuch as the winter solstice period is the busiest ritual season of the year, it is the time that the *Tsave Yoh* are most needed. Beyond these partial considerations, there is probably also some general notion that there must be order and moral purity in the sacred center (village) as the old year ends and a new one begins. This last point will become clearer when I discuss the works of the Made People in the following chapter. Finally, it is equally obvious that the labyrinth itself is also a sacred center, for it represents, like the earth navel, a mode of access to the sacred underworld.

11. To be sure, the *Tsave Yoh* are, like those who impersonate them, somewhat anomalous. Thus, as with the *Towa é*, some measure of confusion has been unavoidable when they have been discussed in the past. I might distinguish them in greater detail from the deities of Category 6 to clarify further their nature and role. I have already indicated in note 9 above that they cannot bestow life; they can only cure illness. The *Tsave Yoh* are further differentiated from the "Dry Food Who Never Did Become" by the fact that they (1) use what the Tewa call "Spanish whips" (strips of rawhide tied to the ends of short sticks), while the latter use whips of yucca leaves; (2) shake hands as a form of greeting, in the Spanish manner, while the latter may not even be touched at all; (3) speak in Spanish (although in a disguised voice), while the latter may only gesture; (4) appear in the open, in broad daylight, while the latter only visit the kiva, and at night; and (5) their impersonators are not required to retreat for four days beforehand, unlike the impersonators of the latter. But they are required to remain continent ("refrain from going into badger holes") during the period they impersonate the *Tsave Yoh*, so the matter is not treated lightly.

From this discussion it would appear that the *Tsave Yoh* might be Spanish-derived, but this is unlikely for two reasons, in addition to those implied in note 10 above. First, among the most common fetishes kept in Tewa homes are pieces of fossilized bone, and these are identified as *Tsave Yoh* bones, the only remains of *Tsave Yoh* who lived in the area in ancient times. In other words, the *Tsave Yoh* are regarded as being among the earliest inhabitants of the Tewa world. Secondly, they are pan-Pueblo, as indicated in chapter 2, although they are not called by the same name or ascribed the same roles in every Pueblo. What is more likely, therefore, is that they adopted the above-mentioned Spanish accoutrements so that they could resemble the Spanish *abuelos*, or masked bogeymen who appear in some Spanish festivals, and, therefore, appear in broad daylight, under the scrutiny of the Spaniards. The adoption of a few Spanish customs may have been necessary to their survival, especially during the Inquisition of the 17th century. In any case, while there is much yet to be learned about them, enough data has been presented here to demonstrate that the *Tsave Yoh* cannot be understood apart from the *Towa é*. A statement about the *Towa é* in an origin myth recorded by Parsons serves as an appropriate closing to my discussion of the *Tsave Yoh*: The Tewa "place their *towae* on the tops of the hills to watch" (1929, p. 149). The *Tsave Yoh* watch too, but from within the hills.

12. The problem is important because the *Towa é* are just the Tewa manifestation of the pan-Pueblo ideology of the "Twin War Gods." The earthly representatives of these gods of Pueblo mythology are found from Hopi (Parsons 1939, 2:867) to Taos (Parsons 1939, 1:178–79). The *Towa é* are, for instance, like the Bow Priests of Zuni in all important respects, just as, in Eggan's words, "The Bow priesthood probably was paralleled by the Kaletaka organization of the Hopi" (1950, p. 220). These officials, whatever they are called, vary in number from four in the little Pueblo of Tesuque (Aberle 1948, p. 91), to twelve in the much larger Pueblo of Taos (Parsons 1939, 2:933). Their actual number is not crucial to understanding their role in Pueblo society; rather, what is important is that there must be at least two, one representing each of the "Twin War Gods," when they act in an official capacity. Among the Tewa, where the moieties are of paramount importance, this is extended to mean that each of the moieties must be equally represented. This in fact is the case; even the Spanish-derived officials have been fitted into this dual alignment.

Why then has there been so much confusion regarding the nature of these officials in Pueblo society? Let me first note the exact nature of the disagreement. Basically there are two points of view represented. With the exception of Kroeber, all students who have ever ventured an opinion believe that the entire ternary system I here describe was Spanish-derived. Kroeber, writing on Zuni, believes that even what the Tewa call "Spanish officials" are "in substance a native institution" in Zuni (1917, p. 178). The answer, as I have indicated, lies in between; the *Towa é* and their counterparts in other Pueblos are indigenous, while the rest, where they exist, are Spanish. It is equally plausible to infer, for instance, from Kroeber's discussion, supplemented by Eggan's more balanced account, that the institution per se is not native; rather, it was shaped to conform to Zuni social structure and culture during the long period since the 18th century, when Zuni has been without direct Hispanic influence. So also, I believe, the institution of the *capitanes de la guerra*, or war captains, was imposed, but it was fitted by the Tewa into their existing spiritual *Towa é* ideology.

I might add, in conclusion, that Eggan actually defined the nature and role of the *Towa é* and their counterparts in other Pueblos exactly when he wrote of Zuni: "The Bow Priests are leaders in war and the protectors of the village; they are the executive arm of the religious hierarchy and take measures against witches" (1950, p. 208). I believe that a systematic and detailed review of the entire Pueblo literature on this problem will serve to prove that Eggan's characterization can be generalized to all of the Pueblos.

5
THE MADE PEOPLE AND THE DRY FOOD WHO NEVER DID BECOME

1. And yet, I qualify this interpretation with the phrase "at least not consciously," because there is a certain logical sense in which the Made People might be thought to be like fish. To explain this point I must briefly explore the ways in which other animal species are consciously equated with human and spiritual categories. First, several societies of Made People are seen as being like certain animal species. The medicine men are called "bears" (*Ke*) because, in Tewa belief, the bear is the only animal which can treat its wounds much in the manner of human beings. Thus, in one myth, a wounded bear is seen pulling out an arrow from its side and applying pine gum to the wound. There are probably other attributes of the bear involved, but the one discussed here does give us a sense in which the medicine men could be thought of as bears. The Hunt chief, in turn, is called "mountain lion" (*Pi xen*), because the mountain lion is regarded as the master hunter in the Tewa world. The medicine men and Winter chief are also referred to by the term *tsiwi*, "those of the sweeping eyes," referring to predatory animals such as the coyote, mountain lion, hawk, and eagle, and carrion-eaters such as the crow and buzzard. The medicine men are regarded as being like *tsiwi* from one perspective, because they are predators against witches. Thus, whenever they perform a cure the

medicine men always wear two tail feathers of the red-tailed hawk on their upper lip so that they may be able to spot witches even in total darkness, and swoop down upon them with the swiftness of the hawk. Yet they also wear a bear paw, complete with claws, on their right arms. The Winter chief, on the other hand, is not called *tsiwi* literally, but *tsiwi ka*, "near to those of the sweeping eyes." He is regarded as being like, or close to, the *tsiwi*, because of the association of the Winter moiety with hunting, a male activity.

Not only the Made People but the *Towa é* also are seen as being like one animal species, in this case the simple yard dog. Dogs are often referred to as *akon gein*, "those of the plain," which is the term used to designate the *Towa é* when they stand watch outside the village. In this case, the analogy is made between dogs and *Towa é* as guardians and protectors of the village against external enemies.

Finally, the term *Po wa ha* ("water-wind-breath") refers to any human, spiritual, or animal category which serves man. The two men who help the *Tsave Yoh* dress at the "Large Marked Shield," the sacred shrine of the east, and who serve as their seconds throughout the period during which they visit the village, are called *Po wa ha*. The term also means "guardian spirit," for every man engaged in ritual also has a spiritual *Po wa ha* to which he prays for aid in his endeavors. Finally, the term is also applied to horses, and for the same reason; they serve as aids or seconds to man.

We have then, in Tewa, at least hints of a fairly well developed system of analogical reasoning relating human, spiritual, and animal species and categories. Applying the logic of these several examples to the Made People, one could easily infer that they, as a category, are, or were once, thought of as fish because they originated beneath a body of water, the primordial home of the Tewa. The problem is that no Tewa to whom the question was posed could "explain" the Made People as fish people in terms similar to the above examples, while these same examples are quite consistently and consciously applied by the same informants. I may appear to be going to extreme lengths to find some logical basis, rooted in Tewa thought, for Bandelier's interpretation, but I do not wish to reject it out of hand simply because it is not conscious today; the fact remains that the term *Pa* still means both "fish" and "made." No more light can be shed on the question here, but the reader interested in this line of analysis is referred to the very provocative article by Leach (1965) which stimulated this discussion. While Leach focuses his discussion specifically on animal categories and verbal abuse, several of the points he makes are very relevant to the general question of the mutual relations between human, spiritual, and animal categories.

2. These eight men, four within each moiety, are occasionally also referred to as *Po wa ha* ("water-wind-breath"), like the seconds to the *Tsave Yoh* and horses, because they are also perceived as aides to others. They are also referred to by a third term, *Maye Tsineh*, which informants could not translate, and which none recognized as Tewa. Those to whom the question was posed suggest it is a Keresan term. This is not unusual, inasmuch as the Tewa use many Keresan songs in their public dances, and several of the medicine men's prayers are said in Keres.

3. The masked deities are brought only when new members are being initiated into the two moiety societies and into the medicine society, for reasons made clear below. Those for the Summer moiety always come from the south and those for the medicine men from the west. For the Winter moiety, on the other hand, the deities may come from either the north or east. But, as indicated in note 5, chapter 3, the Winter deities may come from the east only when a new member is being initiated into the moiety society. This is closely tied in with the fact that one of the activities the moiety society undertakes with the initiate before this final night is to climb Truchas Peak, the sacred mountain of the east. And this is where the deities of the east originate when they are called forth to bless the new Made person.

4. A possible answer to the question of why White Corn Maiden is emphasized in mythology is that she, not Blue Corn Woman, is the one who has to be "explained" somehow, since she embodies the very fundamental contradiction between motherhood and the male force in the Tewa world. In other words, she is both the mother of the Winter moiety and the symbol of the male principle identified with the Winter moiety. The Tewa attempt to overcome this contradiction in myth by, initially, designating her as "maiden" (i.e. one who has not known man), humanizing her, and then proceeding to have her fertilized magically by the Sun or some other transcendental figure. Indeed, at least a third of all Tewa myths known to me have White Corn Maiden as a central character, and all of these are concerned, directly or indirectly, with her impregnation by magical means. Blue Corn Woman, who embodies no basic contradictions, figures in very, very few Tewa myths. White Corn Maiden is the closest the Tewa come to the very widespread notion of a bisexual creator-god.

In ritual and social structure, the Tewa attempt to overcome the same basic contradiction by positing the rule that no woman may succeed to the position of Red Bow Male Youth if she has borne female children. That is to say, she may not be called "male youth," and she may not have a white corn mother if she has too blatantly (to the Tewa mind) demonstrated that she does *not* symbolize the male principle.

But she may do so if she has borne only sons, for in so doing she has only perpetuated the male principle. The same logical criteria are obviously not applied on each succeeding level of thought and action, but, in the absence of an explicit formulation of an androgynous creator, these represent some of the ways in which the Tewa attempt to live with what for them is one of life's unanswerable questions. One really has to review a substantial body of Tewa mythology (i.e. Parsons 1926) to appreciate the originality of Tewa thought in seeking to overcome this and other contradictions.

5. The term "temples," designating this deity as well as his Summer moiety counterpart, refers to the temples of the head. It is difficult to characterize this deity exactly, so equivocal is he and so many are the alternative terms by which he is known. But the reference to "temples" indicates a lack of intelligence and other "human" faculties on his part. Thus, he is also referred to as "The Silent One" because he alone has no distinctive call and, indeed, makes no oral sounds whatsoever when he appears. Other names by which he is known are "Deer Hunter," "He of the Mountain-top," "Rabbit Belt," and *Pishini*, for which no translation could be obtained. He is, for both moieties, a humorously attired figure who shuffles in last during Tewa ritual dramas, and who, after sustaining considerable verbal abuse from the *Kossa*, has ritual intercourse with four young virgins. The numerous terms by which he is known reflect, at the very least, a pronounced fondness on the part of the Tewa for a transcendental figure who, although so dramatically unlike the others, yet manifests so clearly the frailties of the human condition.

6. Richard I. Ford, who has conducted extensive ethnobotanical and ethnozoological investigations among the Tewa, informs me that the *Karawae* is probably the bank swallow, a bird known for its quickness, ability to fly straight up or down, and seemingly continuous motion. It migrates through the Rio Grande area and is said by Ford's informants to arrive each year on April 19, and to stay for "only one day." Whether it, in fact, appears for one day or not, the fact that the Tewa believe it does makes it a plausible and apt symbol for the deity who carries its name. Like the bird, the deity is in constant motion, and he appears only during water pouring. In any case, Ford assures me that the *Karawae* is quite likely some form of swallow.

7. A story is cited by the Tewa to explain why the *Kwirana* is functionally more limited than the *Kossa* today. It is said that once long ago the former challenged the latter to a contest to see who would make the people of the village laugh the most. After each sang and performed his antics, the people gave their overwhelming approval to the *Kossa*. Thus it is, according to the story told in San Juan, that the

Kwirana does not appear in public rituals as often as the *Kossa*. In any case, the *Kwirana* today seems to be only partially fitted into the San Juan ritual system, and only a systematic review and comparison of his role and meaning, not only among the several Tewa Pueblos, but also among the neighboring Keresans, will shed some light on what appears to be his relative paucity of official duties vis-à-vis the *Kossa*.

8. Of the three kinds of evergreens used to designate Tewa *Oxua*, Douglas spruce is *tse*, white fir is *ten yoh*, and blue spruce is *kaañe*. These are the terms used in San Juan, and they are listed here because there are variations in usage from one Tewa Pueblo to another. Richard I. Ford found, for instance, that in Santa Clara *kaañe* is the name for white fir, while blue spruce is *wae k'e*. The ethnographic literature is of little help here, because it, too, reflects this variation. To compound the confusion, *tse* is given in the older literature as referring to Douglas spruce, and in the more recent as referring to Douglas fir. Rather than attempt to reconcile the variations, therefore, I have accepted the views of my most knowledgeable, yet well-educated, informant. He may be proven wrong in the precision of one or more of his identifications if a public opinion poll of all of the Tewa in each village is taken, but that is quite beside the point here. I am attempting only to indicate that six Tewa *Oxua* are named for evergreens, and why this is so, in religious terms. I am indebted again to Richard I. Ford for placing in some perspective the problem of varying usages in the designation of evergreens, for there is probably no other area of Tewa plant-animal classification in which such considerable variation is found.

9. The notion of the liminal period in rites of passage, as discussed in a highly original and very provocative essay by Turner (1967), could also be usefully applied in understanding the *Oxua* "of the middle," from another perspective. For what Turner means by this notion seems to be what the Tewa, in their own unique fashion, mean by their notion "of the middle of the structure." Thus, Turner discusses liminality as referring to the period of ambiguity between structural states, when the neophytes—or even a whole society through one individual —have just left one state and not yet entered another. It is in the rituals during this "betwixt and between" period, Turner argues, that we see exposed the "basic building blocks of cultures" (1967, p. 110). Turner illustrates this point with a wealth of ethnographic examples from around the world, and I can only refer the reader to this essay to grasp the force of Turner's argument. It broadens our perspective on the Tewa data in that the several applications of the notion "of the middle of the structure" illustrated thus far show not only how the Tewa can have unity within the division presented by the moieties, but how they

get from one social, ritual, and temporal state to another. And all of this is, of course, best illustrated by the *Oxua* "of the middle," who appear when it is neither winter nor summer, but "betwixt and between." Here we do catch a glimpse of the basic building blocks of Tewa culture; but only a glimpse, for it is not possible, within the general aims of this work, to single out any processual activity of the liminal period for intensive analysis. For this reason, I retain the notion of mediation, in the common, everyday sense in which the term is used, to designate both phenomena dealt with in greater depth by Turner, and those which do not fit into his framework of analysis. Thus, while I can meaningfully discuss such apparently disparate phenomena as the role of the Hunt chief at water giving, that of the *Kossa* at water pouring, and that of the medicine men during curing by the notion of mediation, they cannot be dealt with as activities of the liminal period at all. But any one of the several life crisis rites of the Dry Food People, the installation rites of the political officials, and the initiation rites of the Made People could be, if I but had the time to do so without departing too far from the general questions posed in this work.

10. When the chief of the Summer moiety passed away in the spring a few years ago, a series of gentle showers began within a week after his death, and continued for several days. This was proof to the Tewa that he was accepted immediately and with enthusiasm by the deities dwelling in the primordial lake home. Had there been a dust storm instead, the Tewa would have interpreted this as a sign that the soul was rejected by the deities, and this, in turn, would have implied that the Summer chief was a witch. The same signs are watched for when a Dry Food person dies. The only difference is that the sign must come within four days for it to be valid, while the period extends to twelve days for the Made People. As one of Parson's informants explained, there are always twelve official days of mourning when a Made person dies (1929, p. 150). If there are no extreme natural signs of this kind, people just do not bother to speculate about the fate of the soul.

11. The phrase used to bring this about in prayer and other ritual speech is *nan fo nuneh, tsin fo nuneh, pin fo nuneh,* "Within and around the earth, within and around the hills, within and around the mountains." This, the reader will recall, is the prayer cited to open chapter 2.

12. It might have occurred to the reader to question whether the Tewa actually believe the souls of the common Tewa rank higher than the living Made People in the hexamerous structure of Tewa existence. If so, this is the best instance I can cite from Tewa ritual to prove that the lowest category of spirit ranks higher in Tewa thought than the highest category of the living. Indeed, *any* ritual can

be postponed for four days when a fully initiated Dry Food person dies. This, then, excludes only children who have not yet undergone the water pouring rite.

13. The only exceptions to this are the two versions of the Buffalo Dance performed in San Juan interchangeably, on the same occasion, during alternate years, or at different times in the same year. And it is this last possibility which provides the exception, at least during recent decades, for both the Tewa Buffalo Dance, which is regarded as native, and the Hopi version, regarded as borrowed, have been performed at about the time of the summer solstice. There need really be no problem in terms of the general picture presented here, because the Buffalo Dances are the only game dances not controlled by the Hunt chief. Therefore, they are not regarded as "native" in the same sense that most of the other rituals presented on figure 10 are. Since the performers do not have to ask for permission of the Hunt chief, there is almost a casual air about when, but not about how, these dances are performed. Equally to the point, the buffalo, not being found within the Tewa world, are not subject to the same ritual proscriptions and hunting regulations as are the game animals in the native habitat. See note 19 below for further elaboration on this point.

14. Three rituals which may occur at about the vernal equinox each year are the Navajo Dance, the Squash Dance, and the Yellow Corn Dance. The first occurs very infrequently; for this reason and because of space limitations it is not listed on figure 10. All are of special interest because they illustrate an extreme form of role reversal, in this case transvestitism, which occurs at changes of season, not only among the Tewa but among most other Pueblos as well. Role reversal in public rituals is a subject about which little theoretical thinking has been done for the Pueblos, so let us take a brief look at each of these rituals.

First, the Navajo Dance is a humorous parody of Navajo dress and behavior, and it is performed by the losers in a women's shinny game. Sometime after the men's ritual shinny game is held in late February (see note 20 below), the married women of the village may play a game against the unmarried. Unlike the men, however, they play over a fixed track running east to west and keep score. It is the losers of this game, usually the married women, who, along with their husbands or beaus, assume the extremes of Navajo dress and behavior of the opposite sex and perform Navajo ritual dances before the entire village for a day as the price of defeat.

The other two dances, in contrast, involve role reversal only by men. In an appearance on the eve of either dance, called *Pu t'an di*, "Painted buttocks thing," several men who are to participate in the dance appear in the plazas and on the housetops of the village. They are dressed in women's clothing and proceed to do an extreme parody of female behavior, even to lifting up their dresses and squatting down on the plaza to urinate, and making sexual gestures at passing men. These female impersonators are called *Pinin Kossa*, "fake" or "temporary" clowns.

All of these transvestite performances are enjoyed by spectators and participants alike, and one or two of them formerly occurred each year sometime in March. Whenever a stern Catholic priest frowned on their performance because of Lent, one or another of them would be performed at Easter. What is of interest for understanding the Tewa ritual cycle as a whole, however, is that all of these rituals represent extreme instances of what occurs when the Tewa wish to mark an interruption in the normal flow of time, in this case the alternation of seasons. Viewed from this perspective all of them may be said to be the spring counterparts of the Harvest and Turtle rituals, which occur at about the autumnal equinox and winter solstice, respectively. In the latter rituals the reversal is marked by the appearance of the sacred clowns, or real *Kossa*, who speak and act in a manner opposite that of normal life. Thus, where the *Kossa* themselves do not participate in rituals at the change of seasons, fake or make-believe clowns do.

The Squash Dance has, in addition, a special place in all of this, one which will serve to prove the point being made. It alternates on the calendar with the Basket Dance so that the two are interchangeable from year to year, but both of them may not be performed during any single year. During a year when the head of the *Towa é* is of the Summer moiety the Squash Dance is performed. The following year, when the head of the *Towa é* is of the Winter moiety, the Basket Dance is performed. Each moiety regards itself as "owning" one dance or the other. However, for some unknown reason, the real *Kossa* may appear only during the Basket Dance. Consequently, since they are interchangeable and since there is nothing in the dances themselves to dramatize or even suggest the change of season, "fake" clowns have to be brought into play for one of them because the real ones are excluded.

Much of the mystery surrounding Pueblo transvestite dances, the role of the sacred clowns, and the very logic in the order of Pueblo rituals can be clarified if we view them against the background of the total cycle within which they occur. What is clear is that there is an order if we but look closely enough. The reader who wishes to ponder this point further is referred to a short essay by Leach (1961, pp. 132–36), who has probably done the best theoretical thinking on the problem. Not all of the implications of his stimulating little essay could be explored here; that would entail a detailed review of the entire ethnographic literature on Pueblo ritual calendars.

15. But these rain retreats formerly occurred at least once during each year. Similarly the Navajos are said by the Tewa to have formerly also made rain retreats to *Tsikomo*, possibly their sacred mountain of the east. So solemn are these pilgrimages, in fact, that as Curtis (1926), Parsons (1929, p. 29), and others have pointed out this is the one occasion on which the Tewa and Navajos will not attack each other, should they chance to meet on *Tsikomo*. Neither side would wish to anger the spirits through violence and, thereby, risk not receiving any rainfall for their crops.

An amusing and not altogether irrelevant note might also be added to the occasion of this annual pilgrimage. During particularly dry years, Spanish-American farmers living within a few miles of San Juan would come to the village as early as April to urge individual Made People to prevail upon their colleagues to "go and get the rain." Although much may have been made of the inimical relations between the two groups by scholars in the past, in this instance the Spanish-Americans exhibited at least as much faith in Tewa ritual as the Tewa themselves do.

16. One of the ponds is about a hundred yards north of the village, and the other about the same distance west of the village. While the Women's society directs the cleaning, other women who are not Made People are drafted to help, with an offering of tobacco. There must be a pair of such women to clean each of the ponds, and both moieties must be equally represented. Thus, members of each of the moieties are paired to carry out the task. After this basic requirement is fulfilled, other women of the village may volunteer to help carry away the trash in baskets. With the drilling of wells in the village proper by the federal government several decades ago, the ponds have fallen into disuse. In still more recent years the ponds have almost dried up entirely because of the steadily falling water table in the area.

17. The coat of the weasel (*Ye*) changes in color from brown to white between November and March. When white is used as a symbol of the winter season by the Tewa, it represents winter moisture, in the form of snow. In this sense the weasel is an especially appropriate symbol for the change in seasons.

18. Geese and sandhill cranes, which come through the Tewa area only in the fall, beginning in October, are also symbols of the change in seasons, since their first appearance coincides with the time when the last crops, corn and beans, are being brought into storage. The Tewa believe that these birds hatch their young at Sandy Place Lake (*Oxange Pokwingeh*), the primordial home of the Tewa in southern

Colorado, and then proceed southward into the Rio Grande Valley. When they return north in the spring, on the other hand, they fly over the high mountains to the west of the Tewa area. Consequently, they can be hunted in the fall, but not in the spring.

It will be recalled, from the discussion of the Winter moiety's water giving rite in chapter 3, that it is the meat of these birds, along with that of mallard ducks, that the Winter chief distributes, through the Hunt chief, to the mothers of the infants undergoing the rite. Thus, the change in seasons, of which these migratory fowl are harbingers, signals a change in life status for the infants undergoing water giving. The prominence of these fowl in the ritual, rather than other fowl and game animals, can be understood in light of this fact. Ideally, the birds whose flesh is to be used on this occasion should be trapped and suffocated so that their blood will not be spilled. This ideal is no longer adhered to, but formerly most animals used in ritual were said to be obtained in this manner.

It should also be clear to the reader, finally, why the migratory fowl do not figure in the Summer moiety's water giving rite, which is held in the spring. On the one hand, these birds are not available and, on the other, hunting is identified with the Winter rather than the Summer moiety.

19. I have indicated, in note 13 above, that there are two buffalo dances performed in San Juan today, one of which is regarded as borrowed from the Hopi. I also noted that both are sometimes performed in June, unlike all other game animal dances, which are performed during the autumn and winter months. I shall now indicate why, in my opinion, the exception is made for the buffalo dances.

First, buffalo were formerly hunted intermittently during September and October, a time not too unlike that during which other large game animals were hunted, although there is overlap here with the agricultural cycle. When a buffalo-hunting expedition was being organized, the members would first go to the Women's society to ask its members "to work" for their success, and "to seek life" on their behalf through ritual. The reason they had to ask for special ritual aid was that they were going to *Sehta Pi Akonge,* "Dry Food Not Plain," or to the land of non-Dry Food People. They were going out of the Tewa world and, consequently, would be among people (Plains Indians) whom the Tewa did not recognize as people. In this ritual exchange, the members of the Women's society then assured the men that they would aid them by making offerings to the sun at dawn, by praying, and by putting out prayer feathers.

Since they had to go so far and leave before the late crops were harvested, the hunters left relatives in charge of their crops, on the assurance that they would share bountifully in anything they brought back from the expedition. The hunters also took large quantities of agricultural products, which they traded with the tribes of the southwestern periphery of the Plains for beadwork and leather goods. They were usually away from home for at least a month.

Upon hearing news of the hunter's approach on their return, members of the Women's society went out to meet them at the edge of the village, and sprinkled a path of white cornmeal for them to follow into the village. After this the hunters were carefully "debriefed" in the kiva on all they had done, said, heard, and seen from the time they left home. They also had to subject themselves to other ritual precautions designed to reintegrate them fully once again into the Tewa world. Indeed, anyone who leaves the Tewa world for any reason has to be debriefed and ritually purified before he can take his normal place in the society again.

How this lengthy disquisition on buffalo hunting helps us to understand why the buffalo dances are performed in the spring is that, as a subsistence activity, buffalo hunting is put outside of the Tewa world. As such, it is not subject to control by the Hunt chief, nor to the special ritual proscriptions placed on the hunting of game found *within* the Tewa world. Similarly, therefore, the buffalo dances also escape the restriction placed on other game dances: that they be performed only during the winter half of the year.

20. The blessing of the seeds is called "putting the mark of the spirits on them." The seed-filled ball used in the game is colored half yellow and half black. The black is symbolic of the rain-laden cumulus clouds of the spring and summer, while the yellow symbolizes sunshine. At noon on the day of the game the Summer chief emerges from his home wrapped in a blanket, his face painted, and the ball carefully hidden from view. He climbs a home which overlooks the "earth mother earth navel middle place" in the middle of the south plaza. Below, the men of the village, from teenagers to the elderly, have already gathered and been divided up into two teams. The Summer chief then utters a short prayer, throws the ball toward the earth navel, and the game begins.

The players must complete four sunwise circuits around the village, although one team always attempts to move the ball in the opposite direction. During this time any woman or girl may grab the ball and carry it into her home to invoke its blessing for the household. The players wait outside in the meantime, and when the ball is returned it is accompanied by a basket of food, both of which are thrown to the players. The ball is usually punctured on the same day, but the game could last as long as four days. If after four days the ball has not yet spilled its contents, it is returned intact to the Summer chief by the head *Towa é*. In any case, the buckskin cover is always carefully picked up after the game and returned to the Summer chief, to be used again the following year.

21. Wheat represents such an outstanding exception to the aboriginal system of restrictions and regulations because its time of planting and harvest cannot be regulated by the Made People in traditional terms at all. The reason this is so is that three different kinds of wheat were formerly grown in the Tewa area. One kind can be planted as early as February, and it is ready to be harvested by the end of June. The second kind, called "white wheat" by the Tewa, is planted during March. It is the only kind grown by them today, and it is the variety which is harvested during late July and early August. The third variety, winter wheat, is planted during October and November, comes up early in the spring, and is ready to be harvested as early as May. Consequently, wheat simply cannot be uniformly regulated by the Made People in the same way other crops can.

This is why the Tewa place the responsibility for its planting and harvest in charge of an external and independent, but parallel, organization, the Spanish officials. This arrangement has several interesting implications and is reflected in several ways. First, the governor receives a portion of the wheat harvest from each family in return for the use of the communal machinery, but he does not, unlike the Made People and *Towa é*, ever receive any portion of the harvest of native crops during ritual redistributions of food. Secondly, he may rent out a portion of Pueblo lands to neighboring Spanish-American farmers. For this he receives payment in wheat, and he may use this himself and/or loan portions out to poor residents of the village, to be paid back to him the following year. Similarly, the governor may lease grazing land to neighboring non-Indian stockmen, for this, too, cannot be regulated by traditional mechanisms.

The only other special prerogative the Spanish officials have they share with the *Fiscales*, and it, too, was introduced by the Spaniards. These two organizations are the only ones exempt from having to work on the irrigation canals while they are in office. Yet the canals are in the governor's over-all charge, and the *Fiscales* have the task of notifying Pueblo residents a month before they are to be cleaned each year. Thus it seems that the non-aboriginal—and often problematical—traits and activities are placed in the charge of the Spanish-introduced officials, and these officials may avail themselves of whatever advantages may accrue to them because of this fact.

22. The reader's attention is especially called to the work "Of the middle of the structure," which is initiated by the Winter chief in

early to mid-November. Ostensibly it was a ritual recognition that nature was dormant for the winter, or in the words of one Tewa: "Mother earth is put to sleep at the work 'Of the middle of the structure' and reawakened at the work 'Bringing the buds to life'; thus you see that plant life dies in the autumn and is reborn again in the spring." But if the first work mentioned accurately reflected the happenings in the natural world, it would begin at least three weeks earlier, since the last crops are in storage by mid-October at the latest, and all other plants used in subsistence except evergreens are also dormant by that time. Of the latter, only piñon nuts are harvested later, but they are not available every year, and, besides, all evergreens, by their very nature, are excluded from the winter/summer classification.

A more puzzling question has already been posed in a discussion of this work; namely, why is it perceived as occurring at the alternation of seasons, "when it is neither winter nor summer," when the Tewa have other rituals (the Harvest Dance and the initiation of *Kossa*) which indicate they recognize the alternation as, in fact, occurring at the end of September? The equinoctial period can be fairly flexible, it is true, but it could not be this flexible in interpretation to a people who demonstrate an ability to make fairly precise solar observations on other occasions. I suggest the possibility, therefore, that the work may have been moved ahead on the calendar after winter wheat was introduced to the Tewa. The reader will recall that winter wheat is planted in October and early November, and the Tewa would not "put mother earth to sleep" while planting was still going on. This, of course, is only a logical deduction, and, as such, may never be proven, since the change would have occurred so long ago that no Tewa living today would know about it.

In any case, two major deficiencies in our knowledge are pointed up which could have a bearing on the problem. First, we need to know whether the aboriginal varieties of corn matured earlier than those harvested in October today. If so, the "Late harvest" work could have been begun and concluded earlier. If not, we might have a false problem, and this possibility cannot be denied. What is clear today is that there are often two plantings of corn taking place about a month apart, and it is the second planting which is harvested as late as October. Secondly, and more importantly, we need to know a great deal more about the intent and meaning of the work "Of the middle." There is perhaps no better time to underscore the extreme difficulty one has in getting detailed information on Tewa ritual, for each time I probed too deeply the Made People would simply reply: "Let us give you water and we shall tell you more." In other words, if I would agree to

begin the process of initiation into a society, I could learn all I wished
to know. I shall let the question bearing on this work stand for now,
and let the reader make his own judgment, on the basis of the evidence,
whether the Tewa ritual cycle might indeed have been altered in this
and other ways suggested below.

23. The ethnographic record is not entirely mute on this problem,
and two suggestive comparative leads bearing specifically on the role
of hunting in Pueblo subsistence may be cited. First, Wittfogel and
Goldfrank (1943) cite a Hopi myth in which a central theme is the
opposition between male and female agriculture. The authors find the
same myth in the eastern Keresan Pueblo of Zia, but with one important difference; here the theme is no longer an opposition between
male and female agriculture, but one in which female agriculture is
opposed to male hunting. This slender lead has never been followed
up, but there is definitely a greater concern reflected in the mythology
of the eastern Pueblos, especially among the Tewa and northern Tiwa,
with hunting. I would suggest, on the basis of the evidence compiled in
this work, that hunting formerly played a much larger part in the
economy of those Pueblos, such as the Tewa and northern Tiwa, where
it could be carried out profitably. Why, then, has this not previously
been recognized by students of Pueblo society? Davis (1959) provides
a clue. Working backward into the recent archaeological horizons
from the available ethnographic evidence, he points out that not much
in the way of animal remains is discovered in ruins dug by archaeologists. The reason this is so, he suggests, is that the modern Pueblos
deposit the unused remains of game animals at shrines which are
usually located outside of the village. Although the Tewa evidence
presented here was not available to Davis, this is precisely what they do.
Now, if this practice also held true during the recent archaeological
horizons, as Davis suggests, then the meager animal remains usually
uncovered in Pueblo ruins would be misleading. Thus, both archaeologists and ethnologists were led astray, since each reinforced the other's
findings because of the lack of detailed evidence at both ends of the
time scale. Consequently, Davis's article has been almost totally ignored
by archaeologists and ethnologists alike; indeed it is difficult to evaluate
without a larger body of evidence.

There is still another aspect to the problem, one for which ethnologists may also be held blameless. It is that hunting was no longer
an important subsistence pattern by the time anthropologists appeared
among the Pueblos, because the Spaniards long ago started its decline.
I can hypothetically reconstruct the process as follows. On the one
hand, the Spaniards brought new crops, a better agricultural technology,
and animal husbandry. And on the other hand, they brought superior

weapons for hunting and, by the sheer force of their number, put increased demands on a limited supply of game. Both sets of factors led to an inevitable and relentless squeeze on hunting, the former by giving the Pueblos a means to live without too much dependence on game, and the latter by disturbing and eventually disrupting the delicate ecological balance between the larger game animals and man. New crops, superior weapons, the appropriation of rangeland, and settlement in new areas unleashed a cycle of forces whose impact on hunting we may never be able to evaluate, but about which we had better begin to formulate some hypotheses.

What bearing all of this has on the general problem of the inconsistencies in the Tewa ritual cycle is that the overwhelming emphasis on the agricultural cycle would soon have reflected itself in the Tewa ritual cycle through the works, and in the period of rule of the respective moiety chiefs. Of these two factors the second is not, by itself, crucial, but the ritual inconsistencies are. And to maintain that they are not problems because most Tewa today do not see them as such would be sheer functionalist evasion. We have the full weight of almost four centuries of Spanish contact to consider, and, while historical records are meager in their detail, we must make some inferences about the consequences of this prolonged period of contact on the basis of what is known about the present. After all, the Tewa have had a very long time in which to bring their thinking into line with the changes in ritual, political, and subsistence practices necessitated by the advent of the Spaniards, and to maintain that they have not done so flies in the face of the evidence from other aspects of Tewa society and culture discussed in this work. And we have such a goodness of fit between belief and practice in these other aspects of society and culture that one cannot help wondering whether the few, but important, discrepancies found today were always present.

Here I can bring the argument down from the abstract by pointing out that some Tewa do perceive and attempt to reconcile the discrepancy between their ritual system as it actually works, and the ideal image of it which they have in their minds. Thus, some Winter informants will insist that the Winter chief actually takes office in mid-September rather than three weeks later, and that, consequently, the work "Of the middle of the structure" actually begins in October. It is a source of some intellectual discomfort to these knowledgeable few that the Winter water giving ritual is held in mid to late November, because it is assumed that it is neither winter nor summer at this time. Yet "The days of the sun," the work at the winter solstice, occurs less than a month later. These same informants will also attempt to camouflage the discrepancy between the times of occurrence of the works to bring the buds, leaves, and blossoms to life, and the occurrence of the actual changes in nature which they are supposed to bring about.

Once again I can only restate the question: Is the problem only mine and perhaps a few informants' creation, or do the several slender lines of evidence cited in this chapter suggest a different state of affairs in the past? I believe they do, although I can carry the argument no further on the basis of present evidence.

24. It is perhaps appropriate, in terms of the unity of this work and of Tewa thought, that the very first and the very last footnotes deal with the same subject, the Tewa classification of plants into categories of "hot," "cold," and "of the middle." In note 1 of chapter 2, I pointed out that the classification of plants into "hot" and "cold" categories is mentioned in the myth of origin, and that I would return to the question in a more appropriate context. I shall take a brief look here at how this classification works out and the basis on which it rests, by presenting a partial listing of edible plants which was provided by one informant, as follows:

Hot	*Of the middle*	*Cold*
red chili	wheat	green chili
pinto beans		green beans
yellow peas		watermelons
melons		amaranth
corn		Portulaca Oleracea L.
		(a wild, succulent green)

The list could be multiplied if time and space permitted, but, in general, the "hot" category corresponds to ripened domesticated plants, while the "cold" category corresponds to unripened and green domesticates and wild plants. The category "of the middle," of which there is only the one representative, is, as in the world of men and of the spirits, a mediating category. This is so because wheat can be planted in the autumn, winter, or spring, and harvested in the spring or summer. Thus it defies categorization on the basis of what the Tewa take to be "hot" and "cold" criteria. The fact that wheat was first introduced by the Spaniards may also be important here. More to the point, wheat unifies opposites, as with analogous categories of men and spirits, by sharing characteristics of both. It is perhaps not altogether irrelevant to this point that the Tewa name for wheat is *t'a t'a*, "seed of seeds."

Let us look now at the same informant's classification of domesticated animals and those hunted for food, to round out the subsistence picture.

Hot	*Of the middle*	*Cold*
cattle	pigs	rabbits and jackrabbits
sheep		deer, antelope, and elk
goats		all game birds
chickens		fish

If we ignore the category "of the middle" for a moment we have here a very clear correspondence between "hot" and domesticated animals on the one hand, and "cold" and wild animals on the other. What then do we do about the pig? The simple answer is that two varieties of pig are known to the Tewa and called by the same name, the penned-up species introduced by the Spaniards, and the wild javelina, found to the south of the Tewa world. In times past, when the Tewa permitted the domesticated pig to run loose in the nearby woods, even it sometimes ran away and became wild. Consequently, the pig is regarded as neither entirely wild nor entirely tame, and, therefore, both "hot" and "cold"; it occupies the interstices between the two extreme categories. Another factor which may be involved here, one of which the Tewa are not consciously aware, is that the pig is the only animal on the list which is omnivorous; it eats the same foods as man. The reader is also referred to Leach's discussion of English and Kachin thinking about the pig, and to the general points he makes about animal categories from another perspective (1965).

These lists of edible plant and animal categories, while not exhaustive, demonstrate that the Tewa do not stop with social and spiritual categories when they classify things as "hot," "cold," and "of the middle." Of these three the last is crucial because it demonstrates how the Tewa overcome the unity within duality problem in the classification of things in the natural world. Looking back over both lists one wonders, of course, whether this classification predated the Spaniards, since both categories "of the middle" and the entire "hot" category of animals represent subsistence items introduced by them. I think that the very pervasiveness of the system of classification, running as it does through social and spiritual categories, games, minerals, and diseases, as well as plants and animals, argues overwhelmingly against a Spanish origin. In any case, more exhaustive lists of both plants and animals are needed, and Richard I. Ford is now in the process of preparing them. When he completes his detailed and precise lists we shall have a better understanding not only of the entire system of classification, but of its ecological implications as well, a large problem area all too lightly touched upon in this work.

Bibliography

Aberle, Sophie D.

1948 The Pueblo Indians of New Mexico: their land, economy, and civil organization. *American Anthropological Association Memoir*, no. 70.

Aberle, S. D.; Watkins, J. H.; and Pitney, E. H.

1940 The vital history of San Juan Pueblo. *Human Biology* 12:141–87.

Adams, Eleanor B.; and Chavez, Fray Angelico, trans.

1956 *The missions of New Mexico, 1776* (by Fray Francisco Atanasio Dominquez). Albuquerque: University of New Mexico Press.

Bandelier, Adolph F.

1890– Final report of investigations among the Indians of the south-
1892 western United States, carried on mainly in the years from 1880–1885. *Papers of the Archaeological Institute of America.* American Series, vol. 3, pt. 1, and vol. 4, pt. 2. Cambridge, Massachusetts.

Chapman, Ann

1962 "Organisation dualiste chez le Jicaques." *L'Homme* 1962, no. 1, pp. 91–101.

Crane, Leo

1928 *Desert drums: the Pueblo Indians of New Mexico, 1540–1928.* Boston: Little, Brown and Co.

Curtis, Edward S.

1926 *The North American Indian.* Vol. 17. Norwood, Massachusetts: Plimpton Press.

Davis, James T.

1959 An appraisal of certain speculations on prehistoric Puebloan subsistence. *SWJA* 16:15–23.

D'Azevedo, Warren L., ed.

1963 The Washo Indians of California and Nevada. *University of Utah Anthropological Papers*, no. 67. Salt Lake City, Utah.

Douglass, William B.

1912 A world quarter shrine of the Tewa Indians. *Records of the Past* 11:159–73.

1915 Notes on the shrines of the Tewas and other Pueblo Indians. *Proceedings of the Nineteenth International Congress of Americanists,* pp. 344–78.

Dozier, Edward P.

1960 The Pueblos of the south-western United States. *JRAI* 90:146–60.

1961 Rio Grande Pueblos. In *Perspectives in American Indian culture change,* ed. E. H. Spicer. Chicago: University of Chicago Press.

1966 *Hano: a Tewa Indian community in Arizona.* New York: Holt, Rinehart, and Winston.

Eggan, Fred

1950 *Social organization of the western Pueblos.* Chicago: University of Chicago Press.

1955 *Social anthropology of the North American tribes.* Chicago: University of Chicago Press.

1966 *The American Indian.* Chicago: Aldine Press.

Eliade, Mircea

1958 *Patterns in comparative religion.* New York: World Publishing Co.

1959 *Cosmos and history.* New York: Harper and Row.

Ellis, Florence Hawley

1964 A reconstruction of the basic Jemez pattern of social organization, with comparisons to other Tanoan social structures. *University of New Mexico Publications in Anthropology,* no. 11. Albuquerque: University of New Mexico Press.

Ford, Richard Irving

1968 An ecological analysis involving the population of San Juan Pueblo, New Mexico. Unpublished Ph.D. dissertation, Department of Anthropology, University of Michigan.

Fox, Robin

1967 *The Keresan bridge: a problem in Pueblo ethnology.* London: Athlone Press.

Geertz, Clifford

1957 Ethos, world-view and the analysis of sacred symbols. *Antioch Review* 17:421–37.

1965 The impact of the concept of culture on the concept of man.

In *New views of the nature of man,* ed. J. R. Platt. Chicago: University of Chicago Press.

1966 Religion as a cultural system. In *A.S.A. Monographs 3, Anthropological approaches to the study of religion,* ed. M. Banton. London: Tavistock Publications.

Greenberg, Joseph H.
1966 *Language universals.* The Hague: Mouton and Co.

Hackett, Charles Wilson, and Shelby, C. C.
1942 Revolt of the Pueblo Indians of New Mexico and Otermin's attempted reconquest, 1680–1682. *Coronado Historical Series,* vol. 8 and vol. 9. Albuquerque: University of New Mexico Press.

Harrington, John P.
1912 Tewa relationship terms. *American Anthropologist* 14:472–98.
1916 The ethnogeography of the Tewa Indians. *Bureau of American Ethnology, Annual Report,* no. 29:29–618. Washington: U.S. Government Printing Office.

Hertz, Robert
1960 *Death and the right hand.* Glencoe: The Free Press.

Hewett, Edgar L.
1930 *Ancient life in the American southwest.* Indianapolis: Bobbs-Merrill Co.

Horton, Robin
1962 The Kalabari world-view: an outline and interpretation. *Africa* 32:197–219.

Kroeber, Alfred L.
1917 Zuni kin and clan. *Anthropological Papers of the American Museum of Natural History,* vol. 18, pt. 2. New York.

Kurath, Gertrude P.
1958 Plaza circuits of Tewa Indian dances. *El Palacio* 65:16–26.

Lange, Charles H.
1959 *Cochiti: A New Mexico Pueblo, past and present.* Austin: University of Texas Press.

Laski, Vera
1959 Seeking life. *Memoirs of the American Folklore Society,* vol. 50. Philadelphia.

Leach, Edmund R.
1961 Two essays concerning the symbolic representation of time. In *Rethinking anthropology.* London: Athlone Press.

Leach, Edmund R.
  1965 Anthropological Aspects of Language: animal categories and verbal abuse. In *New directions in the study of language*, ed. E. H. Lenneberg. Cambridge, Massachusetts: M.I.T. Press.

Lévi-Strauss, Claude
  1944 Reciprocity and hierarchy. *American Anthropologist* 46:266–68.
  1960 On manipulating sociological models, *Bijdragen tot de Taal-, Land- en Volkenkunde* 116:45–54.
  1963a Do dual organizations exist? In *Structural anthropology*. New York: Basic Books.
  1963b Social structure. In *Structural anthropology*. New York: Basic Books.
  1963c The bear and the barber. *JRAI* 93:1–11.
  1966 *The savage mind*. Chicago: University of Chicago Press.

Malinowski, Bronislaw
  1948 *Magic, science and religion and other essays*. Glencoe: The Free Press.

Maybury-Lewis, David
  1960 The analysis of dual organizations: a methodological critique. *Bijdragen tot de Taal-, Land- en Volkenkunde* 116:17–44.
  1965 *The savage and the innocent*. London: Evans Bros. Ltd.
  1967 *Akwe-shavante society*. Oxford: Clarendon Press.

Murdock, George Peter
  1949 *Social structure*. New York: Macmillan Co.
  1956 Political moieties. In *The state of the social sciences*, ed. Leonard D. White. Chicago: University of Chicago Press.

Ortiz, Alfonso
  1965a Project Head Start in an Indian community. Report prepared for the Office of Economic Opportunity, October, 1965 (mimeograph).
  1965b Dual organization as an operational concept in the Pueblo southwest. *Ethnology* 4:389–96.
  1966a A problem of symbolism in the study of myth. Paper read at the annual meetings of the Central States Anthropological Society, Lexington, Kentucky.
  1966b Cold gods, warm gods, and gods of the middle. Unpublished manuscript.

Parsons, Elsie Clews
  1924 Tewa kin, clan, and moiety. *American Anthropologist* 26:333–39.

1926   The ceremonial calendar of the Tewa of Arizona. *American Anthropologist* 28:209–29.

1929   The social organization of the Tewa of New Mexico. *American Anthropological Association Memoir*, no. 36.

1939   *Pueblo Indian religion.* 2 vols. Chicago: University of Chicago Press.

Parsons, E. C. and Beals, Ralph
1934   The sacred clowns of the Pueblo and Mayo-Yaqui Indians. *American Anthropologist* 36:491–514.

Reed, Erik K.
1956   Types of village-plan layouts in the southwest. In *Prehistoric settlement patterns in the new world*, ed. Gordon R. Willey. Viking Fund Publications in Anthropology, no. 23. New York: Wenner-Gren Foundation.

Schneider, David M.
1965   Some muddles in the models: or, how the system really works. *A.S.A. Monographs* 1, *The relevance of models for social anthropology*, pp. 25–85. London: Tavistock Publications.

Scholes, France V.
1935   The first decade of the Inquisition in New Mexico. *New Mexico Historical Review* 10:195–241.

Spinden, Herbert J.
1933   *Songs of the Tewa.* New York: The Exposition of Indian Tribal Arts, Inc.

Stevenson, Matilda Cox
1913   Studies of the Tewa Indians of the Rio Grande valley. *Smithsonian Miscellaneous Collections* 60:35–41.

Titiev, Mischa
1944   Old Oraibi, a study of the Hopi Indians of Third Mesa. *Papers of the Peabody Museum of American Archaeology and Ethnology*, vol. 22, no. 1. Cambridge, Massachusetts.

Trager, George L.
1967   The Tanoan settlement of the Rio Grande area: a possible chronology. In *Studies in general anthropology*, vol. 3, ed. Dell Hymes. The Hague: Mouton and Co.

Turner, Victor
1967   Betwixt and between: the liminal period in rites de passage. In *The forest of symbols*. Ithaca: Cornell University Press.

Twitchell, Ralph Emerson
1912   *The leading facts of New Mexican history.* 2 vols. Cedar
       Rapids, Iowa: The Torch Press.

Van Gennep, Arnold
1960   *The rites of passage.* Chicago: University of Chicago Press.

White, Leslie
1935   The Pueblo of Santo Domingo, New Mexico. *American
       Anthropological Association Memoir* 43.
1964   The world of the Keresan Pueblo Indians. In *Primitive views
       of the world,* ed. Stanley Diamond. New York: Columbia
       University Press.

Whitman, William
1940   The San Ildefonso of New Mexico. In *Acculturation in seven
       American Indian tribes,* ed. Ralph Linton. New York: D.
       Appleton-Century Co.

Winship, George Parker
1896   The Coronado expedition, 1540–1542. *Bureau of American
       Ethnology, Annual Report,* no. 14:329–613.

Wittfogel, Karl A., and Goldfrank, Esther S.
1943   Some aspects of Pueblo mythology and society. *Journal of
       American Folklore* 56:17–30.

Witthoft, John
1953   The American Indian as hunter. *Pennsylvania Game News,*
       vol. 24, nos, 2, 3, 4.

Yalman, Nur O.
1966   Dual organization in central Ceylon. *Journal of Asian Studies*
       24:197–223.

Index

87–88, 106. *See also* Summer
moiety; Winter moiety
Murdock, George Peter, 5, 8, 110,
150–51 n.8
Myth of origin, 13–16, 73, 83, 91,
121, 123–24, 139 n.1, 139–40 n.3,
178 n.24
Mythology, 27–28, 69, 148–49 n.4,
165–66 n.4; numerical formulas
in, 139 n.2. *See also* Myth of origin

Name: birth name, 32–33; marriage name, 47–48; water giving
name, 35
Naming, 30–33, 35, 122, 143 n.10,
154 n.12
Naming mother, 30–33, 56
Navajo Dance, 169–70 n.14
New year ceremony, 102–3
North moiety: color symbolism
of, 109, directional symbolism
of, 109–10; function of, 108–9;
recruitment of, 108; songs of,
109; spirit patrons of, 108, 110
Numerical formulas. *See* Mythology; Ritual, speech

"Of moderation" work, 99–100
"Of the middle": animals, 178–79
n.24; direction, 95; Made People, 91, 96, 101–2, 125, 136;
oxua, 95–96, 136, 167–68 n.9;
plants, 178–79 n.24; work of the
Made People (*see* "Of the middle of the structure" work)
"Of the middle of the structure"
work, 101–2, 105, 107, 112–13,
174–75 n.22, 177–78 n.23
"Of the officials" work, 98–99
Oñate, Juan de, 61
Oxua, 91–97; Dancer, 93; named
for evergreens, 94, 167 n.8; "of

the middle," 95–96, 136, 167–68
n.9

Parsons, Elsie Clews, 3–4, 13. 20,
23, 46, 50, 130, 140 n.6, 144 n.11,
165–66 n.4; on kinship, 150–51
n.8; on Made People, 79–80, 85–
86, 89–90, 168 n.10, 171 n.15
Parsons, Elsie Clews, and Beals,
Ralph, 77
Path of emergence, 40–42, 56–57
Plants, classification of, 118, 128,
178–79 n.24
Political organization: 61–77. See
also *Fiscales;* Spanish officials;
Towa é
Ponds, 112, 170 n.16
Posi village, 16, 37
Prayer, 168 n.11, 173 n.20; in death
ritual, 51, 54; formula in, 23–24;
Keresan, 165 n.2; of Made People 87–88, 107; in naming, 31–
32; in political installation, 66;
in Turtle Dance, 76
Prayer feathers, 66–67, 70, 73, 103,
109–10, 112, 156 n.5, 172 n.19
Primordial lake, 79–80, 85, 88–90,
96–97, 102, 106, 125, 149 n.5, 168
n.10, 171–72 n.18
Punan, 65–66, 155–56 n.4, 156–57
n.6
"Putting in squash," 21, 114–15

Rain retreat, 107–8, 171 n.15
Red Bow Male Youth, 87, 165–66
n.4. *See also* White Corn
Maiden
Redistribution of food, 113–14,
174 n.21
Reed, Erik K., 145–46 n.12
Relay races, 108–11
Re-seeding earth navel. *See* "Put-
ting in squash"